Liverpool Lad

Liverpool Lad

Adventures growing up in postwar Liverpool

Peter Haase

Mother Tongue Publishing Limited
Salt Spring Island, BC
Canada

MOTHER TONGUE PUBLISHING LIMITED
290 Fulford-Ganges Road, Salt Spring Island, B.C. V8K 2K6 Canada
www.mothertonguepublishing.com
Represented in North America by Heritage Group Distribution.

Book Design by Mark Hand
Back cover photo: Hodder Street, rear, 1968, Liverpool Record Office, Liverpool Libraries
Endpages: Bostock Street and Kew Street, 1966, Photography by Harry Ainscough, Liverpool
Record Office, Liverpool Libraries
Dedication page: Three Graces on the Liverpool waterfront in 1920. Royal Liver Building, the
Cunard Building, and the Port of Liverpool Building
p. 13, 50 courtesy of Liverpool Record Office, Liverpool Libraries
p. 116 courtesy of Streets of Liverpool, Liverpool City Group
p. 166 courtesy of Trinity Mirror
p. 278 courtesy of Australian National Maritime Museum, Samuel J Hood Studio
All efforts have been made to locate copyright holders of source material wherever possible.

Printed on Enviro Antique Natural, 100% recycled
Printed and bound in Canada.

Mother Tongue Publishing gratefully acknowledges the assistance of the Province of British
Columbia through the B.C. Arts Council and we acknowledge the support of the Canada Council
for the Arts, which last year invested $157 million in writing and publishing throughout Canada.
Nous remercions de son soutien le Conseil des Arts du Canada, qui a investi 157$ millions de
dollars l'an dernier dans les lettres et l'édition à travers le Canada.

LIBRARY AND ARCHIVES CANADA CATALOGUING IN PUBLICATION

Haase, Peter, author
    Liverpool lad : adventures growing up in postwar Liverpool / Peter Haase.

ISBN 978-1-896949-29-1 (paperback)

1. Haase, Peter--Childhood and youth. 2. Liverpool (England)--Biography. I. Title.

DA690.L8H32 2016   942.7'530823092   C2016-900245-

With love

To Mona, and our son and daughter, Paris and Sophia,

and to my brothers, Fred, Dave and Geoff, three more Liverpool Lads.

Contents

Part One: Born into a Working Class Family

Part Two: Hungry in the Pool

Part Three: Butcher Boy Adventures

Part One

Born Into a Working Class Family

1

26 Cadmus Street, Everton

I was born at home, in 1950, in the same big bed where my three older brothers were brought into the world. My mother had four boys in five years. The house was a run-down tenement, built in the early 1800s, and I grew up there, in that famous inner-city working-class district of Everton, Liverpool 6 until I was eleven.

The Family: Back row, Albert, Dave, Mary, Front row, Fred, Geoff, Peter, Rhyl, Wales, 1954

Opposite: Me and dad, Newsham Park, 1952

Everton was a historic open-door community, full of derelict and bombed-out homes, and a warren-like maze of hundreds of intertwined, wall-to-wall tenement houses on narrow streets and back alleys. The official name given for the old alleyways was back entry. We called them jiggers. We had a nickname for everything and everyone.

A typical row of attached houses presented a front door and a window, and then another twelve feet along was another front door and a window. These doors had a letterbox, street numbers and a big doorknob, all sold brass, which we kept polished nicely with Brasso, to keep the place up to scratch.

Every dwelling on the street had four rooms—two bedrooms up and two rooms down with an outdoor flushing lavvo (that looked like an outhouse) next to the coal shed in the tiny backyard. The front room, which opened right onto the street without a hallway, we called the kitchen (we didn't say living room). Beyond that was the "back kitchen," where we had the old gas stove and the kitchen sink that had only a cold-water tap. To get hot water for any purpose—such as washing your hands and face, filling up the galvanized bathtub that hung on a nail on the backyard wall or doing the dishes—required boiling enough water in the kettle and pots to do the job. The freezing cold water took ages to boil for a decent pot of tea, and as they always said, "A watched kettle never boils." You always had to heat the teapot before making tea, because everything was cold to the touch for most of the year. There were only fourteen houses down both sides of the narrow street, and we lived at number 26, the second to the end. The street was only slightly illuminated at night with a handful of gaslights. I remember when a man would come to turn the lights on with a small flame on the end of a long pole if the automatic switching failed.

Our short cobblestone street was dead-ended with a six-foot redbrick wall that connected the two end houses. We kids would call out to a small dog called Trigger who lived at the end of the street, and as he came chasing and barking after us, we'd jump up on top of the brick wall, being careful not to fall over into the jigger (that particular alleyway had a fall of fifteen feet) because the next street was further down the terraced hill. All of us boys and girls became very deft at climbing up, down and over high walls, using our fingertips where the mortar had fallen out from between the bricks. Alas, not all walls could be negotiated, usually because of the broken glass embedded in cement along the top to keep the intruders and trespassers out. These dangerous walls were everywhere. The hundreds of rows of streets in the old town were designed with simple practicality in mind, hurriedly erected over a century and a half before. There was no elaborate finish, except for the occasional show of detailed patterns of coloured brickwork edging some doors and windows.

Dido Street, Liverpool, turn of the century. It was one street over from Cadmus and looked just like our street.

Hiding within the confines of those cold connected blocks of human habitat was the ever-present silent observation of economical differences between neighbour and neighbour, family and family. It seems almost expected that people in these tight enclaves, should be nosey and curious about each other's private business. This inquisitive-ness was alive and well even though we were all basically experiencing similar life struggles. The veil of privacy was thin between the brick walls. One could sit quietly in the front kitchen and clearly hear the neighbours' raised voices. I remember my mother hearing a personal comment through the wall, from the lady next door, and answering with "Oh aye, I heard that alright!" Then there would be a rebuttal from beyond, either a laugh or a reprimand. You could hear the loud talking, the arguments, the radio or TV shows, the laughing, crying, and as some little old ladies could attest, you could catch up on the local gossip without leaving the house. Partial privacy only came later when we were moved from the inner city to the outlying suburb ghettos, where the walls were thicker.

Even going to the back-to-back toilets in the yards didn't offer much privacy, as you'd listen to all the humorous noises and groans of relief by a neighbour next door paying a visit at the same time. Toilet paper was way too expensive for most people, so the newspaper (the *Liverpool Echo*) cut into nice, handy squares with a string threaded through and hung on a nail fixed that problem. Pull the chain and flush the news. Cutting up newspapers when needed was a small chore for us kids to handle and a picture on a string provided cheap entertainment.

There existed a kinship of warmth and respect in a cooperative community amongst those grotty avenues of red-brick houses in the district of Everton. Working-class stiffs that lined up by the thousands in the mornings at the bus stops, ferries and train stations to get to their jobs, clocking in at the factories, shops, warehouses or docks, then crawling home after their shift. As the buses dropped off tired folk at the end of the day, you'd see the familiar faces chatting and saying fare-well before they headed to their respective houses, and the kids waiting for mam or dad at the end of the street. Many of us were latchkey kids, and neighbours would often offer a cup of tea or a bikky while we waited for our folks to get home.

Every family along our rows of streets paid eleven shillings and sixpence a week for rent, which was happily collected, every Saturday morning, rain or shine, by the bent back Jewish landlord, Mr. Levi. He was an old gentleman with wise observing eyes and a strange European accent who'd sometimes stop for a cuppa if me mam wasn't too busy and they'd chat about the world as it was.

The narrow back jiggers were often filthy, smelly and littered, but the front slate sidewalks were swept and kept tidy. There was no better place to find this brightness of spirit than amongst those dark, dank, sooty streets of postwar Liverpool, where the effervescent smiles of optimism amid the drudgery of daily graft were contagious. Open, uplifting compliments to total strangers were commonplace, and readily returned.

The Liverpool City Council was always in a position of stress, due to the financial difficulties it faced in dealing with broken-down playgrounds and public places, plus the rebuilding of tenement flats and wretched public housing, at the same time as demolishing the remnants of hundreds of toppling bombed buildings, the reward dished out by the Luftwaffe because our town was one of the most important shipping ports in the Commonwealth during the war. It was a major springboard in the Battle for the Atlantic.

Many times, when new equipment for parks or projects was installed, it wasn't too long before the local gangs of menacing idle hooligans had pulled the place apart. Playgrounds were trashed to the point where the kids rarely had the pleasure of a working slide or swing. Back on our street, we kids would run free up and down the road, and because hardly anyone owned a car, the cobblestone street was safe for all ages to wander and play. Tiny tots would sit in the middle of the road playing while their older siblings were nearby having their fun. We'd swing on a rope around the old gas lamppost, play hide and seek, and the girls would play hopscotch, drawing numbers on the slate sidewalks with chalk. Some kids had bags full of marbles we called ollies and would be busy rolling those around. We'd make up our own games, and the older boys would play "nearest to the wall" where you all line up on the road and carefully toss a penny at the brick wall; the closest penny won all the money that was thrown. For young boys, it was a good start to a gambling addiction. Two boys would each toss a penny while alternately one would shout "odds" or "evens." If both pennies were the same, heads or tails, and you shouted evens, you won the two pennies; if they were odd, you lost. "Betty up" was a way of saying Queen Elizabeth's head would show on a toss.

In some areas, you could hardly find a public telephone that hadn't been robbed and wrecked, but if ever the louts were spotted engaged in their thievery or mischief, it was not uncommon to see an average citizen intervene and put a stop to things, even swinging a boot or a fist. The good people, who were in the majority, never tolerated the relentless, mindless goings on. Most took the law into their own hands. Phone the cops you might suggest? Nobody had a phone, and many of the red boxed public phones we sometimes called Dr. Who spaceships were vandalized.

I recall, with amusement, the time when my dad took measures into his own hands. He and I were out and about doing a bit of shopping, and when we were in the greengrocers, another young lad, about my age, lifted a piece of fruit from the counter and began to shuffle off to the door, intending to take off with his prize. My dad grabbed him by the shoulder, clouted him over the earhole, at which moment, the boy dropped the orange and took off down the street, howling and holding onto the side of his head. We both laughed, as did the shopkeeper. In today's world, no doubt, some avaricious lawyer would have a heyday taking my dad to task for child abuse, and the shopkeeper would be charged for allowing his produce to be within arm's length, offering an irresistible temptation to the poor unfortunate child. But in that time and place, dealing with such behaviour, no matter how petty or slight, including a boy's reproof from a stranger, was expected, and it was a character flaw not to get involved. It can never be said that downtown Liverpool was a boring place to walk through. The place was full of life and attitude.

B and Es were also alive and well in most parts of town, and our district was no exception. Predictably, the first thing a burglar would check out on a robbery, whether a rich or poor home, was the electric or gas meters—small square steel boxes in most houses that required coins, such as shillings that were shoved in the slot and the handle turned to keep the power on or the gas going. It wasn't uncommon to be sitting at home, watching a show on the telly, and the power would go off. Then someone would have to make their way over to the "lecky box" in the dark to get it back on. It was the same with the gas. In the middle of cooking, if you weren't on top of things, the gas stove would go off and dinner would stop cooking. There was a thin wire with a seal over the small door on the meter. The meter reader came over once a month and if the seal was broken, you could be up for a fine.

I remember we kids would all hang around the kitchen table as the gas or lecky man arrived. He'd open the box and pour out all the silver coins on the table, and with hands as fast as lightning, he'd count them out, shillings flying this way and that. After reading the numbers on the meter dial, he'd make a quick calculation in his notebook and usually give a few shillings back as a rebate if the numbers didn't add up for the consumption used. It was all pay as you go: no coins, no juice. So, knowing how simple it was to get the loot out of the box, an intruder always hit the lecky box first.

Some Saturday mornings in the good weather months, a rag-and-bone man would turn up in the district pushing his big handcart from street to street, calling out, "Any ol' rags? Toys for rags, toys for rags! I'm the Raggo!" Sometimes he'd become the dancing nutcase with the spoons, as the laughing children would gather around, chuffed to bits at the crazy behaviour of the old git, who'd sing in his nasal voice. Every kid would run into their houses, tell their mams that the ragman was there and run back out with armloads of discarded cloths and rags. We'd line up as he checked them, and more than likely, you'd get one lousy balloon for all your efforts. A special offering would be some small plastic toy, a penny whistle or a tiny goldfish in a plastic bag half full of water. To watch him play the spoons was worth the wait, and he'd prance around and shake those dinner spoons across his legs and up and down his arms in an amazing rhythm—free live entertainment on a Saturday morning. As he exited our street, we little ones would help him push his heavy load along to the next street, where other kids would carry on.

It was handy having the ragman come by now and then. We four boys would go through patched up clothes pretty quickly, and when they couldn't be repaired any more, we'd swap them for balloons. But one day, by accident, we were treated to some new duds.

Our old houses on Cadmus Street were falling to pieces around us, and the unconcerned landlord would gladly pick up the rent every week, but repairing anything was not a priority. The cupboard doors were jammed or broken, the stairs were rickety, and even the plaster was hanging off our bedroom wall.

One morning, as a tiny tot, I was standing at the bottom of the unsteady old stairs, and looking up to the top, watched my dad fall all the way down, breaking his leg, as it went through the bottom tread. Our Humpty Dumpty dad was sent off to hospital to be "put back together again." Now we were without his wages for a few weeks, but the social safety net was alive and well in postwar Britain. So, because of our need, mum rounded us up, and we went downtown to the NAB (National Assistance Board) office to get some help, while dad sat around in a cast. We got all the help we needed, and more. We were given a chit for clothing—four new suits with short pants, all made from the same material—and a pair of new shoes each, which we really needed. We were proud as punch in our new garb, and it became our Sunday best. The new threads were classy, and we had no need to put cardboard inside these shoes to make them more comfortable, like the worn-out ones we threw into the fire.

Peter, Dave, Geoff and Fred in front, Cadmus Street, backyard windowsill, 1952

At home, mam found the old Brownie camera and took a photo of her four sons in a row (just like The Four Tops). As time went by, a lot of those great pictures were lost during the moves in Australia. She'd kept all the family photos in a big, old black purse, and somehow three generations of important pictures disappeared forever. Lost, but not forgotten.

By 1961, the great Everton exodus was in full swing, and 125,000 people from the close-knit street communities began relocating to highrises and maisonettes in the outskirts, as hundreds of derelict homes finally faced demolition. This historic event began seventeen years after my folks had first moved to Cadmus Street during the war, in 1944.

When we finally vacated the old dump, on moving day, as we were humping the kitchen table across the back room, part of the floor between the stove and the sink gave way, revealing a small, filthy crawlspace, about one foot deep, strewn with debris and food scraps, which generations of rats had dragged around here and there for nesting and nosh. It was a health inspector's nightmare. Before falling to sleep, we had often heard the scurrying of rats up and down the hollow cavities of the brick walls. We were glad to get out.

2

Dinner's Served

Most of our family meals were predictable, and we boys—Fred, David, Geoff and I—would all pitch in to help mum with peeling spuds or the vegetables, and she'd show us how to cook this and that as we hung around the kitchen looking for handouts.

Yes, the house chores were done with teamwork, and the place was run like a tight ship. It had to be that way with six people living in a tiny tenement house with four small rooms. Our hardworking mother would teach us as she cooked, cleaned, shopped, sorted out the laundry, darned socks and mended clothes. Both our parents did well in teaching us the ways of frugality, and all the old sayings made sense. Waste not, want not. A stitch in time saves nine. Necessity is the mother of invention. And so on.

In the back kitchen, I remember shedding many tears while dicing onions at the sink. I'd also cut the heads off carrots and put them under the counter in a saucer with water, to watch them sprout as the days went by. We'd use a butter knife to peel everything from carrots to spuds to turnips for the roast dinner. I enjoyed watching mam clean and dissect fresh chicken and marvel at all the organs she'd pull out and put aside for the soup later, after we'd boiled up all the bones for a broth. She always sang a little tune as she prepared the meals like an organized chef. One of her favourite songs began "Speed bonny boat, like a bird on the wing, over the sea to Skye." She had a sweet little singing voice, like a trilling nightingale.

She'd always pass me a small slice of raw liver to chew on, as she cut it up with a little bacon for a meal. Eating all kinds of cooked innards like kidney, liver, heart and tripe was normal at our house. I guess it's what you're brought up with?

On special food days like Shrove Tuesday, the day before Ash Wednesday, we were in for a real treat. Mum would stand cooking at the stove for ages, frying up mounds of thin pancakes, almost like French crepes, and keeping them warm on a large hot plate in the gas oven. We'd line up with our plates, collect a pancake, squirt some Jiffy lemon juice all over it, sprinkle on white sugar and roll it up like a long sausage, devouring one after the other with our bare hands. Pancake Tuesday was a real dinner treat to look forward to. But it only came once a year, and we never saw another pancake till then.

On school days, breakfast was up to you. Toast and jam or marmalade, Corn Flakes or Rice Crispies or Quaker Oats porridge was usual, or a scrambled egg on toast, whatever was quick and simple. But Sunday morning breakfast was the best, with bacon or sausages and fried eggs, and some good old-fashioned fried bread. We used lard for frying most things, and the slices of white bread were brought to a nice crispy brown; a dab of HP Sauce would be the crowning touch to an overflowing sandwich of greasy protein. Lunches at school were hot and varied, and cost us one shilling each. At home on the weekends or on school breaks, it was always sandwiches, or something else fried up with a can of baked beans and always white bread and margarine.

At Cadmus Street, we didn't have a fridge. Instead, a small box, about eighteen inches square and high, with wire mesh all around it, sat on the far table in the back kitchen. It kept the flies and mice out. We'd usually shop daily at the grocer's at the end of the street or at the Co-op on the corner of Dido Street and Everton Road. My mother would send me many times to the Co-op to pick up the messages, as we called a list of groceries. A typical run would be "Peter, go and get a pound of lean rhoded bacon" (nice lean Irish bacon) and so on. I'd leg it down to the shop, pick up the list of food and give our divvie number to the girl at the counter—"seventeen, double nine, four, one." I've remembered that number all my life. Mum would pay the bill at the end of each week.

I think the most used object in our kitchen was the frying pan, and we wouldn't think about throwing any fat away; nothing was thrown away. The fat just stayed in the pan to solidify and be heated up for the next fry-up. Half full of lard, the large fish and chip pan, with its basket for the chips, was left out for the lard to go hard and white, then the pot was hung back on a hook.

Sunday dinner was the most anticipated meal of the week, usually a roast—chicken or a prize leg of lamb or beef—and veggies, and sometimes Yorkshire pud. Plus we'd have a little salad on the side, which we'd smother with Heinz Salad Cream when our frugal dad wasn't watching. Sunday was probably the only day we had a real salad, and my mother would put all the separated lettuce leaves in a bowl of cold water with a large piece of coal to "stiffen up the leaves" as she'd say. We loved the roasted potatoes, carrots and turnip, with miles of oxo cube or Bovril gravy on top, and maybe a little homemade mint sauce over the slice of lamb.

We didn't always have dessert during the week, but always on Sundays. Neapolitan ice cream was my dad's favourite, or straight vanilla, which we'd buy from the sweetshop at the end of the street. Mum could make a good rhubarb or apple pie, and a cheap cake was useful in a trifle, with good ol' Bird's Custard on top. There was also the sweet added bonus, when mum would bring home a big box of broken chocolate bikkies, which she'd get cheap from her job at Jacob's Biscuit factory. As the week went by, she'd monitor how many we were allowed to eat until they were all gone, and you couldn't have any till after you'd eaten you dinner. "It will ruin your appetite," she'd say.

Monday was always Scouse for dinner. The leftovers from Sunday were used up, with some extra spuds and carrots, peas, a little barley sometimes to thicken it, and we'd get stuck into that. The word "Scouse" was probably an abbreviation from "Lobscouse," an old word for a European sailor's stew with meat, potatoes and veggies. I was proud to be called a Scouser.

Tuesday we often had curry and rice. If that's what you'd call an overcooked mush of meat and vegetables sprinkled with curry powder to make it yellow, over a round bed of overboiled rice. Any leftover rice went into the rice pudding the next night, after we had our fish and chips, which mum was really great at. Dad made sure we had fish in the middle of the week and meat on Fridays to show any curious onlookers that we were not Catholics, but instead, "a good Protestant family," as he would say. We also ate fish at other times, like kippers for Sunday breakfast or, one of my favorites, boiled cod with parsley sauce, peas and mashed potatoes. Yum.

All week long, it was meat or fish and potatoes or canned this and that, and especially Saturday night, when it was usually Heinz canned spaghetti with a fried egg on top and some buttered white bread. Good old Wonderloaf. My folks always insisted that we all eat slowly and with good manners. They both detested vulgar behaviour at the dinner table, but we could swap a bit of food around with each other.

Fred, the oldest, was way ahead of us other three in the growing stage and possessed an insatiable appetite. He'd scrape up anything left from anyone's plate and scoff it down. In fact all of us boys would often go to bed hungry as all of Britain was still rationed into the mid fifties. We four would shout down the stairs from the bedroom, "Mam, we're hungry." And she'd tell us to make a sugar butty—margarine on white bread, sprinkled with white sugar—it filled the gap. People found their way around the food shortage by being very frugal and creative with their cooking. Sometimes my mother would send me to the greengrocer's to buy a penny worth of fades (she'd say "a pen'eth of fades"), which was a whole bag of half-rotten fruit for just one penny. I'd take it home, and we would cut off the bad stuff and enjoy a bowl of all that lovely fruit, maybe with a little milk on top. We never bought cream, and my mother never bought whole milk, just sterilized milk, with no cream on top.

3

Cheeky Little Devil

I was a little rebel even at age five.

From our early years, our parents encouraged me and my three brothers—Geoff (b. 1947), David (b. 1946) and Fred (b. 1944)—to have our say, as long as it was respectful.

"Speak up, Peter," my mam would say. "If you don't ask for it, you won't get it, and if you ask for it, you're cheeky. So what are you going to do?"

"Be cheeky," I'd shout back, with a laugh from both of us. It was a little play with words we had once in a while.

My brothers also had a big influence on me to speak my mind. But we'd never talk back or give the eye to our folks, for fear of immediate correction and maybe a belt over the earhole, but on occasion, I crossed swords with me mam over this and that. It was in the genes.

One rainy night, when I was a wee lad, I threatened to "run away from 'ome" when I didn't get my way over something. "OK then," my mam said, as she carried on her knitting, "off you go!" I exited the back kitchen door, and ended up sitting in the coal shed, getting freezing cold and wet. I probably ran away for five minutes that time.

When I was still five, I got lost at Townsend Lane games field on a Saturday morning. The place was a fair distance by bus from our home on Everton Road, and I'd been taken there by my brothers who were playing a couple of school footy games. After the tournament was over, they took off across the street and joined in an impromptu game with a bunch of mates, leaving me to wander around the crowd, wondering where everyone went.

A boy scout, in his uniform, who was about twelve years old, was watching me search for our lads and asked me what was wrong? "I lost me brothers, and I live that way, on the bus." I pointed in some vague direction. He took me by the hand, and we boarded a bus and headed off. I kept watch for my street from the upstairs windows. I remember him telling the bus conductor that he was taking me home, because I was lost so we were given a free ride, as far as we wanted. "We have to go that way now." I said. So off we jumped and quickly climbed onto the next bus, which after a few stops, drove past a familiar spot, the Stanley Park gates, at the corner of Anfield Rd. My Gran lived there, at number 16, just across the street from the Liverpool landmark. "There's Gran's house!" I shouted. We jumped off.

Bang, bang, bang! The boy scout hammered with his little fist, and when my Gran opened the door, he gave a three-fingered salute and told her he'd found me "lost at Clubmoor," and after she laughed a bit at the amusing turn up at her door, and the chivalrous act of our little soldier in short pants, she gave him a thrupenny bit, and some extra money for another bus ride, and directions on how to get me home. When we finally arrived, me mam gave him more money, an extra tanner for being "such a good boy scout." That was big money in them days. I was fed, and the boy scout, who didn't leave his name, took off home. A bit later, while I was playing in the street with all the other kids, my three brothers appeared, sauntering down the street, mud all over them with their togger boots slung over their shoulders. As soon as they saw me at home and having fun, they gave me a piece of their mind for "running off like that. We've been looking for you everywhere!" Our mam told them about the boy in the green cap who did his duty, and how they "should always keep an eye on your little brother when you're out, and not let a five-year-old find his own way home on three busses!"

Thank God for the boy scouts, but they sure have a strange way of saying things?

"We dib, dib, dib, and we dob, dob, dob." Whatever that means?

At nursery school, I was usually well-behaved, but I was also sorely tempted. There I was one day at the Plumpton Street Nursery, standing at the wrought-iron gate that kept us tiny tots from running out onto the main road. As a young policeman was walking past, pushing his bike, I grabbed a good-sized stone and threw it through the gate, hitting his front wheel. "Oy, you!" he shouted, probably amused at the size of the missile-throwing tyrant. "Come back here." I scarpered down the steps, ran inside and quickly slid under the small sandbox that was on a stand above the floor. I stayed there in my bomb shelter for a few minutes, keeping my eye on the door, in case the tall bobby would be coming in to arrest me. One of the women teachers came over and stood right next to the sandbox, and thinking it was safe to come out, I popped out my head and had a moment's glimpse right up her skirt, to her knickers. I dived back under, really embarrassed and would never tell a soul of my first view of a lady's bum.

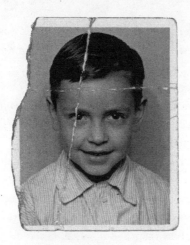

Peter, 5 yrs old, Heyworth Street School

I loved to paint from a very early age, and I had two paintings at the Liverpool Children's Exhibition at the Walker Art Gallery when I was five. I started painting at Plumpton Street Nursery. The *Liverpool Echo* published a photograph of me standing at an easel, with a bunch of kids. I was wearing my little smock and painting a picture of a helicopter; my second watercolor was the children's cartoon character, Bimbo, running away from a copper. The colourful character had a big sack over his shoulder and gold coins were falling out of a hole in the bag. I remember it distinctly. I guess I've always loved bank-robbery movies since I was a kid.

Always inventive, one winter morning at the nursery, I found a picture of a man skiing down a snowy hill, and asked if I could make a pair of skis. "Of course you can Peter." I was given two pieces of wood, about a foot-long each, plus a small ball of string. After twisting and turning the string into some kind of spider's web, I'd finally tied the blocks of wood onto each foot and was attempting to ski down the back stairs, just like in the picture, right? Only there wasn't any snow around. Down I went, head over heels, and after howling for help, I ended up sitting on the staffroom table getting my bloodied head bandaged. When me mam came to pick me up after work, the comment was probably something to do with me moving to the Swiss Alps.

That night I was treated to a trip downtown by a couple of teen-age girls from our street, Annie and Shirley Tatloe. They took me to the Christmas Grotto at Lewis's department store, where all the lights were set up and thousands of toys were on display. A veritable kid's wonderland. The smell of roasting chestnuts and toffee apples outside wafted through the doors and filled the place. Here was probably the first time that I consciously took something that wasn't mine. Inside a small sliding glass cabinet, just at my head height, was a small blue car. A Dinky Toy. The glass was half open, and in went my hand, my eyes looking this way and that, as I gently lifted it and put it into the big pocket of my oversized hand-me-down raincoat.

We walked past the lineup of a dozen kids waiting to see Father Christmas, only to find the jolly old fat fellow in the middle of a huff with a parent whose kid had upset the big man in the red suit. We could see that the front of Father Christmas's legs was all wet, and he was telling the store clerk that he was heading out for a tea break and a smoke. I never thought Father Christmas smoked ciggies or got mad at kids my age. I didn't want to get near that sod, never mind sit on his knee, and I refused when the girls asked me.

On the bus home, I pulled out the little blue tin car, and the girls both burst out laughing, knowing they had not bought the thing for me. I hung my head in shame as they asked me where I found it. "It was behind the window." I said. "Well we'll tell your mam that we bought it for your Chrissy present. OK?" "OK," I said, as I cheered up and enjoyed running its tiny wheels up and down the empty bus seat, across the aisle. The girls enjoyed their smokes and laughed some more as the double-decker made its way up to Breck Road on that dark, rainy December night.

There was a sorry sight: a shoplifting five-year-old with a bloody bandage wrapped round his head, playing with a stolen car, and a new, uneasy feeling about Father Christmas.

At home we celebrated Christmas in a fairly subdued way even though there was very little money to go around, we each got a present. I got a cowboy outfit one year, and some other kids down our street also got the same. The hat, the riding chaps, the silver six-gun and the caps that went bang, bang. It was the fifties, and cowboy movies were very popular in England. We'd pretend to ride horses and fire at the bad guys, but nobody wanted to be the bad guy. Only the good guy rode off into the sunset.

There was also the annual jigsaw puzzle as a gift to the family, and we'd sit around at the kitchen table and put it all together. Mum had the sharpest eyes, and she'd have the pieces placed quicker than anyone. We kept all the decorations from the previous years, like the Chinese paper streamers and colourful paper bells that we'd fold open and pin all over the walls. The three-foot plastic tree was pulled out of its box, stuck on a table and hung with the ornaments and trinkets. We'd also carefully unwrap the pressies on Christmas morning and fold up the paper for next year's presents or maybe a birthday gift. No tearing up paper with abandon at our place. We never really got birthday gifts ourselves, but we'd take something along if we were invited to someone's party, and we'd have a bit of fancy paper for that reason.

With four boys in the house and two parents working and struggling to make ends meet, we kids didn't really expect much at all for Christmas or birthdays. The morning I turned ten, I was presented with a small plastic two-inch racing car from the bottom of a Kellogg's Corn Flakes box, and a thrupenny bit. That was my pressie, and I was made up. Maybe mum made a sponge cake that evening? I don't remember.

Easter was the next celebration, and we'd each get a tiny chocolate egg, but my dad also had other ideas. He was never left in the dust. On

Easter Monday, he'd give us a couple of pennies and tell us to go to the same sweetshop on the corner and buy a bag of broken chocolate Easter eggs. It was the same chocolate as the day before, but a quarter of the price, and we could enjoy a little extra chocolate after teatime, throughout the week. He was frugal all right.

4

When I Was Good: Sunday School

Once I had a Bible, a small, compact full edition of the King James Version complete with a shiny green vinyl cover and gold leaf edging on its rice-paper thin pages. My small magical book contained not only hundreds of pages of book, chapter and verse, but also a handful of strikingly colourful pictures, each depicting the well-known "Old, Old Stories of the Good Ol' Book."

This beautifully illustrated miniature Bible, securely held in my small eight-year-old hand on the way up our dirty, wet, cobblestone street to Sunday school, just twenty minutes walk away, was my very own sword and shield in the battle between good and evil.

Within the pages of my mini-tome, many vibrant pictures were spaced throughout, including the familiar image of the Garden of Eden, with all the animals hanging out in perfect harmony and the lion with the lamb lying down together in the lush green grass. The lion with his well-groomed mane, licking his huge paws with his large vegetarian tongue, enjoying the grassy herbs and fallen fruit in the field; for as yet, the Fall of Creation had not occurred, and he had no desire for the delicious delights of fresh leg of lamb or a nice chunk of beef brisket. The dear little lamb, daydreaming with his big brown pantomime eyes, chewed slowly, while a new commotion seemed to be going on a few feet away in this haven of rest.

That first dramatic picture, forever branding itself into my mind, also had an overweight Santa Claus-like character leaning over the clouds with his big white beard, enraged and shouting at the poor fellow with the Mister Universe body cowering behind a tree. God pointed at the half-eaten apple on the ground, and the terrified Adam, in turn, pointed at the new help-meet, as she was called, who was also crouching behind a bush. While, lo and behold, high up in the adjacent tree, the familiar diamond-patterned questioning snake, wearing an almost hideously human grin, melted into the foliage.

This colourful image is of what happened to the first innocents. As the old story goes: Adam (meaning red) was the first man formed from the red Middle Eastern clay of the Earth, and Eve, his help-meet wife, was later cloned from a rib, which was removed from Adam by magic, while he was deeply sedated. Enter the world's first navel-less couple. She was apparently an afterthought of the surgeon God, when God observed how lonely Adam was feeling in Paradise. From the outset, poor Adam had probably felt a deep curiosity about why all those beasts, birds and fish surrounding him, which he'd personally named, had their respective mates and partners, yet he was left companionless, talking to himself all day, awaiting the arrival of his only conversant contact, his god-friend, that mysterious illusiveness who appeared each evening to have a brief chat and then leave poor Adam to curl up in the meadow to sleep alone.

Oh, how a young mind can swim when exposed to the harsh stories of good verses evil, and as they say in the Catholic church, "Give me a child until he's seven, and I'll give you the man."

One of my favorite songs at Sunday school went like this, "Dare to be a Daniel, Dare to stand alone, Dare to have a purpose firm, and Dare to make it known." Another was "Onward Christian soldiers, marching as to war." We were always taught that it was normal to compare following the faith with war and battle, death and victory. And as the hero of my young life was my dad, the old war veteran, it made sense to behave as a steadfast soldier as I walked, Bible in hand, past onlookers, young and old, some mocking, as my three older brothers and I trudged along Heyworth Street, past my junior school, up to the crest of the hill to arrive at our Sunday school. We went three times on Sundays for years, till we were in our early teens. Fred was the first to stop going, then in sequence down to me.

The upper room, called Berean Hall, was run by an old brother and sister who lived together on Dido Street, which was the next street to ours. The bachelor and spinster, Mister and Miss Howard, as they were respectfully called, were just as old as my dad. Mr. Howard was a First World War veteran, like my dad, and, as time passed, he'd become one of those celibate men who had found some semblance of purpose to his life by helping society in his own humble way, which was to work as a carpenter all week long, and deliver the Good Word on Sunday.

Mr. Howard had a storefront carpentry business just around the corner from us, on Breck Road, and his only mode of transporting his tools and materials was by pushing it along on his large two-wheeled handcart. On Sundays, the two siblings would run a small church group located on the second floor above Mrs. Cartmel's sweet shop on Priory Street.

Each week, after we'd polished up our shoes and were ready to leave for Sunday school, our dad would give us four boys a couple of pennies each to put into the collection box as it was passed around the one-room gathering place. The meager amount barely paid for anything, but these old folks were givers, not takers.

Another special old geezer by the name of Mr. Young was always the first to meet everyone as they came up the rickety old stairs. He was a war vet; there were lots around, but this one had lost his right arm. With his coat sleeve neatly tucked into the pocket of his suit jacket, he would shake hands firmly with his left hand, give you a nudge and a wink, and look down at his pocket where he would always keep a handful of toffees or sweets, and quietly tell you to reach in and take one. He was a kind man, short and bubbly. We knew the jolly man loved all of us kids, and we loved him back. He was like a granddad to us. Mr. Young was a retired man who lived alone, and as the story went, he'd lost his wife and family in the Second World War in a particularly fierce night of bombing in Liverpool, down by the docks.

A sad event happened one night in the summer of 1960. Our family was away on holiday at Lake Windermere in the Lake District. When we returned, we were told that on the previous Sunday, Mr. Young had died. He had been sitting in the back row at the old hall when a bunch of young louts scampered up the stairs into the middle of an evening service, shouting abusive language at the minister and the small group of people gathered. The boys were reprimanded and told to leave, and as they were racing out of the building, one teenaged boy purposely knocked the old fellow over. Mr. Young fell to the floor and had a heart attack. His close friend, Mr. Howard, held him in his arms as he passed on, forgiving the lad who had knocked him over. As was said at his funeral, "If anyone goes through those Pearly Gates, without question, it will be good ol' Mr. Young. A kind, Christian man to the very end." Everyone agreed.

We would sometimes pretend to go to Sunday school, and instead, would buzz off elsewhere and spend the few pennies on sweets or ice cream, making sure to get back home at the usual time. One time when it was just the three of us, Dave, Geoff and me, they wanted to take off to play with their friends, so I turned up with Bible in hand, on my own. Mr. Howard asked me where the other two where, and I lied and said they were sick. My brothers met me after church was over, and I told them what the subject of the meeting was, something like Noah's Ark or David and Goliath, etc. We knew the stories backwards, so when dad asked what the story of the day was, we all had the same answer. Things went fine until Sunday afternoon arrived, and the Howards came by our house to see how my sick brothers were. They said, "We missed them this morning. How are they?" They were met with my dad's response, "What? They're not sick. What do you mean?" It came out that I'd lied, and Dave and Geoff were playing the truant game. After my dad apologized for our absenteeism, and the two enquiring siblings went home, we were all given a good sorting out, and told we'd be going that night, even though we protested that the place was boring, and the People's Church down on Village Street had more kids going there and it was closer. After a week of listening to more of our bellyaching, he let us change churches to keep the peace and closer tabs on us.

We loved going to this new church, and we particularly enjoyed the big, slap-up meals that were served at one fellow's house every Sunday afternoon. When the three o'clock service was over, a pile of us would clamber into the back of Mr. Rowland's huge removal wagon (that was his business), and we'd jam in shoulder to shoulder, hanging onto the ropes around the inside as he slammed the big doors closed, leaving us all in the dark, and drive off at a hair-raising speed to his place on Lower Breck Road. We'd fill our faces and get back in the wagon again to go to the church for the evening service. I know the ride in the back was a good excuse for some of the boys and girls to hang on to each other for a few minutes in the dark, only to reveal their embarrassment when the doors swung open. The young charismatic Pastor Kaye of the People's Church was idolized by the youth, especially the young ladies. He was a handsome man with the gift of the gab.

Each year, on a special day, all the kids in the Sunday school would be called up to the front, one by one, to be congratulated for various things—our good attendance, the accomplishments of our memory of verse and scripture, our tidiness and our good manners—and then be presented with a brand-new small Bible about the same shape and size as the one given out the previous year. By the age of eleven, I'd accumulated about five of these, but the little green tattered and torn book with all those lovely colourful pictures and my pencil under-lines was my all-time favorite. Later, as an enquiring adult, I learned the book I studied was actually a compilation of sixty-six books that spanned three millennia of Pagan, Jewish and Christian history. The best-selling composition of all time, replete with plagiarized Sumerian, Assyrian and Egyptian mythologies.

At morning assembly in school, we'd sing a hymn, listen to the reading of some scripture and always end with the Lord's Prayer. At home, because my father was an enthusiastic student and expounder of the Biblical way, he encouraged his four boys to also understand, study and memorize scriptures from the Old and New Testaments. It was almost like living with a dictatorial bishop as a dad. Everything seemed to revolve around that Big Black Book on the table. One year, he'd heard that they were teaching the memorization of the Ten Commandments at evening classes down the road at St. Benedict's. He asked if we'd like to go. Nobody was interested, but I agreed, so he sent me two nights a week, where I studied, rehearsed and memorized perfectly, word for word, Exodus, chapter 20.

My dad would often quote book, chapter and verse. Even when he was explaining something non-religious, he'd still quote something. I think he reveled in the fact that he'd been a well respected part-time preacher, and probably missed those youthful days of being up on the podium. Someone once told me, "If anyone could bring you to your knees, it was Albert."

On our living room table, we kept our humble family library. There would be three or four different translations of the Holy Bible, as we were told to call it. "Holy" being emphasized. The King James Version was the one we read and memorized. My dad, who emphasized its

poetic pungency, would stand me, when I was little, on the table to recite a few verses to impress anyone of like mind that visited our house.
After that big old family Bible, there was the Tyndale translation, a
small copy of a Latin Vulgate. Two interlinear Testaments; Greek to
English New and Hebrew to English Old. We also had a variety of
other books: a large *Oxford English Dictionary*, *The Pilgrim's Progress*, then
Eusabius, Josephus and Herodotus, all early historians and philoso-
phers. A small collection of classics like *King Solomon's Mines*, Dickens
and a couple of Boy's Own Annuals, *Gulliver's Travels* and the like. Kids'
adventure books, such as *Treasure Island* or *Tom Sawyer* were on a side
shelf, away from the "important" reading material.

When Fred changed from the old Upper Room to a Methodist
church where he had a few mates, he asked me to join him one
Sunday morning. They were selling tickets for their annual church
picnic to be held at a campground in the country, and my big brother Fred mentioned that his ten-year-old brother could recite the Ten
Commandments, so I was offered a picnic ticket if I could recite this
passage of scripture in front of the church. I didn't know this crowd,
and was a bit nervous, but after proving my memory skills, a free ticket
was put into my hand, along with a cheerful applause from the con-
gregation.

In my junior class at Heyworth Street, I was also known as the
memory man (as I was reminded decades later by an old classmate,
Alan Bruce). Sometimes the teacher would have me recite some of the
well-known psalms at the front of the classroom. I was a determined
boy.

5

Laundry Day on Everton Road

U sually on Tuesdays, my mother would pile up all the family's dirty laundry in the old pram that had served us as babies, and off she'd go to the public washhouse to do the weekly load. Yes, that big black pram took up a lot of space in the back kitchen, and the large wheels made it a bit easier to push over the front steps and through the house to where it was parked in a corner until needed. Pushing that pram down the jigger was nigh to impossible because it was narrow, and the rubbish all along made it awkward even for two people to pass.

My mum mentioned that sometimes when she pushed little me around in the pram, off to the shops or elsewhere, people would smile and look at me and ask her "Is his dad a Spaniard?" and she'd laugh. I was the only one of her four boys that had jet black eyes and black hair. Dave and Geoff both had blue eyes and were blond, and Fred had hazel eyes and brown hair like both my mam and dad. When Geoff and Dave were little, she'd have the two of them in the pram at the same time, because they were only eleven months apart. She took a photo once and called it the "two Prime Ministers" because chubby Geoff looked like Churchill and David was like Macmillan.

While we were small, we wanted to show our mum what strong boys we were by helping her push the big heavy load of laundry along the street, across Everton Road and then down Rupert Lane, past the old round Everton Lock-up, built in 1787, which became the insignia of the famous Everton Football Club. Then we'd roll the pram further down the steep hill to Netherfield Road public washhouse, where dozens of hard-working mothers would gather everyday except on Sundays.

While all the women washed the dirty laundry in the large tubs of steaming-hot soapy water, some singing the old familiar songs in unison, we kids would run around the place or go back up the hill to Rupert Lane park, kick a ball and play on the swings or sail around the old wooden maypole, killing time until our mums were finished. After doing the hot wash, they'd rinse and put the piles of soaking wet clothes through the hand wringers, then fold it all, still wet, and press it back into the pram. We'd get behind it together, the load weighing twice as much as before, and push our squeaky wheeled pram home, back up Rupert Lane's hill. Our mam would hang it out on the two washing lines that stretched across the grimy old backyard. There, the laundry flags, from bed sheets to the dozens of boys' undies, flapped away, and sometimes the chilly wind would dry everything up like hard cardboard. We'd rush to pull them all off the lines if it looked like serious rain was coming; otherwise we'd judge the moment to fold and bring everything in.

The later years of drying clothes in a machine could not be compared with the smell of fresh, wind-dried clothes and towels. There was life in them, if you didn't mind drying yourself on a towel as stiff as a sheet of plywood. Our mam never owned an electric dryer in her long life; it was always the washing line. I can only imagine the work and difficulties my mother had in having four boys in five years and raising them in that environment.

Mum and her boys, Lake District holiday, 1955

6

Ancestors and the World Wars

I grew up in a family of working-class survivors, way back through my stalwart grand-folks, Charles Edward and Annie on my dad's side and Ethel (Ettie) and George on my mum's side. A northern European mix, stretching from Danzig, Prussia, on the Baltic Sea, where Charlie was born and raised by his dad, the gun maker, and then, at age thirteen, ran off to sea, as a cabin boy; to the origins of George and Ettie—Aberdeen, Scotland, and Liverpool.

Both my grandmothers were born in Liverpool, Annie the orphan and Ettie with the Scottish blood. Because Annie Warburton was adopted, her last name Cardwell was added, and she probably met Charlie when he sailed into the port of Liverpool, in his merchant seaman days. This was in the late 1880s. So, when Annie and Charlie tied the knot, her father disowned her, and she was ostracized from the family because of his dislike for Germans. Her dad apparently owned a large warehouse and hardware business, but the mean-spirited fool later lost everything to his gambling habits. After the young couple married they rented a small house at 32 Crete Street, Kirkdale, raising ten kids in that four roomed shoebox.

Albert, my dad, the third child, was born on June 4, 1896, the very day Henry Ford test-drove his first car, the Quadricycle in Detroit, and seven years before the Wright brothers introduced the first plane. So, to me as a young boy born in 1950, my dad was an old man. The technological advances in his lifetime were staggering and he died in 1988 at age ninety-two.

After Charlie quit the sea, he found a job at the docks, rising to a good position of foreman stevedore. He also found work there later, for his sons, my dad and his brother Ted when they were teenagers. My dad was previously apprenticed to a brass foundry at fourteen, but soon left and went to the docks with his older brother.

Granddad Charlie was a dapper fellow, as his only picture shows, and during those late 1800s and even after the First World War, the Prussian and his English wife, Annie, suffered their fair share of discrimination. For many years in Britain, there was a boiling antagonism toward the Germanic tribes, whose background, historically speaking, enveloped all the localized nations of Saxon origin. England often conveniently forgets its own ancient connection to Saxony, especially with the royal family, who changed their name from the House of Hanover to the House of Windsor in 1917 to appease the British public at that time.

Sometime in the 1920s, as the story goes, my Grandmother Annie came home from the shops to find Charlie collapsed in the house, flat out on the floor, with the oven leaking coal gas into the house. She ran outside and turned off the main gas tap and dragged him out, feet first onto the street, as the neighbours ran to help, and some scarpered for cover in case the place was about to blow up. Charlie barely recovered, and had a bad set of lungs for the rest of his life. My other granddad, George had a similar problem with his chest, except his was due to the mustard gas in the First World War. Both my granddads died at middle age due to pulmonary emphysema.

Ettie was now left alone with four kids to raise, my mother being the oldest at eighteen when her dad passed on. A few years later, Ettie remarried another man with a heart of gold, Big Henry he was called.

Poverty and the heat of wars had molded my resilient family. At the beginning of the First World War, Charles Edward, who'd been living in Liverpool for twenty-five years, since 1890, was interned in 1915 at a camp in the Isle of Man, by the British government because of his Prussian background while at the same time his three oldest sons, Ted, Albert and Johnny were signing up to fight for Britain against the Hun in France. Ted and my dad both fought at the battle of the Somme, Ypres and other places. Dad was severely wounded, and Ted, just a hundred yards away, lost his life for his country of birth and never met his new-born son back in Liverpool. My cousin Lewis.

To avoid further discrimination, these three Liverpool brothers talked among themselves and signed up under a different last name— Hayes, a good English name that sounded close to their real one. They would certainly be ridiculed in the trenches, and many English lads changed their foreign sounding surnames. Most of my aunties, uncles and cousins were buried with that adopted name, but some of our clan, my three brothers included, reverted back to our original name, Haase, later in our teens.

My dad entered the First World War at the age of eighteen, telling the recruitment officer he was nineteen, which was the proper call-up age, and getting the nod and a wink in response as he was signed up. He was one of so many young boys who were given a "dead man's number." Six months later, and three months after he'd entered the heat of things, he received his real service number. After signing up, he was sent for his three months of training and then to the troop carrier, across the English Channel to the Western Front.

My mother Mary was born in 1920 in Walton, Liverpool, the eldest of four. It was her job to keep her brothers—Johnny, Harold and Henry—in line and make sure they behaved. After early schooling at Major Lester Junior, Liverpool, she graduated from Evered Avenue, where she excelled in all her classes. Mary was a well-rounded person, attractive, smart, loving, witty, brave and hard-working. Calling a spade a spade, she never minced her words. She and my dad never swore but returned idiocy with statements like "You need to get your bumps felt!" referring to a person who'd been hit in the head, to a point of acting stupid or were uttering foul words. Where others might swear for some reason, my dad would usually say, or shout, "Dear Doctor!"

There was quite a difference in my parents' ages. When they met in 1943, Mary was twenty-three and Albert was forty-seven. She was working at Bibby's, a manufacturing place that was supporting the war effort, and he was working for the city council, on the roads. He and his brother Tommy were also part-time preachers, and Mary began attending their services in a small hall. She was impressed with the young raconteur who sported a pencil moustache like Errol Flynn. My uncles mentioned to me many years later that their sister Mary had a steady boyfriend from Wales whose name was Idris. Everyone thought they were going to tie the knot, "till Albert came along." They married and were together for forty-five years. Mum died in Australia, in 2014, at ninety-four. She outdid dad by two years. Both my parents died peacefully in their sleep.

Albert was also a man of eloquent speech, a lay preacher from his thirties, and quite an orator for a man with a poor education. Dad liked to get his point across, but fell short with patience and emanated a dogmatic stance when he knew he was being out-smarted with religion versus scientific conversation. On occasion he would argue, but never seriously quarrel, with my three atheist communist uncles, Johnny, Harold and Henry, when they visited us. They'd corner him on his unwavering faith, and he'd always conclude the meeting with his usual evangelical message for them all to repent and get saved. The three of them would laugh at his stubbornness, while my mother, their sister, would try and keep the peace. We never got to see much of our relatives because of my dad's stubborn religious ways. No one wanted to come over to be Bible bashed. I had lots of cousins I unfortunately knew nothing about.

7

Everton Before the Demolition

The name Everton is derived from the Saxon word *eofor*, meaning "wild boar that lives in forests." Everton was settled in 1094, and until the late eighteenth century, it was a small rural parish. By the early nineteenth century, with an increase in working-class population and demand for housing, Everton began to be built up with back-to-back terraced houses and hundreds of connecting streets. By 1835, it became part of Liverpool. By 1850, the Irish Potato Famine had furthur increased the teeming population and expanse of slums. Over 90,000 Irish settled down in Liverpool out of the 1.3 million who passed through the port to the New World in the USA and Down Under.

Our short cobblestone street in Everton was named after the Greek mythological character Cadmus. He was the man to whom Homer, the ancient Greek poet (we also had a Great Homer Street), attributed the founding of the city of Thebes. Cadmus was also credited by the ancient Greeks with introducing the original alphabet, another of one of the many feathers in his cap.

Everywhere in our town, roads and streets had colourful names derived from lists of famous people, countries or historical events. Across from our street was Rupert Lane, probably named in remembrance of the Siege of Liverpool in 1644 by Prince Rupert's Royalists against Oliver Cromwell's Roundheads. And just up the road on Heyworth Street, on the Everton Brow, Liverpool's highest ridge, the primary school we four boys attended was built on the site of one of Cromwell's barracks and cavalry stables. The height of the brow allows an extensive panorama of the city of Liverpool, including a distant view of the River Mersey.

Another street nearby was Scotland Road, affectionately known as Scotty Road; it became part of the stagecoach road to Scotland in the 1770s. Hundreds of Scottish masons and bricklayers came to build the docks and city centre during the Industrial Revolution.

In the early development of Liverpool, the building of many of the streets came with varying levels of pomp and ceremony, like baptismal services. The naming rituals of thoroughfares, especially historically important names that had a patriotic flavour, touted the value of commerce such as Liverpool's shipping background. One example was Beacon Lane, where, in the old days, a light set high up on the heights of Everton guided the ships in and out of the River Mersey's entrance. Battles and commerce have often given birth to street names. There's an old standard in Britain that a town only becomes a city when a cathedral is built. Liverpool has two cathedrals, one Protestant and one for the Catholics, which we called 'Paddy's Wigwam'.

Liverpool was established by decree in 1207, signed and sealed by King John. Its handy little port was recognized as a useful departure point, along with northern Wales, for sending soldiers across the Irish Sea to the Emerald Isle, to take on those "Wicked, hairy people" who understandably had a big problem with the interfering English, much the same way the early Americans had a problem with the Empire.

As the centuries passed, the small town stretched her arms and legs from the water's edge, in very determined and meaningful ways. The Pool, as we affectionately call her, also had the longest continually running ferry system in the world. Operating for over eight hundred years, it carries passengers and goods back and forth across the River Mersey to the Wirral Peninsula, a short distance by land from Wales.

8

Bombs Away

A lot of the Everton area was slums. The district had endured Second World War bombing and destruction, night after night. During those raids, if there wasn't enough warning to get to a more secure bomb shelter, my folks would cuddle up together under the old staircase until the sirens sounded the all clear when the Jerry planes had passed.

On some heavy nights, when the Luftwaffe came to visit the many miles of docks, warehouses and ships, the bombing would stretch way up the hill into our district. My mother told me that one night our kitchen windows were blown out and a few nearby houses were flattened. Each morning after a raid, the news spread quickly about who had suffered loss of life, limb and property. But through the misery and torment, it was "Ye Olde English Fortitude" and sense of humour that pulled the people through.

A large bomb shelter was built on the Wirral side of the Mersey, in Tranmere, where up to seven thousand people a night would gather into the long tunnels. When the air raid sirens sounded, usually at night, the multitudes would hurry into the tunnels and camp out till morning arrived, when the bombing scares were over. The throngs of sheltering folks would intermingle and muck in, laying out their sleeping bags, blankets and pillows; share cigarettes; sing, dance and generally support and cheer each other up. The Air Raid Precaution Squad would keep order, and the noise would be limited so everyone along the subterranean passageways could have a good night's kip. There were no strangers in those crowds; everyone was in the same boat till it was time to pack up and get off home or to work.

Some families didn't see their homes for days, because the routine was shelter and work, the same, day after day. When there was respite from bombing, people finally discovered if their luck was good or bad, as they stood on their street and saw their houses either standing or destroyed.

While my dad worked as a road labourer, he was also being retrained as a machinist. This new skill enabled him to start work on aircraft engines, and because he had served in the army during the First World War, he also signed up as a captain with a local Air Raid Precaution squad. Here, at the ARP, he was again thrust into war. Dad and others were of the opinion that there was only one war, with a twenty-year interlude, when Britain and her allies slept—unprepared for the new nightmare that was to come.

The ARP was similar to the Home Guard elsewhere, except they were also trained as firemen. Part of their duties would be directing people towards the nearest shelters, and then they'd remain on duty outside, as the bombing continued, working on the hoses, putting out burning buildings, helping the injured and removing the dead.

My dad, received many medals for his service in both world wars, but his ARP medal was the one I looked at the most. He kept some of his medals in a small box in the sideboard drawer, but others he'd thrown away earlier, like thousands did in protest over how the veterans were treated, and the political games that were played with people's lives. This particular big bronze medal for bravery in the rescue of injured people in the raids was the one with the Britannica helmet on the one side, and his name written around the edge. Later at eighty-five, he wrote a letter to the Queen, asking if he could get replacement medals, and he received duplicates.

He once spoke tearfully to us boys of the time he had to carry two dead little girls over his shoulders, down a ladder from a burned house. He was reticent to talk too much of his experiences in the wars, but we lads would bother him enough to get a story once in a while.

9

Bommie Night

B ommie night, as we called it, a slang term for bonfire night, was the exciting annual celebration of the unsuccessful assassination attempt on King James 1 on November 5, 1605.

The would-be assassin, Guy Fawkes, alias Guido, was a discontented man, born in York, England, who fought for the Spanish against the Dutch and returned to England, where he tied in with a bad bunch of lads who wanted to send the King heavenward with the help of a few barrels of gunpowder.

Poor Guy (no pun intended) was roped into guarding the "gunny" in the basement of the House of Lords. The King was to be there that morning for the grand opening, but as the building was swept with inspection, before the arrival of His Highness, the silly lout Guy was discovered sitting in the corner, with his feet up, filling his face with Yorkshire pudding and a tankard of home brew. He was nabbed, tortured and after spilling the beans on his buddies, sentenced to the greatest punishment of the day: hung, drawn and quartered.

It's always interested me how the whole Bonfire Night thing evolved from celebrating a thwarted assassination of an early monarch to burning an effigy on top of a heap of old discarded furniture and wood. Depending on which part of town you lived in, the burning effigies bore striking resemblances to Guy Fawkes or other identifiable figures like the Pope or King Billy or a disliked politician. Here was an annual event when religion and politics went up in smoke on the same raucous night. No wonder the people of Britain celebrated with unbridled festivity.

On November 5, in the hours after school and before the bonfire was ready to be lit, youngsters would wheel around their homemade Guy Fawkes, stuffed dummies in prams or barrows, asking for "a penny for the Guy," which went into the collection for fireworks for the evening. The effigy was placed as securely as possible on the very top of the fire, usually with a few fireworks—rockets, bangers, Catherine wheels, Roman candles, rip-raps and the like—blasting away as the heat and flames released them.

Fireworks, of all kinds, were sold to anyone who wanted to buy them. Little kids would pour into the corner shops and hand over a few pennies for some bangers or other explosive devices, and no questions were asked. Some kids would light the fuse and push them through the front letterboxes of people they wanted to alarm or wake up at night. We'd throw lit fireworks at each other on the way to school, stand across the street and fire Roman candles in a duel. I was one of many kids who lit a banger or firecracker and waited for the fuse to burn down a bit before throwing it, only to be surprised with a short fuse and a burned hand. During that first week of November, there were always reports of some kids succumbing to harsh burning injuries, which sent the message throughout the schools and homes to be extra careful with these recreational explosives.

As the fires subsided and became low and manageable open-air infernos, we'd throw potatoes into the edge of the red-hot cinders to cook and be eaten with butter in your gloved hand. A "hot potato" with a little ash and butter is a tasty thing. Amazingly, the cities of England lived every year with the anticipated workload of having to repave and repair hundreds of roads in the following days, due to the fires destroying the surfaces of the streets. The bonfires in parks left large burned piles of debris and ashes for the parks crews to clean up. A little bit of overtime boys?

"Remember, remember the fifth of November, gunpowder, treason and plot. I know of no reason why gunpowder treason should ever be forgot."

Part Two

Hungry in the Pool

10

At the Evvy Picture House

e lived just opposite the run-down movie house gloriously called the Everton Palace Movie Theatre. It was here, at the Evvy Picture House, as we called it, where we kids would line up with our pennies to buy a ticket for the Saturday afternoon matinee. Sometimes a bold boy or girl, after paying their way in, would run through to the bottom of the aisles and open the exit doors to let a few sneaky kids bunk in for free. Yours truly being one of them when I was about eight. Some of us would bring along an apple or orange and, if you had the means, maybe a chocolate bar or bottle of lemonade to share with your mates. Our most favourite snack food was a bag of crisps. Each bag would have a small amount of salt, separately wrapped in a square piece of blue paper, twisted together, two if you were lucky. You could have the crisps with or without the salt. But we all know, kids love salt.

Besides madly filling our hungry gobs, we'd scream, laugh and watch wide-eyed as the noisy old projector ran through the new episodes, dancing its speckled light and spotty images across the battered old screen: black-and-white movies like *Flash Gordon*, Gabby Hayes, *The Lone Ranger*, the Three Stooges, Spanky and the rest of the Little Rascals, Frankenstein's monster, Laurel and Hardy, etc., intermeshed with a selection of colourful cartoons, Tom and Gerry, Popeye and

Opposite: Dido Street No 16, 1966

Olive Oil, ad infinitum. More than once, when the film broke and had to be re-spliced, the big white-silver sheet, which normally displayed the movie, became the object of a spontaneous target practice for the unruly in the front rows, hurling apple cores and wrappers as hard as they could to make it shake and bounce. One Saturday afternoon, a big lad, named Lenny Gaskell, from our street, about fifteen or so, threw a half-empty bottle of Coca-Cola, splattering the brown liquid across the middle of the already weatherworn screen. He made his quick escape through the side exit. This mess on the screen returned us to a show where everyone in the middle of the picture appeared with shiny brown stripes down their faces, even the lily-white English heroine on the Tarzan movie.

We loved the calamity and wild chaos allowed once a week in the dark, basically unsupervised theatre, which also became an opportune place to pass the ciggies amongst ourselves, slowly turning the atmosphere into a blue haze. The smoking age was sixteen, and if an usherette shone her light here or there to see who was lighting up, the loud response from the older kid would be that they were old enough to smoke and to put out the torch and mind their own business. We'd cover the red end of each lit ciggie with our hands to screen it from view as we took deep drags and passed them along the line. There were always some kids we didn't know who'd try to steal them from us, but the big lads from our street would sort that out. In the fifties and sixties, smoking anywhere and everywhere was allowed and expected. It was even tolerated in hospital beds. All the seats in planes or theatres had ashtrays. Public transportation allowed smoking (only upstairs on buses, of course) and in all restaurants and cafes. Teachers smoked in the staff room or the outside playgrounds, and we'd also be hiding in the corners of the schoolyard, sending up our smoke signals. Needless to say, every pub was clouded with blue smoke. By contrast, lighting up anywhere in the West now usually gets a different response, mainly disapproving, and today's youth would be amazed at how common it used to be. Yet, all you need to do is take note of how much smoking and drinking was done in the old movies; all the actors and singers smoked. Everyone was hooked on nicotine. We had many names for cigarettes in those days: fags, coffin nails, penny loosies, stumps or dog ends, ciggies, cheroots and smokes.

11

My First English Bobby

At the ripe old age of eight, I was booked by a young English bobby for starting a fire in a bombed house and then giving him a false name. The most exciting places to play were the bombed houses and alleyways. I'd begun smoking already, and most days after school, a crowd of us patched-up ragamuffins would frequent some of the familiar bombed sites and pass around a ciggie or two. We'd quickly exhaust our meager supply that we could buy at the corner store for only one penny each, which we called penny loosies. We'd buy smokes and say we were buying for our parents. No questions asked.

Sometimes if we had no money, which was usually the case, one of our mates would steal a couple of smokes from his parents; others would cruise the cafes or shops and pick up the discarded smokes from the ashtrays, take out the tobacco and reroll it in small squares of paper, usually newspaper. We'd all puff it back, get dizzy, laugh, cough, and our sore throats would make us spit a lot. If our parents had known what we were up to, boy would we be in for it.

One cold afternoon while we were gathered in an old three-story shell of a house, we decided to light a fire in the middle of the main floor to heat the place up a bit. As we all gathered around the large blaze, warming our hands, it began to get bigger and bigger till we had to run the hell out. As we scarpered, my mate and I both ran into the path of this cop who was parking his pedal bike outside the smoking house. He grabbed us both by the jacket and apprehended us right there. After he'd stood us to attention, he pulled out his little black book and asked me first for my name and address.

This was the first time I'd been booked by a boy in blue, and I'd been coached by my older brothers and friends never to give your real name or address to a rozzer, as we sometimes called them. The cops would usually book you and send you on your way, and you'd most likely never see the same one again, so you didn't risk much by lying. So my immediate response to his question was "Peter Thomas, sir." I suddenly realized that my mate, standing right next to me, was the real Peter Thomas. We looked at each other in some kind of disbelief.

"Thomas?" said the cop, as he knew something was up. "Are you Peter Thomas?"

"No, sir, I am," called out my mate.

"And your name, young fella?"

"Peter Hayes, sir."

"Mmmm, I see".

After he had written down our particulars, we walked a few blocks, dropped the real Thomas off at his house, then, walking alongside the policeman as he wheeled his bike down a few more roads, we finally arrived at my house. On the way through the streets, people gazed and stared at us. Someone even shouted across the narrow road, "Caught yourself a bank robber, bobby?" I held my head down as we passed people I recognized and shuddered as we reached the front door. He knocked: bang bang bang. My mother was home cooking the dinner, and when she opened the door and stood there in her apron with her hair pulled up in a scarf, she couldn't believe the embarrassment of me being part and parcel of a bunch of louts who'd set fire to a bombed house and then, crime of all crimes, sin of all sins, lying to a policeman?

"Just you wait till your dad gets home," she shouted and then politely bid the cop goodbye and closed the door. Then all hell broke loose, and she began to chase me around the house with a wet towel. I faced the bigger consequences later, when the old fellow got home. After a good spanking and a talking to, it was teatime, but I just sat there, carving pictures in my mashed potatoes with my fork.

"Eat up, you! Do you think your mother comes 'ome from work and makes dinner so you can sit and sulk and play with your food? There's a million hungry boys in Africa who'd kill for that meal. Eat up and get to bed, all o' yeh."

We did as we were told, and were off to bed. My brothers thought it a great laugh and knocked me around a bit and made me laugh too, which, thankfully, distracted me from my sore, red arse. Our house was so small and cramped that Dave, ten, Geoff, nine, and I still shared an old double bed, while lucky Fred, the eldest at twelve, had graduated to his own single cot, near the gas fire, in our tiny upstairs room.

We'd slept two at each end, so you can imagine the tickling and grabbing, before we'd finally settle down and pass out, in a tangled mess of legs and arms. Sometimes if the bedtime craziness got louder and boisterous, my dad would come stomping up the stairs, pull back the blankets, as we struggled to hang on to our safety net, and give us a couple of hits over the backside with his old army belt. That would soon shut us up, and there's nothing like a sore rump to put one into a silent mode. Most nights, if we remembered, we'd line up at the kitchen sink and scrub our teeth with powered peppermint toothpaste, which came in a tin, till our gums bled. We thought our teeth weren't cleaned properly till we spat a bit of blood. After we brushed, we'd stand in a line outside the back door and see who could piss the farthest across the backyard, aiming at the grid in the middle of the ten-by-twelve concrete slab. If it was a cold night, we'd warm up our pillows in front of the coal fire and run up the dancers, (the stairs) to bed.

The next morning, after my encounter with the bobby, was a new day. My parents weren't the type to harp on. When it's over, it's over.

12

The Dentist's Chair

I remember watching a black-and-white movie, where an old fellow was strapped to his chair, a string tied between a doorknob and his bad tooth. The door was slammed closed and out flew his tooth. Well, a visit to the dentist in the mid-fifties in our town was just one step up from that, and not always the most comforting moment for a seven-year-old whose teeth needed attention. I was sent by the school one day to see the dentist about pain in my gums because my baby teeth were not falling out easily enough. I'd pulled a few loose ones out myself, but there were some hangers-on. I'd cleaned up my collection of tiny teeth and checked on them every morning and night to make sure they were still under my pillow, but four boys in a bed usually meant pillows move around a lot and you don't want to be sleeping on a small cluster of teeth. So no pennies were ever found from the tooth fairy, which my dad would scoff at anyway. He told us, from an early age, that these ideas like Easter bunnies, Santa Claus and tooth fairies were all just made-up stories to make people spend their hard-earned cash. So it was futile to shove a tooth under your pillow in our house, but we did it anyway. Mum was more lenient and softer, and sometimes would slip us a few pennies for sweets. When dad wasn't around, she'd sometimes say, "He's not like our crowd. He's a bit hard." But that wasn't completely true. He was generous when he was in the mood—ice-cream on Saturday night.

So, with a note in my pocket from school, I took a walk by myself down Everton Road to see the dentist, with an appointment to turn up in the afternoon. I arrived with the expectation of a quick easy visit. My first visit ever to a dentist. I was unaware as to what lay in wait for me behind the door on the second floor.

I entered the office, and was led into the large cold room with a dentist's chair in the middle. I sat in the oversized seat, and my arms were tied with straps to the armrests to keep me from moving while he worked. The dentist took a keen look inside my mouth and decided to remove four troublesome teeth, two top and two bottom. Now that I was immobilized, the dental assistant put a large square rubber block in my mouth, and the man dressed in white pulled out the problem teeth. It was done in less than five minutes and without anesthetic. Not too bad after all. I rinsed my mouth out, was given a cloth to hold over my mouth, then sent home. I was a tad disappointed, thinking they gave you sweets for needles across the street and ice cream over here at the dentist. But not so. I arrived home with a bloody rag over my sore gob, and was met by Peggy, the next-door neighbour with the heart of gold. She caught sight of me heading home a little early before the rest of the family and ushered me down to the corner shop, bought me a chocolate ice cream to calm things down and took me in, out of the cold, till my mum got home from work.

Her son, Jimmy, was my age and suffered with epilepsy. We'd often walk to school together, and one day I helped him when he collapsed and went into a fit on the street. I loosened his tie and belt, and when he recovered and got back to his feet, I took him back home to his mam. At school I'd keep a watchful eye on him and helped him through more of his fits. I knew how to tend to his problem, and Auntie Peggy, as we called her, was very thankful for my help and treated Jimmy and me to a day out the fairgrounds at Southport beach. We went on a few rides, like the helter-skelter and the roller coaster, and Jimmy didn't have one bout of an epileptic problem with all the spinning and hurtling around. Fish and chips on the bus home sent us both to sleep, along with the exhaustion of an exciting day. It was even better than most trips to New Brighton, and it was a great time, even though it rained buckets.

I grew to be a bit leery of dentist visits after that, and when I was fourteen, I had to get some teeth drilled and filled at a dentist in Lee Park. His name was Dr. Butcher, of all things, and he did the whole nerve-wracking job, drilling and filling, without anesthetic. But one time in between these two mentioned hair-raising visits, I do remember a blue gas mask coming down over my face to knock me out and the familiar words, "Count down from ten, Peter." And when I got to seven, I went into a dream. Why do they always ask you to count down and not count up?

13

A Case for the Cane

My next initiation that year, was my baptism into the harsh reality of corporal punishment in school: the cane.

For countless years in Britain, striking across the hands or the backside, as a means of bringing attention to a child's disobedient or disruptive ways, was the norm. In the school system, laws guided a teacher in the process of correction. They allowed only a certain number of strikes, and no more, for such infringements as fighting, stealing, swearing, insolence towards the teacher, lying, disruption of the classroom and on and on. Each violation awarded a different number of hits, usually based on the discretion of the teacher or headmaster, depending on how sadistic they felt that day.

Up to about the age of seven, children who were out of hand sometimes got a smack across the hand or the backside, or even a clout across the earhole, but after that age, it was assumed by the law of the land that a more severe and effective method would be in keeping. Hence the introduction of the three-or four-foot-long rattan cane. The strap was mainly used elsewhere in the world such as the States or Canada, but in Britain, the cane was the main instrument of correction. Unlike its Asian cousin, bamboo, rattan is solid and not hollow. It is also easily bent and shaped, and sometimes the end of the whistling stick had a curved handle, like a shepherd's crook, that the wielding administrator held firmly while whipping it through the air at the target, the victim's hand or arse. Whack, whack, whack.

On one bright, happy day, my friend Georgie Miles and I had arrived back at the classroom earlier than usual after school dinner. We were still pretty hungry, and to our delight, lo and behold, there sitting in the middle of the teacher's desk was a half-eaten sandwich. We didn't think twice about it, and before you could say "Ow's yer father?', the cheese and tomato sarney, which we thought was disguarded, was gone. Gulp! Half each! Soon the class was full, and we were all sitting at our desks waiting for the teacher to start, when the visiting student teacher from Malaysia, who was assisting for a short while, whispered something quietly to our teacher, causing Mr. Simmons to halt his talking and address us in this manner.

"Class, sit up and pay attention. Our guest teacher, Mr. Woo, has just informed me that before we left this room, at dinner break, he had left a sandwich on this desk, and upon returning, found that it has disappeared. We have a thief in our midst."

He continued, "I'm going to go around this classroom, from desk to desk, and you will stand, one after the other, and tell me, yes or no, did you take that sandwich from this desk? We'll start with you, Driscoll?"

"No, sir!"

"Sit down. You, Carlisle?"

"No, sir."

"Sit down. Brown?"

"No, sir."

"Sit!"

And on it went. The question circled right round the class, and none of us admitted to anything. The next utterance from Mr. Simmons was a threat: "OK then. If none of you will admit to have taken it, then all of you will receive one of the cane across the hand. We'll start with you, Church." Simmons knew what he was doing. The very boy he knew was the weakest link in our chain of silence was going to be the first he'd scare. And it worked. George and I had bragged to a couple of lads about what we'd done, and half the class by now knew it was us two. Johnnie Church held his head down and coughed out my name.

"Hayes took the sandwich," he squealed.

"Stand to your feet, Hayes! Did you steal Mr. Woo's sandwich?"

Oh god, I thought, not more trouble? And just as I was about to speak and reach down and pull the word Yes from my guts and out of my mouth, George sprang to his feet and blurted out, "Sir, it was me, sir." The class broke out in an uproar; seldom did we enjoy such drama as this.

"No, sir, it was me," I shouted to the front. "I was hungry, sir, after lunch and…"

"No, sir, it was me," George insisted.

"Class, be quiet. Both of you get here. NOW."

Stamping his foot, he turned around to reach up on the wall for one of his favourite tools of correction, his three-foot-long, half-inch diameter rattan extension of his masculinity. We were stood to the side and glanced at each other as brothers-in-arms about to face the firing squad. The command was given.

"Hayes, you first. There's a punishment in this school for stealing. Hands out. Out straight! Out straight, I say, man!" Man? I thought. Maybe this is how we become men; we turn into men through pain, like soldiers. My father's words rang through my young head, "Yes, son, I joined the army. It made a man out of me."

Both my arms were stretched sideways, highly stretched out like a tiny young fledgling bird, standing on the edge of its nest, about to try its first leap into the unknown. As he lifted up the cane towards the ceiling, he accidentally hit the old hanging light, and it made a clinking noise. He looked up and repositioned his feet and giggled a bit to the class in a hideously crazy voice that was new to us. He was enjoying this. The class response was total silence, as every eye was on me as I stood, shaking with my eyes jammed closed, ready for the first hit.

WHACK. "Ow, ow, ahhh."

"Now the other hand, hold it up. Up!" As he tapped at my knuckles with the stick, my palm facing the ceiling, and my very sore finger tips of my right hand were in my mouth to ease the pain.

"That's it, hold it there." WHACK.

"Now back to your seat. Miles, hands out." And so it was dished out to George too.

We both slumped over our desks. Two small eight-year-old boys, crying onto our exercise books. The message was delivered, loud and clear. You'd better behave, cause this punishment hurts like hell.

We were then split up, having occupied adjacent seats. George was sent to the back, and Church was put next to me for the remainder of the year. The class snitch, the traitor, the grass. Mr. Simmons continued with the lesson, allowing us to sit quietly in our seats. The young student teacher appeared a little withdrawn over the whole commotion, and he probably felt responsible for the way in which the war vet, Mr. Simmons, had got his enjoyment for the theft of a measly half sandwich. When Mr. Woo had first arrived and shared some stories of his tropical country; the rubber trees and jungles, etc., we all thought he was a great fellow. After this, George and I didn't much like him anymore, and he knew it.

After school, Church took off down the street in a hurry, but I caught up with him and offered him out; I wanted to get even with the weasel who got me into trouble. He wouldn't have any of it, so I just gave him a hard boot to the shin, and he limped off home. Most of the lads wouldn't talk to him for a long time, knowing he had become the teacher's pet. That night, at teatime, I had throbbing sore hands and could hardly hold onto my knife and fork with my swollen fingers. I kept my problems to myself, and my folks didn't notice anything; only we brothers shared these stories. Our parents were excluded from that kind of information—we'd probably get more punishment from our folks, so we knew to keep our gobs shut.

A few weeks later, before school was about to break for the summer holidays, George and I decided to play a trick on our mean teacher, Simmons. While he was out and about, we snuck back to class and took down the thinnest of his three canes, which he had mounted horizontally on the wall behind his desk. It barely made it, but we shoved the rattan rod into the largest hole in his old pencil sharpener at the edge of his desk, rotated the handle, and after shaving its end to nice little point, we put it back on the two hooks on the wall.

On his desk, Simmons kept a small pile of pink blotting paper, a little box of extra nibs for our wooden pens, a bottle of blue ink for the inkwells on our desks and of course the handy sharpener to keep a good point on our pencils. Ballpoints hadn't come out yet, so our writing was carefully done with the old pen, dipped in the inkwell, and then carefully blotted so as not to make a smudge. If you got caught using a pencil as a drumstick, you were punished. It broke the lead in the middle, and pencils were sparingly given out.

A couple of hours had gone by since our little moment of rebellion, and we were in the middle of our arithmetic exercises, when Simmons's shrieking voice broke the silence.

"By Jove!" as he often exclaimed. "What has some imbecile ape done to my discipline rod? Everybody, stop what you're doing and stand at your desks. Webb, go immediately and fetch Mr. Maschetter."

Maschetter, the headmaster, had a good reputation as a fair man, but not one to mess with, as he could dish it out when needed. We all stood still behind our desks, staring at the front, while our angry teacher grumbled to himself as he examined his prize possession, and opened the pencil sharpener, shaking out the shavings.

"Yes! Oh yes!" he gnashed out. "Somebody's going to pay very dearly for this." And he glanced around the classroom, glaring intensely at the half-dozen usual suspects.

Then turning his back, he looked out of the window and began waving the stick like a swordsman flexing his rapier. We all began looking at each other and shrugging our shoulders. Who could have done this crazy thing? I stared to the back of the class at George and crossed my eyes, but no reaction; we were in our poker-faced mode. We had learned the hard way to keep our gobs shut. "Loose lips sink ships."

In walked the headmaster, like a wild monk, his long black robe flowing around him. He was the only one in the school who wore the pretentious garb, and he flaunted it down the halls like a peacock.

"Yes, Mr. Simmons, what's the order of the day?"

"It seems sir, that again, we have idle hands in the Devil's workshop. And some young sprout can't tell the difference between a cane and a pencil." He held out the upturned pencil sharpener containing rattan shavings.

"Yes! I would say very interesting." As they both examined how tightly the cane fitted the largest hole on the hand-cranked machine.

"And what do you suggest we do with such a pair of idle hands, Mr. Simmons?"

"I suggest we apply this, now pointed, instrument of correction to the hind quarters of whomever has the courage and wisdom to own up and receive due punishment, or we may have to issue a stroke each for the whole class." Now we were all in animated mode, looking around and eyeing each other.

Maschetter continued his comment: "It's milk break right now boys, off you go, and we'll expect someone to be standing at this desk," as he whacked it hard with the cane, "when the bell rings. Off with you all."

We lined up at the downstairs doorway that led to the schoolyard for our daily ration of a third of a pint of milk, in a small glass bottle, a government-sponsored offering to every pupil.

Besides the milk rations at 10 AM, we were also given government-susidized dinners at noon. The first thing on Monday mornings after assembly, we'd line up and give the teacher five bob for our school dinner. Nobody was allowed to bring a packed lunch or snacks to school; you had to eat the provided lunches like everyone else, or go home. The school had a large kitchen, and a few women worked there every day making the meals. We had a good variety. One day we'd get stew, and the next day a thick cheese and onion pie. Every dish always had watery mashed potatoes with it and was followed with a desert or custard. They were good meals for only a shilling each, and the teachers could also buy the same lunch, and sit at their own table in the dining room, but lots of them brought their own grub and sat around the staff room. Anyone would be punished for eating food in the classroom. Usually it was the stick.

During our break, there was a buzz of excitement mixed with trepidation about who did the mischief, and why we should all get it across the arse if the perpetrator didn't own up. Two boys knew, and two boys kept mum. We all returned to the cold room and sat in our seats. With his usual insane smile on his face, Simmons walked in, turned his back to us again, grasped the long windowsill with his large merciless hands and, looking up at the chilly cloudy sky, spoke: "Now there's a dark marauding sky, if ever I saw one. I believe a storm is about to break the silence."

Some monsters seem to have ease with eloquence. Here were thirty young boys, their scared eyes glued to the man who weeks earlier had openly relished his license to physically hurt children: yours truly and George. We all lined up down the hall, in alphabetical order, as one at a time we were called in to take our medicine. He gave each of us the choice: one stroke on the left hand, right hand or backside. How generous of him. How democratic. I chose the left hand, because I was nearly finished a nice painting I was going to bring home for my mum, and I needed to keep my right hand in working order. Some got a hard hit and some got it lightly. Half the class cried a bit, but they were all angry that everyone got the belt and nobody owned up to the prank. I had the sickening feeling that I'd betrayed the crowd, a feeling that took me a while to get over, but I knew that to confess would bring down the Gates of Hell on my head, as well as on George. Maybe I thought one whack of the cane wouldn't be much of a problem for us to endure? There were other ways of punishing the class, like detention or writing lines, but this teacher, Simmons, made his decision, and he became the most hated teacher in the whole school, even amongst his peers. Within the whispering classroom, the general consensus was that one of our rebellious group had done the small act. It was either Miles, Ryan, Tate, Naylor or me, the handful who were always stirring the pot.

14

Fisticuffs and Fear

Violence and verbal abuse were not scarce in my world, and the very first time I can recall seeing a couple of adults fighting was back in Cadmus Street. I was just a little lad, playing in the street with my friends, when an altercation took place between the coal man and the old curmudgeon Dougie Smith, who lived a few doors down from us with his young adult son. Dougie's son was a cheery, quiet fellow who would once in a while come out to the street and pass around a box of digestive bikkies to us crowd of hungry kids. His dad was completely the opposite, grumpy and short-tempered.

It was coal delivery day, and the coal man was carrying his hundred-weight (112-pound) sacks of coal to the customers along the street. It was quite a task as the many sacks had to be carried way down the jiggers to the coal sheds at the back of the houses. These men moved tons of coal each day by hand, one heavy sack at a time, and it was hard graft. The delivery days were always a fun time for us to chase the wagon and grab a nice big piece of coal that fell off as it turned the corner of our street. Sometimes, as the men were busy hauling the sacks around the back lanes and out of sight, one of the big boys would jump up onto the flat-deck truck and tip over a sack, spilling a pile of big, shiny Welsh coal onto the road. We hurriedly grabbed it and, using our pullover sweaters as bags, would carry the pieces back to our houses for free fuel. We were careful not to get caught, or else!

The old fool, Dougie, came out with a smart remark as one of the men walked past him, humping a sack of coal on his back. But his poorly chosen words directed at the tall strapping man with a face black with coal dust proved to be a big mistake. The words possessed such an arrogance that the young fellow took immediate grievance and dropped the sack of coal at the old man's feet. A loud exchange of abusive language ensued. This caused the nearby neighbours to run outside and order the peace-disturbing fools to shut the hell up, but to no avail. So, as some of the kids were quickly rounded up and moved out of harm's way, a spontaneous crowd of eager observers gathered as the two combatants squared off and hove to.

Dougie, the old retired docker, made his move. With his old worn-out walking stick, he took a swing at the young man, who was a bit slow to duck, resulting in a good whack square across his face that opened up a wide bloody gash. Gasps and mad shouts of disapproval arose from the crowd, accompanied by the yells of encouragement from others to strike back. The old fellow went crazy, flailing his stick and swinging his arms and legs about like a tattered sail in a storm. The young fellow, after throwing his leather shoulder guard and donkey jacket onto the coal wagon, examined the colour of the fresh blood dripping off his chin, and wiping his face and stretching out his arms, took the provocative stance of a veteran prizefighter about to exercise the Marquess of Queensberry Rules against his formidable opponent. An old man with a limp. So what was expected to be a casual lesson to the old man with the unbridled tongue escalated into a very unnecessary lesson in humility and pain. A left, a right and a boot sent the geriatric warrior back into a sitting position onto his doorstep with a screaming howl. As the brief swinging and flailing ended, the two casualties were attended to by the local self-appointed Red Cross housewives, who were quick to deliver cups of sweet tea and bandages. The young coalie was offered a lift on the back of a motorbike, and ushered off for a few stitches at the local clinic, while the ol' git, Dougie, just sat on his arse, in his doorway with a cup of tea in one hand, a blood-stained fag in his mouth, and what looked like a double whiskey in the other hand. It was just another day in the life for this worn-out sailor-boy.

At the beginning of the scuffle, when the kids were hurried out of harm's way, I managed to slip into an empty doorway and saw the whole dramatic show from start to finish. So for me, at six, that brief exposure of first-hand adult violence, in full view on our street, caused me to realize that grown-ups actually did fight in real life. Just like in the cowboy movies. It wasn't just us kids who did it. Wham, Wallop, Crack, Bang. I also took note that when the odds were against you, either by age, size or numbers, a little help from a handy weapon was allowed. The old man used his walking stick to even the odds, and the young man didn't take Dougie seriously enough to anticipate the swing. Age before beauty.

15

Young, Tough and in a Gang

Earlier that year, a boy named Dennis Duffy and his two older brothers pushed me around as I was walking home up Breck Road from Sunday school. One of the big boys butted me, hard enough to give me a bloody nose. They warned me, "Keep away from our road, or else!" My brothers Fred and Geoff got home later, and after hearing about my bloody shake down, took off and sorted those big lads out pretty well, but I had to deal with Dennis at school the next day. You do what you have to do. Dare to be a Daniel.

On an average day, a few of us little boys would hang out—playing on the street, kicking a ball, climbing the jigger walls, playing hide and seek, sneaking a look at the older boys and girls chasing each other and kissing in the back lane. We would also wander around the district exploring the grimy world of bombed houses, playing our Tom and Jerry war games with sticks and broken pipes for rifles.

One afternoon, a small group of us were mucking around down the jigger, when a friend of mine, Billy Gaskell, a little boy with a propensity for causing trouble and going a little bit wild, was reiterating what had happened on the day we'd witnessed the adult altercation on our street. He started wielding a small piece of rusty old gas pipe around and around through the air shouting, "....and Dougie swung his stick, and hit the coal man like this," at which moment, he belted me right across the ear with the pipe. Boy did that hurt, so I pulled the pipe out of his hand and belted him twice over his head. We were both pushed together by the bigger boys to carry on, and as little boys do, we grappled on the ground only to jump back to our feet and run off to our respective homes, blood running down our faces.

At home, as I was lying down on the sofa, my mother mopping my bloody head with a damp rag, Billy's mum darted into our front room and started on about her boy being hit with a pipe by yours truly. My mother's response, pointing at my bloody ear, was, "Look at his head, will you. Your boy started it. He's a little terror, your boy is." My mother often had the last word.

Mrs. Gaskell, like the rest of her crowd, was a well-known head case. A hard-faced busybody, with half a dozen crazy kids living in a Mad Hatter's house. But all the kids on the street liked her invalid husband, and when we'd be at Billy's house, which had two floors above the Co-op grocery, his dad would tell us wide-eyed children all sorts of stories about his time in the navy. War stories were usually withheld from us, by the old veterans, but occasionally they mentioned heroic adventures that captured our imaginations.

The most frightening story from old Mr. Gaskell was when his ship was torpedoed and quickly sank in the cold North Sea. The few sailors that were not blown to pieces were bobbing around in their life jackets in a sea that was on fire from all the ship's fuel. Many men were burned in the rolling waves, and the back of Mr. Gaskell's neck and head was one shiny mess of wrinkled, hairless skin. Sometimes, after the story was told, we'd ask him to take his wooly hat off so we could see his scars. Here was another war veteran reduced to sitting in his armchair, staring out the window to the street below with a beer in one hand and a cigarette in the other. His fingers were so nicotine stained that half were white and the other half dark brown.

His wife was a bag of nerves and kept on at him to "get over it, will yeh?" Then one day, as this usual palaver was going on, she turned to us ragamuffins, with her wild eyes dashing between us, and said, "I told the last husband I had to 'Drop dead.' Which he did, right in front of me. Ha, imagine that. Right there in the kitchen, straight to the floor, Bonk! Dead." Our eyes popped out of our heads.

The second hubby responded. "Go on then, tell me to drop dead too, will yeh. You think you're God. Go on. Ah, shut yer trap, will yeh?"

"Will yeh? will yeh?" That was always the added question to their idiotic yelling and quarrelling. Will yeh? No wonder Billy was turning out a bit odd.

As in any town in the world, there were territorial rules to abide by. Stick to your own district, or you might be noticed and harassed. Districts with hard reputations sometimes had to maintain their name with a challenge to another district. "We're the Dingle." "We're Everton Road." "We're Scotty Road." "We're Toxteth." Lots of districts had bragging rights, and a "we'll take you on" attitude.

These things happened all the time. Trouble here, retribution there. There seemed to be no end to young restless kids looking for some action. Groups of little preteen scallywags, just small boys, running here and there, antagonizing other young packs of snotty-nosed whipper-snappers. We started early, and we soon thought nothing of using a weapon; the big boys did it, and we learned from them, right? Among the bigger teenage boys, some names became notorious for mischief and fighting: Lenny Gaskell (he was good with the head), Tommy Kelly (he'd stick the boot in), the Hayes brothers (their uncle Vinny was the Lancashire welterweight boxing champ), Mike and Lenny Brown (took on a gang of Micks with bicycle chains), the Duffey boys, Harry Taylor, Colin Smith (he'd knifed a lad and went inside for six months), Bryn Jones and many more hard knocks, all out to make a name for themselves. Rough lads with tough upbringings.

And the stories went around, about what they'd done and who they'd taken on. Who'd done time. Who's dad was a bad egg. On and on. The stories became so exaggerated, you'd have thought some of them had taken on an army of giants with a rusty fork and one arm tied behind their back. Catholic and Protestant scrapping teams carried on with their usual historical hatred of each other. St. Patrick's or Paddy's Day, March 17, and King Billy's Day, the 12th of July, or the Glorious Twelfth, as it was called, were good excuses for some rumbling on the streets and parks. In certain areas of town, when a gang ran into another gang, a common question would be called out, "What are yer? Catholic cats, or Proddy dogs?" not "Who are yer?" Similar antagonism was experienced in Glasgow or Belfast, between the Orange and the Green. Extreme attitudes were held among the fanatical devotees, and I knew of a family that wouldn't have a scrap of green clothing in the house. Not a pair of socks or shirt or hat. Nothing Green. But they possessed many Orange ties, shirts, sweaters, anything, to denote what religion they followed. Small bronze statues of William of Orange abounded in people's living rooms on tables. A large, bronze statue of King Billy stood on our doctor's windowsill. Every 12th of July, stalwart Proddy men would dress up like the Dutch prince who invaded Britain to dethrone the Catholic King James II.

The central moment of decision being the famous Battle of the Boyne in Ireland, when William III sent James packing. It was the big day for the Loyal Orange Lodge parade, which wove its way through our district of Everton, along Netherfield Road, to the downtown core where hundreds of loyal followers climbed on busses or trains for a day's excursion to Southport and some fun at the seaside. Many returning to Liverpool, inebriated to the gills after swilling it back and cursing the Pope and the Fenian hordes all day, finally passing out in their beds or bus stops later that night.

16

Singing, Dancing and Acting Up

Among my friends' families, some folks liked to display their insatiable appetite for entertainment with singing, dancing and joking. Just walking down the street, you could hear a wide variety of music ringing out from radios in the close-knit houses. People singing, laughing and carrying on while all the world watched and listened. The doorways were only twelve feet apart along the road, and in the summer, those front doors were wide open with just a curtain pulled over on the inside to keep the peeping eyes out, but allowing the listening ears and the fresh air in.

So, if it wasn't rock and roll from one house, it was classical music next door or someone in their front room, taking a bath, bellowing out an operatic howl, while they scrubby-dub-dubbed away. Bathtubs, remember, were galvanized large plant pots that hung on a nail, on the backyard wall until they were used in front of the living room fire, where it was cozy.

On bath night, mostly Saturdays in our house, we'd boil kettle after kettle, pot after pot, to get enough hot water to half fill the small tub, where you sat and bathed with your knees bent. A big pot of warm water placed next to you provided enough clean water to rinse after you'd shampooed your hair etc. In a way, it was kind of comfortable to spend a few minutes in a warm living room in front of a coal fire and relax in the suds. When the bath was fresh, hot and ready, my mother was the first one in, after we'd vacated the house and locked the front door. I'm sure she enjoyed that wonderful time of complete privacy and warm luxury. No noisy kids running around, no chores to do, maybe a little music on the radio and a cup of tea within reach? A bathtime treat.

Then my dad was next in for his weekly scrub, then sometimes the two oldest, Fred and Dave, or each on their own as they got bigger, then me and Geoff. We all used the same water, with a little replenishing and heating up now and then. When it was time to get rid of all that water, we used a couple of buckets to haul it out. Because our front room was close to the street, we'd throw the hot soapy water across our slate sidewalk and give it a good brush off. This left the front of the house nice and clean again. The sandstone front step was washed and scrubbed, and the backyard was also swilled clean.

It was convenient that the school we went to took us swimming at least two times a week; with all that showering afterwards as well as going swimming again at Margaret Street baths on Saturday, we lads often didn't need a bath, and the folks had the whole thing to themselves. Considering our grimy environment, the kids in our area were not too dirty at all; in fact some of us were pretty shiny and well-groomed.

This was the overt world of Liverpool, a town where I'd often join the queue at a bus stop as someone started up with a well-known song, to entertain, and others joined in while we waited for the next bus.

This behaviour was probably a happy-go-lucky residual leftover from the war, where people were compelled to mix year after year, sheltering in the church and school basement bomb shelters, thus developing the unabashed talent of communicating with total strangers. Another reason for openness was that Liverpool was one of the main seaports of the world, and there's nothing more gregarious as a drunken sailor.

Open, funny behaviour is probably a working-class trait, sometimes to the point of being a tad too much in your face for shy and withdrawn folk. To try to cheer up the crowd, was applauded and encouraged. Sometimes on a late-night ride home, one might find some entertaining drunken character, hopefully with a good voice, crooning away to a crowded bus, and receiving requests for more, or demands to "Shut the hell up!" Not forgetting that every pub enjoyed a good singalong over a few pints, during and after a footy or rugby game, and it's always heartwarming to be among thousands of cheering footy fans all singing in unison.

In the old days, crowd singing was part of the deal at the movies before the show started. It wasn't a time to be shy. Songs like "Roll out the Barrel," "It's a Long Way to Tipperary," "Daisy, Daisy," "If You Were the Only Girl in the World" and so on.

Some adults, spotting a budding talent in a kid, would ask for a tune or a dance. Anything to keep the spirits up despite the embarrassment for the conscripted child.

From age six to ten, Graham Waring, or Gray, as everyone called him, was a good mate of mine, and he was lucky enough to have a pair of bouncy, fun-loving parents who were into all the modern music. My folks had more conservative tastes, and my older dad, sixty-four when I was ten, was from a different era. We were forbidden to listen to the "Devil's music."

War had turned Albert into a serious man, but he'd had his years walking on the wild side as a sailor and a pro footballer, with all the drinking, gambling, smoking, swearing and carrying on. At about thir-

ty years old, he got converted to fundamental Christianity at a Welsh
Revival meeting and became pretty fanatical about everything, which
included, in later years, the music his sons wanted to listen to. He regarded rock and roll and pop music as frivolous, vulgar and too rebellious for his liking. His whole path in life changed after the First World
War, and he stayed on the straight and narrow for the rest of his life.

The Breakers: Fred, George, Tom, Rod, Brownlow Hill, Liverpool, 1965

Our Fred led the vanguard in the music rebellion department,
playing drums in a local rock band, The Breakers. In his late teens,
he'd picked up a five-piece kit, with the usual snare, bass and tom-tom
drums, along with the high-hat and crash cymbals. Fred practiced upstairs in the bedroom he shared with Dave, a tiny room where things
had to be stacked in the corner when practice was over. The kit had to
be reassembled again and again, so he could hammer away when dad
was out. Fred gave me the occasional lesson (I liked the brushes a lot),
and I'd also jam with him on my recorder, pretending to be Acker Bilk
on the licorice stick, the famous Trad Jazz "Stranger on the Shore"
maestro.

In the sixties, The Breakers was patterned after the usual four-member ensemble: Tom on lead, George on rhythm plus vocals, Rod on bass, and Fred was the good-looking guy on drums.

When Fred left grammar school, he scored a job doing general office duties at Lime Street Station. One day his office received an unusual letter from a tobacco farm in North Carolina. A young girl sent it with the hope that she could find a pen pal in Liverpool, someone her age. She was my age, so Fred brought the letter home to me. We sent letters back and forth about three times, and she invited me over to the States to visit them on the farm. They'd pay for the whole trip. I was about twelve or so and slightly interested, having received some photos of the nice-looking girl, her family and the farm. My dad told me there was no way I'd be going across the Atlantic on my own, and when I told her that, the letters stopped. I'll never know who she really was, and dad's decision was obviously the right one.

My mother didn't mind Fred's drumming practices too much, if it was within certain hours: not too late and especially not when the folks were taking a quiet break themselves. It wasn't like we weren't allowed a bit of music around the house, but the Devil's music was only allowed when dad was out.

Most days we'd put on the BBC radio and listen to "Music While You Work" in the afternoons after school. The show played everything from classical to the old familiar tunes, and on Saturday mornings, when we were just little kids, we'd usually put on "Children's Favourites" and sing along with all the old kids tunes: "The Big Rock Candy Mountain," "Little White Duck," "High Hopes."

We finally got a really small black-and-white television when I was about ten, and after a while, when it became too well used and distracting, my dad would walk by it and lightly give it a kick and say, "Devil's vision."

We also had the old worn-out wind-up gramophone that played 78 vinyl records, but the only stock of musical selections we had was a bunch of scratched-up Christian tunes. We'd crank up the old music box and play "Abide with Me" so many times that the words on the poor old record sounded like, "A bribe big bee, brass balls the dreaming slide…" Hardly a word could be understood, but we lads knew all the words backwards anyway, and our dad would remind us when we played it, "That was the song they played when the Titanic was going down"—hammering us with more religious indoctrination whenever the opportunity arrived. The old machine with a worn-out needle provided a little noise, and that was it. When the folks were out, we four boys would make a lot of noise, pretending rolled-up newspapers were clarinets and trombones, a paper and comb was a harmonica and the usual saucepan was a drum. Despite the din, we did have rhythm, and we knew all the lyrics.

A great escape for me was when I'd visit my friend Graham at his place, on Lloyd Street, after school. His mother always asked me to sing or dance around for some live entertainment, and often for the reward of ice cream or sweets. A wooden spoon was usually the pretend microphone, and someone tapping on an old pot kept a mean drum rhythm. I think her intentions were to bring her shy son Graham out of his shell and exercise his hidden talents, of which he had lots. Most of the time, he'd sit there giggling away, as I'd follow orders from our stage director, Jean, being allowed to address her in that way.

At that time, early 1960, a popular song on the radio was the American tune "Running Bear" by Johnny Preston. When I sang the song, everyone joined in with the chorus, as Graham's crazy mother would dance around in a circle like an Iroquois Princess, pretending to swim the raging river like "Little White Dove." She encouraged me and Gray to sing together, probably dreaming in her silly head that we'd be the English Everly Brothers, just like Cliff Richard was England's answer for Elvis. "Pass the Brylcream. 'We're all Going on a Summer Holiday' with my 'Living Doll,'" as Sir Cliff would say.

We harmonized pretty well with some of those tunes, like "Til I Kissed You" and "Bye Bye Love," as well as some Buddy Holly songs like "Peggy Sue" and "Oh Boy," etc. I only wish Gray had stayed around long enough for the arrival of the Mersey Beat—we could have done something with that—but my best friend immigrated to Australia later in 1960, and after one or two letters, we never wrote again. His old grandma stayed back in the Pool on her own, and when I ran into her on the street, she would tell me they were all wearing straw shoes down there in Aussie. I laughed when I heard that, until a few years later, I was doing the same thing, when our crowd moved down there too.

Since the time that Gray and I were tiny boys, we'd played footy together on the street and at school, enjoyed a good chess game, went swimming at Margaret Street public baths and liked the same music and mischief. We probably shared our first cigarette at age eight. His mum and dad smoked, so it was easy to score a smoke or two when they weren't around.

It was Gray's place that provided one of those special venues for some wild fun. His mum was a real live wire, and very lovely to look at, by all the eyes on the street. She could have been on stage. But instead, she was this bubbly mother of two happy boys, Gray and his older brother, Derek, and her lot in life was to hold down a job at the local co-op grocery shop and tend to the family needs. But she was a star when she got home.

We three boys would sit around their back kitchen, playing chess or cards, or gluing together a model aeroplane, which was one of Derek's hobbies, while sipping tea on a cold day, or lemonade when it was hot, always with ginger biscuits with jam on top. Their mum would usually be cleaning up the house, prancing around, with the radio turned up high, and the top hits blasting away, one after the other. A real "Hit Parade Momma." My mother didn't care for her too much "'cause she's full of herself," and barely thirty years old, having had kids in her late teens. Gray's dad was also a young fellow, late twenties again, like a big overgrown kid himself. Tall and fairly handsome, he worked at some factory down at the docks, and when he got home, he and the missus were all over each other, like two reunited lovebirds. He often brought a treat home for his lads, like a packet of sweets or toffee, and I never saw an angry word between any of them. I hated leaving their place to go home; it was such a fun place to hang around, and she made me feel so important, with my singing and dancing. I craved her attention, in my little boy way. She was my first crush. Once after school, I was asked over to Gray's for tea: home-made steak and kidney pie, with chips and peas. Man! What a treat. That night, while we were eating, we saw Cliff Richard and the Shadows on the telly, singing "Living Doll," one of his biggest hits. That was it; I was going to be a rock and roll singer, with a band, and see the world.

A few days later, during dinnertime at school, some of us were playing tennis on the concrete playground. Tennis? What a joke. We didn't have a net, just a rope tied off between two short poles stuck in holes in the ground, and if the ball went below the rope, a small crowd of spectators would all shout "Net!" in unison, so there was no mistaking a clean hit from a bad one. After the bell rang, before we returned the battered-up rackets to the teacher, four of us started pretending to be Cliff and the Shadows, with our "Living Doll" act, doing all the step routines, like they did on the telly. The teacher was leaning back on the wall finishing his ciggie, and began to clap wildly with approval. So, at his suggestion, we did the same show-biz gig in front of the class that afternoon, pretending the rackets were guitars. A big lad in the class, who was a bully, asked if he could join in with the Racket Band. We told him where to go, which was one of the highlights of the year, watching him sulk off with rejection.

17

Eleven Plus and on Top of the World

In 1960, our class at Heyworth Street was given lessons on the skills of the Holger Nielsen method of artificial respiration (AR) in the small gym, just upstairs from the subterranean swimming pool. About the size of a large living room, this was where we all piled into on Duck-Apple day, diving down, and just using our teeth, retrieved the apples that were thrown in by the teacher.

Our instructions in AR were quite involved, and incorporated a bit of first aid, such as loosening belts and ties, making the subject warm and comfortable, calling for assistance and staying calm under a stressful rescue. Some of us even learned how to bounce a person with their outstretched arms over the side of a swimming pool, and to check their air passage. This was a lot for ten-year-olds to gather, but we all did it and received small bronze medals after passing the practical tests. It was a proud moment for us, and we wore our medals pinned to our jackets for weeks after.

Our old school was only a twenty-minute walk from Margaret Street swimming baths, down Everton Road, were we'd go a couple of times a week for swimming lessons and racing heats with other schools. I don't remember anyone in our school who couldn't swim by the age of ten, unless they had a physical problem. We just had to learn, and there was no choice. We'd all march there in pairs, with our swimming togs rolled up in a towel tucked under our arms, like a troop of soldiers off for exercise.

Peter and mates off to Margaret Street Baths. Peter-front row right, Ronnie, with glasses,
back row, 1957, courtesy of Ronnie Marshall

Margaret Street baths was a pretty old and simple building. The changing rooms were small cubicles running down the sides of the twenty-five-yard pool, girls down one side, and boys down the other. Their individual doors were a foot or so off the tiled floor, so if you were already in the pool, the first one to break the jelly (the first one into the still water) as we'd say, you could look up at the row of doors and see people dropping their drawers and putting on their swimming costumes. Nothing was locked up because you could always see your little closet where your stuff was. One day a crazy boy called Danny Lawrenson got annoyed with someone and ran into the other kid's changing room, grabbed all his clothes and threw them into the pool. He paid the price for that nonsense and was not allowed back.

The old facility also had a handful of deep bathtubs in private rooms, where me and one of my brothers paid thrupence to share the deepest, hottest bath we'd ever had, complete with a big bar of carbolic soap and a clean towel each. What a treat to loll around in a massive clawfoot tub. A big difference from the Saturday night squeeze into a tin can at home.

Then, I turned eleven. Eleven! This was a year where I seemed to excel in more ways than one.

Firstly, I'd won the Liverpool Schools Chess Congress for my age group, held at the Liverpool Collegiate on Shaw Street, receiving a large book on astronomy as my prize. That was quite a weekend, where hundreds of boys and girls, of all ages up to sixteen, played game after game for two days.

Next, our class won a painting competition, which was a poster for Ceylon Tea. I'd always enjoyed art, and for a poster, I painted a ship tied up at a dock, in a jungle setting, with people walking up a long plank onto the ship, carrying tea leaves in their baskets, while others walked down another plank with empty baskets on their heads. The poster was a large watercolour, and one of our teachers at Heyworth Street, Mr. Jones, one of the better teachers, told me my poster may be used as an advertisement for the tea company, but I never witnessed that or met anyone who had.

Mr. Simmons, our main teacher for the year, had the class read the famous book *Reach for the Sky*, written by the Second World War flying ace Douglas Bader. Although Bader had lost both legs in a flying accident before the war ended, he fought for Britain and became an RAF hero of the highest order. Simmons had the class read out, one by one, a page each, until the book was finished, and he always had a nice way of putting things: "Hayes, you can quote scripture like no one else, but you do not read very well."

Another item of importance that year was that I passed the Eleven Plus Examination, which meant I would be going to Alsop Grammar School—where my big brother Fred was finishing his last year. I was excited, then came my big disappointment! Because we were moving to the outskirts of Liverpool, to a new district, I was enrolled in the new experimental system called the comphrehensive school at Gateacre. There I was sentenced to 5 years of mish-mash in the house of chaos. At the Comp' I was put into a top-level classroom where grammar-type lessons were taught, including French. In the comphrehensive system, all three streams of education met. One could climb within the grades, if you did well, or slide if you were lazy. To me, it was a place of distraction and personal struggle. My first report card comments for that year were: "Peter must take life more seriously. He tends to day dream, scribble away with pictures and make up silly songs, which distract the other students." I really missed all my mates from the old school and the Everton district.

Most of us who'd arrived at this new modern place called comprehensive form school had never before shared the same classrooms with the other gender. We found this a novel arrangement and greatly amusing, but to some, it became intimidating and uncomfortably competitive. After all, who wanted to sit next to a girl who was twice as smart as you and was constantly illuminating how dumb you were? This rude awakening usually delivered a blow to the solar plexus of any stripling who was under the illusion that he was some kind of junior scientist. The usual things boys and girls shared in school activities were morning assembly, where we sat on different sides of the hall, a mirrored seating arrangement like a synagogue. We also shared the classrooms, the library and some of the field trips.

In the comprehensive school, it was hard for young lads to keep to themselves in a co-ed classroom, especially when it comes to private comments and conversations about the most important subject on our minds, the girls. In every class, there were one or two lassies that really attracted our attention, and some of them realized this was a new opportunity for them to ply their female skills of charm and beauty. This caused division amongst the ranks. They'd ask certain boys for special assistance with homework and difficult mathematical questions, when they probably knew more than us poor, naïve and excitedly nervous knobble-heads in short pants. All of us boys wore short pants, sometimes till we reached fourteen, and blue jeans were never allowed in our schools till the late sixties. Not even at school camp.

Lots of drama went on in the classroom, while some "rosy red cheeks of the little children" were turning green with envy at their desks. Envy and jealousy came along with the mixing of the sexes. Boys vied for the favour and attention of certain girls, and vice versa. Brains challenged brains, and threats challenged threats.

Monday mornings in school, as I imagine in all schools worldwide, was a time of teenage storytelling frenzy. Who was out with whom on a date? What was the band like at the local Saturday night dance? Was there a scrap or two over the girls? Did someone break up? Did someone get lucky? Gossip, left, right and center.

With regards to academic achievement, if you behaved yourself in class, you'd probably do well; if you misbehaved, you were left behind and suffered the consequences. That's probably why most of the girls and a few quiet boys excelled, and the rest of us mad monkeys got the stick, served detention after school and did lines: "I must not do this, and I must not do that."

What was the Eleven Plus? Before the tumultuous teenage years arrived, all school children in the UK at the age of eleven–in the last year of primary school–were condemned to sit for a life-directing exam, which was called the Eleven Plus Exam. Passing or failing this paper on English, math and general knowledge determined what level of schooling was to be your lot for the next five years. This also determined your future in the working world. If you got high marks, you could expect to go on to grammar school–the top level–then maybe later on to university, and thence a higher academic and well-paid career. An average mark sent you off to technical school–the 2nd level–where you could be groomed in the trades; but if, for instance, a bright and intelligent youngster had a moment of bad nerves on the big day, received a poor result in this culling exam, they were sent off to secondary modern school–the 3rd level–where, upon leaving, after a few years, sometimes at fifteen (as was the case with my two middle brothers, David and

Geoff), the world of the laborer and low-paid skivvy could be your reward. In other words, one's status and financial future, with its benefits
or struggles, rested heavily on that one memorable day. If the results
were unacceptable, then dodging this bullet could be achieved if one's
parents were determined and/or influential lollipops that contested
their child's results, demanding a rewrite for the perplexed youngster
or had pull so they got into a better school. This exam was just one
example of how narrow and rigid the early British education system
was with its strong class bias. The upper crust was rife with nitwits who
continued to climb the ladders to the top. Toss a coin: heads, you're a
banker; tails, you sweep the streets.

By the late sixtiess, things changed, and more opportunities arrived
for all types of kids, as finally, after decades of much discrimitory treatment, it was accepted that the Eleven Plus exam was the failure, not
the child.

This test, with all its consequences, arrived for my three brothers
and me before our slowly deepening voices, and the anticipated arrival
of hair in the northern and southern latitudes, not forgetting of course,
the accompanying know-it-all teenage attitude.

In the fifties and sixties, British schools spared no expense on cul-
tural education and excursions, and we were the better for it. We went
on biannual visits to the Walker Art Gallery, museum, philharmonic
orchestra and other places of interest, like Speke Hall. Yes, this unusual place full of hidden passageways called Speke Hall was where
once lived the "Childe of Hale": a nine-foot-three-inch-tall reclusive
giant, who was taken to London to wrestle the King's Champion and
"put out his thumb." The giant, on his return home to Lancashire,
was robbed of his twenty pounds prize money and spent the rest of his
strange life "behind the plough," as the story goes.

Every year, the government subsidized our annual escape from
Liverpool to the countryside of North Wales. Here were hundreds of

acres of countryside that most of the children growing up in Liverpool seldom enjoyed, except for the summer holidays with their families.

Busload after busload, filled to the brim with wild screaming youngsters from different schools barreled through the Mersey Tunnel and we'd have the upstairs windows pulled wide open and be taking in deep breaths of exhaust fumes as we hurried through the two-mile stretch of the four-lane, badly lit highway to hell. Ah, that wonderful smell of carbon monoxide. The gas that kills your brain cells. Kids are crazy. As the double-deckers entered the beautiful countryside of Wales, the destination was good old Colomendy Camp, at the village of Loggerheads, Denbighshire.

Local farmers beware—the children of Bedlam have just arrived! But it was a fat chance we'd be stealing horses or cows; the only thing on four legs any of us had ridden would have been a thrupenny beach donkey ride in New Brighton or Llandudno.

We were lucky that lots of schools from Liverpool had that Colomendy connection. The camp had long bunk houses and an assembly hall, where one night in '58, we sat glued to our seats watching the great new kid's movie "Tom Thumb," and I learned a bit of "The Yawning Song," which my brother Geoff often asked me to sing to get him to sleep.

We were given the usual school meals in the camp dining room, and every day, after an early rise, we'd go on long hikes through the hills, and race to the top of Moel Famau and Moel Fenlli, the Iron Age hill forts. There was also the notorious Cat Walk: a narrow winding pathway that weaved its way along the edge of a cliff face with a steep drop-off. We negotiated the dangerous fifteen-minute trek for a couple of years until one day we found the trail was closed because a hiker had foolishly raced down the path, missed the sharp turn and hurtled over the edge, breaking a thick branch off a tree as he flew through the air. That was the end of him, and the end of any more school treks up the Cat Walk. This event happened in the morning, and we could see his belongings scattered on the ground as we were quietly ushered away.

At the base of the Cat Walk was a quirky-looking entertainment area, a small fairground, where we'd gather around one of those electric shock machines that was fitted to a wall. The square contraption had a brass knob on one side and a brass handle on the other, which you could turn to see how far the needle on the voltage dial would go, after making a complete circuit with both hands. For a penny in the slot, you could shock yourself silly with direct current and show how strong you were by withstanding a lot of juice in front of the awestruck onlookers.

We'd make a circle of three or four kids, hold hands and see who let go first. Sometimes a couple of bullying boys would take hold of an unsuspecting younger kid walking by and include him in the shock treatment. The attending teachers would be looking out for this terrorizing, but when they weren't watching, many little kids had a shocking experience.

18

Footy and Ten Needles

As the old song goes, "For he's football crazy, he's football mad. The football, it has taken away the little bit of sense he had." And footy, or togger as we called it, was in our blood from the time we could stand up and kick at any object: a tennis ball, a small rubber tiny-tot beach ball, a tin can and, of course, the heavy old brown leather regulation football, kept in millions of homes, schools and clubs all over Britain and the world. The hides of millions of slaughtered cattle provided enough leather to keep the glorious game supplied with the stitched-up object with the air bladder inside. The spherical icon was inflated with a bicycle pump, where the proper pressure was noted when you dropped the bouncy thing from shoulder height and it bounced back up to a certain distance. This old way of measuring things made sure the game was enjoyed to its fullest and the players got their greatest pleasure in the fine art of dribbling, passing, juggling, heading and generally blasting it at the desired target, the goal.

Probably the first round object I wellied, before I was out of nappies, was one of a few small soft plastic things that our dad would buy for us lads to kick around the backyard, without doing too much damage to windows or doors. There we were, smacking it around our ten-by-twelve-foot training ground. Four little boys, knocking the exhausted, half-inflated thing from wall to wall, on our own private football pitch. Fred, the seven-year-old coach, with his younger-brothers-team, including me, the wide-eyed one-and-a-half-year-old, learning from the older pros, yet barely able to stagger, never mind run, and now prepping for the street games, where the bigger boys bashed and belted away in their daily competitions, their goal posts laid out with piles of coats and jumpers.

Back in the fifties and sixties, when we were out playing on the real grass fields at Towsend Lane or later in the city outskirts, and not the inner-city cinder pitches, we wore ankle-high leather boots with six rounded studs nailed on the bottom—four studs in a square fashion at the front half and two at the back, under the heel. Later there came the screw-in studs and then the molded boots with about ten plastic studs and the low sides below the ankle bone. The nail-on studs we used were made of layers of small round circles of leather with four sharp nails that went right through, which you hammered on to the sole, and replaced when they came off during a game. Sometimes you were unfortunate enough to go into, or take, a tackle and end up sliding across the ground where the tiny nails in a lost stud would cut your leg or your arm. It was all part of the game anyway, to get a bit battered and bruised, so not many complaints were made. It's not an exaggeration to say that the game of football, also known as soccer around the world, not only is a fanatical pastime, but to umpteen millions, it's their religion.

One spring day in 1962, we were having our usual noon-time game of footy after school dinner at Gateacre Comp'. I was standing in front of our goal about to block a shot from this older lad twice my size. (All ages mixed in with the games, the big and the small, but the teams were evenly picked.)

I was successful in blocking the heavy leather ball all right, but in not the way I intended. The big fellow was one hell of a player; he was powerful and could belt the ball a mile. When he slammed it, with the kick of a racehorse, I collected it smack dead center of the family jewels. Man! That sent me into lunar orbit, and I collapsed, the wind knocked right out of me, gasping for air and holding onto you-know-what for dear life. The big boy came immediately to my assistance and told me what a regular sports coach would say: "Sit on the steps here, put your head between your knees and slowly take some deep breaths." After a few minutes of following his advice, the colour began to return to my sheet-white face; the yard-duty teacher took me into the gym and told me to lie down on the coconut mats and get some rest before the afternoon classes started.

I was really hurting when I got back to class, sitting next to a good mate of mine, when I began to get very dizzy, and went into a fit of pain and turned to Joey and punched him in the gob, knocking him out of his seat, onto the floor. The teacher dashed over, thinking we were getting into a scrap. At that moment, I fainted across my desk. When I woke up, I was too embarrassed to tell the teacher or anyone about my problem with severe pain in the lower regions, and the teacher simply told me to go home, because I wasn't looking too good. With my satchel packed up with all my gear and books slung over my shoulder, I started out on the long walk home, taking each agonizing step slowly, in a daze. I got home before every one else and checked myself out. My balls had now swollen to the size of bright red oranges, ready to explode, and all I could think to do was to strip off, make a cup of tea and go to bed. A good cuppa usually helps fix a problem, as we all knew.

My brothers were the first home, and Geoff told me to put a cold wet towel over the expanding area and wait it out. When my mother finally got home, I had to disregard any embarrassing reserves that I had and show my shocked mother what an old leather football could do. She hit the roof, helped me get dressed and took me off to the doctor's a few blocks down the road. I walked like John Wayne all the way to his house, which was joined to his surgery. He was always available morning, noon or night, and his diagnosis was not only inflammation, but the onset of a possible infection. He gave me a couple of Aspirins for pain and a week's regime of antibiotics. I was to continue treatment with the cold wet towels. Then my ears sprung open with joy when he told my mam "probably ten days to two weeks off school." Yes, I was delighted until I heard the next announcement: "Ten days of Penicillin injections. One every day, administered by the district nurse." Good God! I thought. Ten needles?

"Yes, doctor," my mother agreed.

"And we'll start with one right now," he whispered in my ear, with a wink of the eye. "OK, Peter, lower your pants and lean over the chair."

"What? Over the chair?" I said.

"Yes, lad. The best way to get the medicine into the body is with an injection in the rump."

"What about my arm?" I looked at my mother.

"It's OK, son. It only hurts for a second. You have to have it. Come on: 'Doctor knows best.'" My mam smiled at him.

I'd had my fair share of needles before now, and as small boys, we'd have to walk from Heyworth Street School, all the way down Everton Road to Mill Lane clinic to get our polio shots. We walked half an hour there and back on our own. There was no problem with that, and the nurses would give you a sweet on your way out the door. One time after taking the needle in the arm, I asked for four sweets, one for me and one for each of my brothers. They laughed and gave them to me. I made those four toffees last two days.

Here we go, I thought, as I bent over the doctor's old wooden chair, and stared at the small statue of King Billy on his windowsill to give me courage as I grabbed onto his desk. What scared me the most was the size of the needle with the big glass tube full of liquid that he was going to jam into my rear cheek. I felt the heavy weight of the pointed object hit the side of my hip and the damn needle push into me and inject what felt like acid into my flesh. That really hurt, and while me and my mam walked back home in the dark, I expressed my concerns about the next nine days.

"That was pretty sore, mam! Boy did he jab me or what?"

"It's OK, son. It only hurts for a second. You should've seen all the needles I've had. Ha!" This was the second time she said that in fifteen minutes. I wasn't looking forward to the district nurse's visits. I'd heard from others that these witches, dressed in black, who rode bicycles, were a wicked breed, and especially loved to inflict a bit of pain on the boys, because we deserved it for being bad and mischievous. The girls got it easier 'cause they were "sugar and spice, and all things nice."

Sure enough, about nine in the morning, as I was looking out the window, scouring the horizon for a pirate's flag, she arrived on her black government-issued bike and parked it against the wall downstairs at the neighbour's. She looked up at our window with a forced smile and a wave in my direction, untied her bag from the back of the bike and headed for the stairs. My mother stayed home from work on my first day of injections and opened the front door after the heavy Bang, Bang, Bang.

"Morning, Mrs. Hayes." The nurse stepped in, removed her rain hat and Macintosh coat, turned and gave me a cheery "Well hello there. You must be that World Cup Football player, Peter." She was short and chubby, had badly kept yellow teeth and sported a pair of rain-splattered bottle-end glasses.

"Morning, nurse," I returned.

"Yes, nurse, he likes to kick a ball. All my boys do," Mum added.

"Well, we'll just get a little medicine into you, and I'll be on my way. Shall we go into the kitchen?"

This, as I've mentioned before, is the living room anywhere else in the universe. So there she was rifling through her bag, pulling out this small bottle and a wad of cotton wool, a syringe tube and finally a small tin, which contained her reusable needles. These weren't the throw-away jabbers that came along later; these needles were used over and over again on different patients. They screwed and unscrewed them onto the ends of the glass tubes, and before use were put into some boiling water to be sterilized. A small pot of water was put onto the gas stove to boil along with the kettle.

"Cup o' tea, nurse?"

"Ah, yes please, love, the cup that cheers. OK, Peter, let's go in the front room and get this over with, and I can get on to my next visit. How about over the sofa?" she held the needle high, and followed me into the front kitchen.

I'd probably seen too many Jekyll and Hyde movies, and as I studied her face, it began to squint and twist in some hideous manner, and she started to bare her jagged teeth at me. Her tongue slithering and sliding across her gob with some kind of speech impediment, like a wild-eyed cannibal, salivating over the next meal. Man, she looked dangerous.

"I want it in the arm, mam," I called out, like the night before, beginning to roll up my sleeve, and keeping away from the two of them, but no, they started cornering me, and I finally agreed to the shot in the cheek. There was a large bruise from the night before, and so she now aimed for the other side. She didn't say a word of warning. Wham! She jabbed me hard, like sticking a pig, and when I jumped with surprise, the needle snapped in half, leaving part of it stuck in my raging rump.

"Fuck!" I shouted.

"Watch your language, Peter! Stay still. Stay right there." She went to her bag and produced a small pair of tweezers to pull the bit of needle out.

"There, that's got it!" she sighed with relief. "Don't move when you're getting a needle, sonny boy. Look what happens. She dropped the broken bit on the small metal tray.

"Now we'll have to do it again."

Oh God! I thought, as she placed a new needle into the syringe, filled it to the mark, while I stood by the coal fire, my pajamas down at my knees, rubbing my sorry arse. I could see my mother was getting annoyed with her, but encouraged me as per usual.

"There now, Peter. It only hurts for a second, then you can do some more painting." I always did a pile of watercolours or drawings when I was at home sick with bronchitis or the flu. Common illnesses in smoggy old Liverpool.

The second attempt with the sharp instrument was successful, and after they'd had their tea, I was left alone to carry on with another masterpiece, probably a painting of a hideous sea-hag carrying a big black bag.

I lay down again with another cold damp towel over the oranges, praying to God to send some relief, and promising to serve him in deepest Africa, and also asking for a more empathizing nurse the next time. After the first couple of days, things started to improve quickly. Mum couldn't afford to miss work to be home with me, and, so from the second day on, I stayed home on my tod, and let the nurse in to do her target practice. Ten days of needles, fried eggs and beans on toast, telly, painting and boredom went by, and things became right as rain. Mum would say goodnight with her little sayings, like, "It'll be a 'pig's foot' in the morning."

Back at school, I presented the doctor's note to the teacher, and handed him my five bob for school dinners for the week. His eyebrows raised as he saw the explanation for my absence.

"Yes, the gentleman's game of football is known for its painful injuries to the nether regions," he whispered. "Dixie Dean, our famous Everton player, lost his left testicle in a tackle during a game."

"Yes, sir, I heard that, and my dad played a few years before for the same team at Tranmere Rovers, and knew Dixie."

"He did? That was back in the twenties, Peter."

"Yes, I know, sir," I continued. "And my dad scored the winning goal for Tranmere, on Boxing Day 1922, against Ashington, at home."

"Oh! Well play safe, lad, and maybe you'll be inside right for Everton one day."

"Yes, sir, and maybe my brothers will join me; we all love a game."

I later told the ten needles story to my mates at morning break, and mentioned that our footy hero, Dixie, lost his left ball in a tackle. "OOOHH!" We all groaned, and then someone started up with a familiar war song we all knew. Everyone joined in.

"Hitler has only got one ball. Lost it outside the Albert Hall. Himmler, has something similar, but old Goebbels has no balls at all."

It was the gear to be back at the game after school dinner, but I made sure I wasn't in the wrong spot when the big boys were blasting away at the target. I had bruises on both sides now—another football term, five-a-side, and maybe I should write a song, "It's OK, son. It only hurts for a second." The world owes a gold medal to that great, Scottish inventor, Jock Strap.

19

Moving to the Outskirts and Immersion in Nature

Until the age of eleven, I'd lived in the stark treeless inner city with its occasional grassy areas, Newsham Park, Townsend Lane, Sefton and Stanley parks. The really nice big parks we enjoyed visiting were out a bit, Otterspool and Calderstone's, for example. The downtown streets, generally speaking, were so tightly arranged that all we had to view were rough cobblestone or tarmac, slate sidewalks and roofs, red-brick houses and sandstone windowsills and steps. As far as greenery was concerned, there was very little. Some people with a talent for growing things would have window boxes that sat on the sills in their backyards, full up with the usual array of daffodils, tulips and hyacinths in the spring. And those lucky enough had small garden allotments further out of town, provided by the city council, for a small fee per year. Here the avid city-bound horticulturalists would visit their little plots of soil and tend them for endless hours, developing their miniature gardens of Eden, sometimes full to the brim with veggies and lots of flowers, of course with the always well-maintained stone pathways, compost heaps and cold frames.

In late 1960, my mother visited the local council housing offices to inquire about our position in the long lineup for a new location in the new districts. She was astounded to find out that, if she'd inquired a year earlier, our family could have moved out of the rundown, rat-in-fested slum district we were in, sooner, into a brand-new row of flats that had inside toilets. In the new dwellings, which had been under construction for a few years, there was even hot water in both the kitchen and indoor bathroom, with a real built-in bathtub, not like the old tin can we hung on a six-inch nail outside in the weather. Boy! My poor mother realized we could have been living in luxury all this time. So, upon her last visit to the bureaucratic office of "The Relief from Human Misery Department," she was told to get the family prepared to move, as soon as December, to the new development known as the Childwall Valley Estates. Estates? I thought, an unusual term for a grouping of high-rise flats, maisonettes and some adjoining houses. In simpler terms, "a new ghetto" a distance away from the slums we presently lived in. To call these grey square cells Estates is like placing a sign over a hot-dog stand, Imported Delicacies.

Our lot was drawn from all the numbers, and we were to move to the two upper stories of a maisonette, a French name given to the two-level house above another two-level house in a long block formation.

We were thrilled with the idea of change, but for me, the big move was bittersweet, because nobody I knew from our district would be heading that way, and none of my good friends that I'd grown up with would be joining me at the new school. For the last few months of the school year, after we moved house, I had to ride a couple of buses each way to school in the old district before starting at Gateacre Comprehensive, which was just a bike ride away.

My oldest brother, Fred, was leaving his school to start work in the office at Lime Street Station, but my two middle brothers had a few months left at their school and would be joining me part of the way each morning, on the bus, and then jumping off the number 25 bus near their destination, Prince Rupert Secondary Modern on Margaret Street. I'd get off the bus at Heyworth Street and always arrive early because of the bus connections. It was fine by me, giving me extra time to play a bit of football in the schoolyard before class.

Looking back, that time of separation from all things familiar probably prepared me for future times of leaving things behind and starting all over again, often on my own, an experience that I would repeat in the years to come, from country to country. The demolition of the Everton streets also dismantled a long established community where generations of families were uprooted and separated forever. Where once there was a safety net for the elderly, now family and friends were scattered by the winds of unwanted relocation, which often brought loneliness and isolation.

As the days neared for the move, we grew excited with the prospects of a new community and home. "Just imagine," my mother kept saying, "an inside toilet, and a real bathtub with hot and cold water." Yeah. Wow! The removal van arrived and parked next to the newly painted block of flats on Hartsbourne Avenue, and the family started unloading and carrying our goods and furniture up the three flights of stairs to the long landing, where we turned left, to find our new front door next to the coal locker at the end. Imagine, we were now living on an avenue? Not a atreet, not a road, not a lane, not a close, but an avenue. It all had a fancy ring to it, "Une maisonette dans une avenue." Bon voyage, mes amis d'Everton Road.

Mum at the new place, The Childwall Estate Maisonettes, 1963

Along the second-story landing, there lived six families. The crowd next door had an older boy and girl. The girl, big and tough, thought she could pick fights with everyone, and we once had a go at each other halfway down the stairs. Her dad was a nice quiet fellow who opened his front door one day, only to be butted in the gob by the terror of a neighbor who lived downstairs. That was his reward for asking for peace and quiet. In the next apartment after that lived a girl named Debbie who was the same age as me, and we'd sometimes walk to school together. Deb's dad had lost his wife and was raising the girl on his own. He was a great guy who spotted me running, skipping and shadowboxing down the back by the bins and bought me a fabulous book on *The History of Boxing* to encourage me to keep my dukes up.

Beside them lived Linda, about two years older than me, and quite tall and good-looking. She'd sometimes invite me into the house when her folks were out, so we could neck on the sofa, and have tea and toast. I think she may have had a fling with a few lads on the block, but she particularly asked me around, 'cause I liked to dance her around the living room to the radio and crack jokes.

Later on, when she was seventeen, and I fifteen, she kindly introduced me to some delicate intimacies of human relations, for which I was grateful. "Come into my parlour, said the spider to the fly."

Linda's next-door neighbours were from Hades. The place was a wild collection of asylum escapees. Ronny, who was about the same age as our Dave, kept a pet monkey in a cage in the living room. The green-looking monkey was about the size of a small cat and looked a bit dangerous if you were to hold it, as Ronny often did. It had a hell of a set of teeth, and was always showing them off. It looked like it could bite your ear off, so I always refrained when he held it out for friends to hold. The place stank to high heaven, and when we sometimes visited to see the incarcerated creature, it would go crazy, screaming and shaking the cage, trying to get out. Well, one day it did, when everyone was out, and what a mess it made of that house, from front to back, upstairs and downstairs. Ronnie's parents had the poor thing destroyed, much to Ronny's dismay; he left home that week, and we never saw him again. I spotted him once getting off a bus in London when I came back from Australia in 1971. He was a long-haired hippy by that time, and was still laughing his head off, as he always did.

There was only one door leading into our new place. You entered a tiny hallway where we hung our coats and straight ahead was the living room, which overlooked the street. The other room off the hallway was the kitchen with a large walk-in closet for the portable washing machine, which was rolled out on wash day and parked in front of the sink with the hot and cold taps. What a luxury! Upstairs were three small bedrooms and a separate toilet and bathroom. Fred and Dave shared the back bedroom, while Geoff and I had the front one. Finally the bonus of having our own new beds.

We moved from Everton by Christmas 1960, and a few months later, dad would turn sixty-five and begin collecting his old age pension, but he enjoyed his job as a fitter/turner so much that he didn't want to stop working. Also, he no longer had to take a couple of busses to his job at Lucas Brothers, and now could enjoy a half-hour walk instead, which suited him fine. He kept on working for another couple of years, and then they called him into the office one day and told him his time was up and he had to quit. Fortunately they said they needed a grounds man for their sports center (knowing he was an ex-professional footballer and trainer), and he was delighted to take the position. It involved maintaining the fields and running track, plus the indoor facilities and recreation areas. It was right up his alley. He took to it like a duck to water, and some days after school, I'd pedal a couple of miles to the grounds and meet him as he'd finish his shift. We'd walk home together along the Valley Road, and share some news of his or my day.

The old athlete encouraged us lads to do a lot of running, which was a passion of mine anyway, and most times, I had the whole track to myself. At the end of one day, when he was locking the chain across the entrance of the driveway, he spotted two lads about my age hanging around the back windows of the center.

"Hoy! You two. Beat it! Get outta here!" The boys started sauntering away. "Move it!" My dad waved his arms.

"Ah, fuck off, yeh fat bastard," one shouted back.

"What? You fuckin'…," I shouted back, but quickly stopped myself. He grabbed my jacket as I was about to run after them.

"Hey! Enough of that! Don't you start your swearing like him."

Then, as they began to leg it out of the field, they both slid into the muddy ditch and shouted again, "Yeh fat bastard!" At the sight of them, my dad started laughing. When the old fellow laughed like that, tears would run down his face and his oversized tummy would bounce up and down. It was one of those bonding moments. His laugher was contagious.

Later, I kept my eyes open in the district for those boys, but they weren't from our way, so I never saw them again.

20

Flowers in the Childwall Valley

At our new home in Childwall Valley, a small piece of mud, about fifteen feet by fifteen feet, was allotted to every household. It was down the stairs and around the back, past the rubbish bins to get to our prized garden. Mum and I were the only ones who showed any real interest in this area given by the housing corporation. So as the weeks went by, I dug our little patch over, pulling out the rocks, roots and weeds. Finally, with a little guidance from a green-thumbed obsessive gardening neighbour (who I once spotted trimming his tiny lawn with scissors), I divided our patch with a diagonal pathway of gravel and flat stones. A dry pathway was much needed so my mother could hang out the laundry. One side I raked smooth and planted grass seed, and on the other, flowers and a couple of veggies: some sad-looking carrots and a few peas, which were knocked off one night just as they were ready to pick. My choice of flowers, and the ones I found easy to grow, were gladiolas, dahlias and irises, but of my favorites, the tall golden vanguard of spring, daffodils took the lead. I didn't need to buy any of these, they were aplenty at an old wooded park, past our district, at a magical place we all called Bluebell Woods. I wanted my own group of golden flowers, so I just brought home a pile of daffodil bulbs, on the back of my bike, and shoved them in the ground, and as the years passed, they multiplied and spread out nicely.

At the Bluebell Woods, the blue carpet was so thick, it was hard not to trample the flowers. These woods was divided down the middle by a wide and high stone wall with a big old screechy wrought iron gate at the centre of its hundred-yard length. Throughout this area were clusters of tall horse chestnut, oak and other deciduous trees, spaced well apart with a colourful undergrowth of tall rhododendron bushes. An amazing psychedelic experience was had when one walked from one side to the other, through the ancient gate. On the blue side, there was not a tinge of yellow, and on the other side of that dividing wall, hardly one bluebell was to be found, just a million daffodils.

These woods became a part of my own biological laboratory, where I'd examine different plants, bugs and the occasional animal. I once shot a rabbit with my homemade bow and arrow and took it home for stew. One winter I thought I was doing a hedgehog a favour. It was already in a state of curled-up hibernation on the path, so I buried it under a thick pile of leaves in a spot I could remember and came back in the spring only to find the skeleton. Maybe my choice of a winter hideaway was not as smart as the one found by the tiny prickly baseball. Still, I did get a few good remarks from the biology teacher when I turned up to class with my carefully glued project for winter: my hedgehog skeleton.

21

Collecting Birds' Eggs

Being uprooted from the inner city of Liverpool, and moving out yonder, I started to embrace and develop all sorts of new outdoor interests: fishing, gardening, sketching birds and trees, collecting seed specimens and keeping a small journal on what I was finding in the high grass, ponds and woods.

One interest, developed with the motivation of a few new school friends who'd grown up in the country, was collecting birds' eggs. At one boy's house, he showed me his fabulous collection, which was kept meticulously in two drawers in his room. A variety of eggs were displayed in neat rows, gently set in a thin layer of dry sand. Each egg had a small label below it, just like you'd see at a museum. Dozens of beautiful specimens he'd actually taken from the nests, with an awareness not to take more than one of each type. I immediately began to start my own collection, and some of us lads would go on special rambles here and there to score more for our hobby. There was a certain ingenuity to handling, collecting and especially climbing down a tree with a delicate egg. If it wasn't too big, it went in your mouth and was carefully held there till you reached the ground, or you wrapped the larger ones in a handkerchief and put in a loose pocket. I began to fill up my own collection drawer with colourful specimens. I'd spotted a blackbird's nest up in Bluebell Woods, set back in a deep thicket of low-lying bushes. Its four neatly placed eggs were warm to the touch. The mother bird was nearby, making a bit of a noise, and trying to distract me away. There was some contrived mythology among us kids that a bird can only count up to three, and so taking away the fourth egg wouldn't be too alarming when it got back to the nest. I wouldn't place too much credence on that idea, considering many birds only lay a couple of eggs.

On this occasion, I took two eggs, one for me and one for my friend, who was searching other bushes and trees, further in the woods. In the back of the lapel on my coat, I kept a small needle, which was used to make a hole at each end of the egg so you could carefully blow out the contents, and end up with a hollow egg for the collection. Some eggs were so tiny, like the tree sparrow egg I scooped out of a small nest, high up in a horse chestnut tree. The nest was inside a hollow, too small for a hand to get into, so I used a twig to roll one out. The egg was the size of your smallest fingernail.

Once while checking out a tawny owl's nest, I was dive-bombed by the bird, and not liking the idea of getting a talon across my face, I scurried down the tree, protecting my head from the mad mother, who swooped at me 'til I left the area.

I grew more interested in my other new hobby, fishing, and a while later, sold my egg collection to a mate for a few bob. But I still carried on drawing and painting quite a few watercolours of birds and fish. I also had an extensive stamp collection, full of all kinds of interesting pieces that I later gave away to an orphan boy I met in Australia when I wanted to help his future. He's probably bought a nice house by now. I also had a few Roman coins and a couple of English Silver Pax Pennies that were about a thousand years old. I don't know where they ended up.

22

Home Alone and Terrified

On September 9, 1962, at the beginning of fall, some horrible news struck our district. A girl, who lived just a mile down the road from us, right next to the railway line and the adjacent road tunnel, was murdered one evening, while she was home alone. The description of the crime was particularly savage, and word was out that a young man was seen by some neighbours running along the railway tracks at the same hour of night. After a couple of days, the police narrowed down the suspect to a description of a teenage boy. His height and build was similar to one of my brothers. After dinner one evening, I answered the front door to be met by two plain-clothes police detectives. They'd arrived to question Geoff about his whereabouts on that terrible night. Within minutes, he was dismissed as a person of interest, and they left. I briefly witnessed the police as they questioned my brother, and it revealed how serious some sides of life can be. As the days went by, the realization that the murderer was still at large caused my imagination to give me some anxious moments, especially with those dark, foggy streets with few people out and about.

We lived not far from the same train tracks, and our district had had its fair share of violent nutcases, and certain types of unpredictable people were to be carefully avoided. Gangs of restless? Hooligans out to make names for themselves in the new mixing bowl of council housing? From an early age, I'd witnessed harsh street fights and knew of a few locals who had done some jail time, but for someone to take a young girl's life so violently? Well, that had to be the most abhorrent of crimes. Commited by the lowest of the low.

At the end of the school day, I was usually the first to arrive home. I was twelve, and my older brothers had to take their buses from school across town, and my folks, were at work, miles away. Nobody was expected home for an hour or so after me, and I usually made a couple of jam butties with a cup of tea, and sometimes peeled some spuds to get things started for dinner.

By the time I got to our place, all the streets were dimly lit. A dark creepy atmosphere awaited me as I climbed the stairs to our front door. The house had sat cold all day, and it was the duty of the first one home to light the coal fire. None of these houses had any form of insulation or central heating, and it was like living in a fridge until the living room fire was rocking. Back in the kitchen, I put the radio on and tuned it to Radio Caroline to listen to the tunes as I poured myself a cup of tea. Suddenly a hand reached in from the hall, flipped the light switch off, and, with a hideous, muffled laugh, quickly closed the door. I went into what I can only describe as a state of shock, and yelled something like "Go away! Help!" as I grabbed the milk bottle. My heart beat fast, and my fear escalated as I began to imagine that the murderer was loose in our house! I became so frightened, thinking I would have to fight for my life against some horrible-looking creep with a huge knife, that I shouted again, "Get out, you bastard!" Suddenly the door swung open, and there stood my brother David, laughing hard, but trying to consol me over the trick he'd just pulled. I couldn't think straight, and my immediate reaction was to strike back, and I threw the cup of tea at him, missing him by inches. The cup smashed against the door. I leaned over the sink trying to collect myself. I'd been reduced to a lump of scared meat, and as he approached to calm me down, I growled and kicked at him like a disturbed animal. After a few moments of half laughing and half shouting, I shook it off. David apologized for scaring the shit out of me, and we cleaned up the broken cup and wiped the tea off the wall, and he agreed never to pull a stunt like that again. The prankster had come home early from school without letting me know, and was upstairs in his room lazing around when I'd arrived, and he crept down the stairs to surprise me. It was a terrifying moment for me, and another mischievious trick by my brother who was always up for a good laugh. We four brothers were good to each other, and always got along. But sometimes a laugh can go too far.

A couple of days later, on Saturday night, my folks were heading out to see a movie, and I was again to be home alone. My older brothers were out chasing skirt most nights, and I was usually very relaxed about having some time to myself to watch whatever I wanted on telly, as well as treat myself to a snack and do some art work. More news had travelled around the neighbourhood that an old person had been viciously attacked in their home days earlier, again, not far from us, and the girl's murderer was still at large. Feeling a bit nervous and uneasy about being left alone in the house, I asked my folks if they could stay home instead and we could all watch the telly together. Mum was all right with that, and asked dad. He came out with the expected reaction, that not only was I acting like a baby, but I'd also ruined his night. But they stayed home. My aunties and uncles mentioned to me, years later, that when we four were tiny babies crying in the crib, he forbid my mother from picking us up for comfort: "Don't pick IT up, you'll make IT soft." It was the old way of doing things, and our family was not the exception. Hardness was everywhere.

23

Holiday in Wales à la Great Train Robbery

n August, me and the folks took off for a couple of weeks' summer escape to a bed and breakfast in Llanrug (pronounced Llanrig), a small village near Caernarfon, North Wales.

Caernarfon Castle was the well-know place where Queen Elizabeth crowned her son, Charles, the Prince of Wales on July 1, 1969, before four thousand guests within the medieval walls. My older brothers stayed home and had their wild fun while we took off to see the great sites of the Welsh countryside, to visit castles, the mountains of Snowdonia and golden beaches. Our favourite beach was Benllech Bay on the Isle of Anglesey.

The big wide and cold Irish Sea has an abundance of fabulous beaches, ringing Scotland, England, Wales and Ireland. We first took a charabang from Liverpool, then the country bus from Caernarfon through the sleepy hills and dales to the farmland of Llanrug. We were greeted at the garden gate by the burly landlord Illtyd, his wife Bronwyn and their two lovely daughters, Anna and Caryl.

The landlord welcomed us in his beautiful Welsh language, then English. (My father always told me, "The Welsh speak the best English. Just listen to Dylan Thomas read his work *A Child's Christmas in Wales*.") After we'd put our bags away, we were invited for an afternoon snack and a cup of tea while our jolly sheep farmer entertained us with a couple of local North Wales songs, sung in his fabulous rich baritone voice.

The farming family would be using the downstairs areas of the house, and we had the two bedrooms upstairs. Every morning, they dished out the best breakfast one could ask for. Most days, we'd take off on our daily excursions and eat out a lot—sandwiches here, fish and chips there—but one night, we were invited for an evening with them, and treated to an enormous feast of roast lamb, with all the trimmings.

Peter in Llanrug Wales, 1963

On August 8, as we got back to the farm at the end of a long day out and about, the landlord and his wife met us, and told us he'd heard on the news that a big robbery had happened in England that morning, and millions in cash taken. This was later known as the Great Train Robbery of 1963. A bunch of guys had stopped a train, belted the driver over the head with an iron bar, sending him off to an early retirement. A London boy, Ronnie Biggs, was the most notorious robber, and ended up in the clink, only to escape and spend a few years in Australia and Brazil. I had a picture taken outside the barn on the day of the heist, so have a cast-iron alibi that I was in Wales on that particular day.

Funny thing about remembering jailbreaks, when we were driving across Dartmoor in a bus, a year later, there was an escape from the famous prison, and our bus was stopped and pulled over for an inspection. A copper came on board and took a couple of serious looks at my dad, asked him to stand up and said, "Nah, too short. Sorry, sit down please." The whole bus began to laugh, including me dad. "That was a close one, Albert!" me mother puts in.

Years earlier, we had taken a two-week summer holiday to a farm in Towyn, a small town east of Rhyl, in Wales. We were four young boys from the inner city, and the whole lively environment of the country was a wonderful adventure for us. Here was a typical variety farm, with a handful of sheep, goats, chickens and veggies for market.

The caravan we rented from the farm was a bit small for the six of us, so Geoff and I shared a double bed in the main house, which was very comfortable, and each morning, at the crack of dawn, we'd have a cup of tea with the rest of the house, while our crowd were still snoring across the yard. One day my folks asked the farmer if we could have a chicken for our teatime that night, so the man-of-the-house asked if I'd like to come along to choose which chicken was destined for the pot. On the way to the chicken run, he picked up a small sickle, licked his thumb and tested the blade for sharpness. "Which one shall we get, Peter? A brown one or a white one?"

"That one," I said, pointing at a frisky bird running madly around the pen.

He plunged the tip of the sickle into the fence post and grabbed the howling fowl, secured it tightly under his arm and quickly, with the flick of a wrist, rung its neck. We next walked out of the pen and across to the garden.

"Here, Peter, you hang on tight to its legs, and I'll take its head off."

"What?"

"Here! Hold on tight." And he thrust out the two dirty claws. I held onto the chicken's legs, he grabbed its head, cutting right through the neck with the curved sickle, and then the chicken swung down splattering its blood all over my legs. He told me to hold the bird over the roses right next to us, which I tried to do. The headless chicken was flapping, blood flying everywhere. Then he grabbed it from me, and I ran off. I don't think our folks were very happy with his thoughtless blundering.

This was the same week Geoff badly cut his ankle on a bike chain, and mam rushed him off to hospital. It turned out to be a bloody eventful week, to say the least, and every time we went on holidays something unusual happened, but it gave us things to talk or laugh about on the way home.

24

Crazy Rellies

An interesting religious moment came when I was about thirteen. One night, we were all home, watching the telly, or doing this and that, when a knock came to the door. Up I jumped and opened it to find this curious-looking couple, who appeared to be in their sixties, standing there, dressed up in real fancy colourful clothes. The woman was all dolled up with a funny floral hat on, and her husband was wearing a loud checkered suit that you'd imagine in an old James Cagney movie.

"Hi there, sonny. Is this the residence of Albert Hayes?" he chuckled.

"Yes. That's my dad."

"Well 'Glory Be!' Hallelujah! And what's your name?"

"Peter," I said, backing away as they reached out to give me some kind of hug.

"Hey, dad." I shouted, as I stepped back. "There's these crazy people at the door. A religious man and a woman. They sound American."

I turned around, and they were already in the house, howling and shouting.

"Lord Jaysus, Hallelujah. Glory be!" And on and on, like I'd never seen before in my life.

"Albert!" "Tommy!" "Florry!" "Mary!" They were all shouting.

"This is your uncle Tom and auntie Flo from America," Dad said. I even heard my dad say "Praise the Lord." Not a usual expression from him.

"Surprise!" shouts his loud brother with the overt Yanky accent. They'd only been in the US for thirteen years, yet they were talking like perfect Yanks. Not a Scouse word between them.

This bubbly couple had arrived unannounced and were here to see their extended family, my invisible cousins and relatives, who lived in the same town. I was soon to be meeting a couple of them. Two lads, David and Eric, my own age, that were Tom's grandchildren, making them second cousins to me. And there were many more relatives out there. Enough to start a couple of football teams.

Tom and Flo, thank goodness, would be staying with their daughter Gina and hubby, Eric Jones. I felt spared. We were to all meet on the weekend at their house, just a ten-minute walk from our old house back in Everton. I couldn't believe it. They lived just down the road, and I knew nothing about any of them.

After Sunday dinner, we went to some church to watch our stomping, Bible-thumping evangelist, called uncle Tommy, preach hellfire and damnation, American style. I fell asleep in the back row during his rant. I guess roast lamb and potatoes for dinner will do that. I was informed by my newly discovered family members that they were returning with Tom and Flo to America shortly, to be with the rest of the crowd. I only had that one encounter with Dave and Eric, and they ended up (after trying out Mississippi) returning to the old country and living on the Isle of Man, in the Irish Sea. Uncle Tommy died many years later in Mississippi at one hundred years old.

I was soon to learn more of my father's secretive past. To draw a family tree of our crowd would wear out a pencil, but our dad knew where they lived—aunties, uncles and cousins, like the tribe of Israel—but he had no desire to contact anyone. He had nine siblings, and they all had kids who had kids. My brothers and I had inquiring minds, and shortly after learning this, realized that our auntie Edna, who we'd visited for years at the prefabs in Lee Park, was in fact our half-sister Edna from his previous marriage. Auntie Edna, really?

She was not much younger than our mother, and way too young to be dad's sibling. So, after putting things together, it also became obvious that her two daughters were not our cousins, as we were always told, but were in fact our step-nieces. I went to school with one, and had once belted a guy for making her cry.

But more explosive than any of these revelations was when I later found out, at sixteen, that our family name was not Hayes but Haase.

Before graduating from school, every student was required to bring their birth certificate in, to verify the spelling of their name. As my dad handed the certificate to me, my eyes lit up.

"Dad, look, they've spelt my name wrong."

"That's your real name, son. It's a long story." And so it was. There were other "long stories," and his secretive ways were beginning to really annoy me.

He was a typical Victorian Brit—stiff upper lip, and all that rot. "Children should be seen and not heard." Keep the children and the wife in their place. Unfortunately I'd begun to mistrust him about a few things from an early age, and that was a disappointment.

Shortly after the initial meeting with the Pentecostal preacher and his wife, I tied a few more loose ends together in my head. I had a cousin about forty years old, Uncle Tom's son, who didn't live too far away, and once in a while, he'd pop by, and dad would talk privately with him, always out on the street. He never invited him in. I was sent on an errand one day way down Breck Road, to give Young Tommy a ten-bob note. I'd seen my dad give him a little cash before, and it seemed the guy was never doing too well. He was "the Preacher man's" oldest kid, and he and Gina, his sister, had stayed behind in Liverpool when the rest of the large family immigrated to the States in 1950.

My eyes were opened, for the first time, to the flamboyant and bazaar world of the Pentecostal way of doing things, when Tom and Flo passed around some photographs of people laying around and jumping all over the place at their church meetings. "Under the Power of God." It was shocking, to say the least, when I thought church was a place of quiet respect, and not a showy circus act. Then out came the picture of another unknown cousin of mine in the US army. Dad's remark, as he turned to me was: "Look at your soldier cousin here. I joined the army. It made a man out of me." Later, when I was nineteen and living in Australia, I had to register my name for conscription for the Vietnam War. The old fella said the same thing again, "It made a man outta me."

"Yes, dad," was my response, "but I don't believe in this war. It's not like taking on the Nazis. I'd sign up for that, but not for this bullshit."

"What? You're a pacifist?" he inquired.

"No! You know I'm not. If somebody attacked Aussie, I'd join up and fight. But we won't be taken over by the Commies, like all the liars tell us. It's fearmongering to get us scared for nothing."

He walked away.

My cousin, young Tommy, had had a tumultuous life, and was at sea for years, and I heard from others in the clan that he'd done some serious time. But I guess that comes with the territory of combat, zealous religion and poverty. I never saw any of that religious crowd again. They all vanished as quickly as they arrived. Amen.

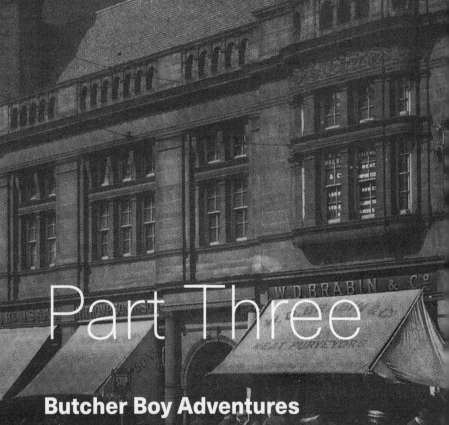

Part Three

Butcher Boy Adventures

25

Scoring at St. John's Market

When I was fourteen, I made a decision that it was time to quit the run-of-the-mill, yo-yo jobs that young lads start off with to get a bit of pocket money. It was time for bigger and better things. As a twelve-year-old, my brother Dave had helped me score a paper round, where I'd earn a miserable six shillings and sixpence for delivering two large, heavy bags of newspapers, five nights a week after school. A little bit of money, in fact a very slight amount of moola for the trouble of hand delivering the *Liverpool Echo* through the letter boxes of all the houses and three-level flats that lined our streets. There wasn't the luxury of riding around on a peddle bike, hurling the rolled-up news rags onto rich folks lawns like you see in the American movies. No, we had to climb the stairs and slide the papers through the mail slot, making sure not to tear or mess up the folded missive, and when Saturday came around, we paper boys would now have to go from house to house, door to door, to collect the money for our miserly boss. Any customer withholding payment from us usually blamed it on the delivery of a dirty or wet newspaper. The unpaid money came out of our measly pay, but now and again, we also got a small tip from a grateful person, for our services. I couldn't wait to leave that god-awful, thankless job. For all that effort, I hardly made a Yankee dollar in a week. It was the tips that kept me there for the best part of a year.

Opposite: St. John's Market, Brabin's Meat Purveyor's, 1909

Liverpool's town center was where I started my search. That's where all the action was. And as fortune would have it, the very first place I went to was not only one of my most favourite and exciting places to hang out, but also the spot where I was lucky enough to score a great part-time job. The name of this hub of activity was St. John's Market. Here was a bustling location where I could apply my skills, but at what? Some people mistakenly called this market Paddy's Market, but the real Paddy's was on Great Homer Street.

St. John's, built in 1822, was further downtown, on Great Charlotte Street. This huge monolith of a building was one city block of ornate arched stonework, blackened by 150 years of soot that had billowed out of the thousands of chimneys from our coal-burning homes. If one was looking for a great laugh and a good time, this area of town was one of a few marketplaces to be on a Saturday morning. It was nonstop action and entertainment. A real market!

An amazing potpourri of stalls represented everything including greengrocers, flower shops, dairy shops, butchers and fishmongers. Further up the street, at Queen's Square, a lineup of fly-by-night, silver-tongued salesmen had their stalls and carts. One of these regular guys would demonstrate magic kitchen knives. He'd cut through a three-inch nail and then perfectly slice an over-ripe tomato with the same knife. Amazing! Another tinker in a borrowed oversized suit would be flogging "genuine gold" watches, beautiful objects of European engineering, completely guaranteed, of course, to last a lifetime. The warranty only fulfilled if you could ever find this guy called Joe again. Good luck. Another fellow with a strong Glaswegian accent sold crystal glassware imported all the way from Naples, Italy, while his buddy alongside, with the Geordie accent, offered the ladies exquisite silk cloth, by the yard, which, of course again, had just arrived by sea from China. These two clowns, who'd obviously kissed the Blarney Stone, looked like they'd spent a few months in the same room together, otherwise known as a cell, rehearsing their eloquent pitch.

The old market was a mixture of grand hallways and stooped passageways crammed together in a mishmash of organized confusion, smelly, dank, dirty and old. Everyone was shouting out the prices for this and that. There were the extroverted singers and joke tellers, people laughing loudly at the general goings-on of all participants, customers and venders alike. It was alive with the aromas of fresh vegetables and fruit and the sharp primitive reek of unrefrigerated carcasses of lamb, pigs and beef, as well as geese, ducks and chickens all hanging by their necks, and of course, turkeys at Christmas time. On most Saturdays, the crowds were graced with the effervescent performance of a gentleman vendor, who always sported a showy dickey-bow-tie. He kept live chickens and rabbits in a few cages, and you made your choice; he'd take the poor creature around the back of a screen door, dispatch it and return to the counter where he'd wrap it up in newspaper. All this in less than a minute. You'd take it home where you would have to clean, pluck and dress hoppy or henny for dinner.

I must not omit mentioning the in-house bakery with its bread, buns and cakes fresh out of the oven. You could buy a fresh buttered barm cake, a small bun for only a couple of pennies, and everyone would line up patiently as the hot trays were pulled out of the big ovens.

Hundreds of people of every shape and size, age and ethnic background were milling around. Their arms sagged under the weight of trophy purchases; the only thing missing was the cash they'd spent, and the cares of the world. Ah, peace of mind, a laugh, a cup of tea, a buttered barm cake, a bag of fresh groceries and a dead hen, wrapped in newspaper under your arm for dinner tonight. Who could ask for more?

I had to find work; my dad's wages and my mother's part-time jobs kept our ship afloat, but they had no possible way of dishing out pocket money to us four boys each week—we had to find our own resources. At an early age, my brothers and I had learned the realities of frugality with our patched-up clothes and secondhand shoes. We did get the occasional treat of ice cream or a piece of chocolate, and our family always had a two-week summer holiday somewhere in the country-side, usually in Wales or the Lake District. Dad did his best with what he had, and his was a long, hard life of graft. He finally retired from drudgery when he was seventy. When I worked on the paper round, and got my pay of six and six, I'd take it home, give it to dad, and he'd give me back one shilling and sixpence. He kept five bob for himself, and told me he was proud of me helping out the family. It wasn't long before I didn't feel like helping out so much, when I began to realize I was working hard each day and getting nowhere fast. The old fellow's ways didn't stimulate a climate of trust, and I learned at an early age not to tell him everything. He'd always reach out to help himself, so I always told him I made less than I really did. The less he knew, the better. Once, when I was tiny, after I'd shined up a few pennies with some Brasso, and hidden them away in, of all places, an empty Pond's Vanishing Cream jar, which he found, he said, "Whatever money comes in this 'ouse, son, is my money. OK?"

I'd tried other menial jobs in my search for some dosh. Usually I found hard and tough work. Yard work, washing windows, cleaning up at the boys' club. Small labouring jobs for a shilling here and there. These were all mindless jobs to me. There was also the annual Boy Scout slavery for seven days, called Bob-a-Job Week, where scouts and cubs would be hired by anyone to fix this or shovel that for a lousy shilling, or bob, as we called it. Some unlucky kids got lumbered into working their arses off for a lousy twelve pennies, and then taking it to the scout hall and handing it in. This was all to raise funds for the scouting events throughout the year. I was a cub for a short while, but didn't like the old folks who ran it. They were a bit weird. After a stint of doing the three-finger salute, standing at attention in the rain for two hours on parade day and promising to "do our duty to God and the Queen," etc., I was finally dismissed and sent home for not cooper-ating with the big noisy old bag, the 'Our Kalah' or whatever her name was. She'd scream and shout out all the orders as we'd run around in circles, leapfrogging over each other, climbing ropes and doing all the exercises, preparing us for the Navy Seals. There was hardly an empty spot on her shirt, it was so full of badges for everything from rubbing two sticks to make a fire to darning a sock. Boy, she must have had more decorations than Field Marshal Montgomery, and could have won the war all on her own. "'Tention! Stand easy!"

Nothing, as yet, seemed to offer any kind of interest or a future that I could aim towards. So, in 1964, I felt that my moment to discover something really new and exciting was there for me to find and grab. A part-time number that maybe had a promising foundation in a trade or a good-paying future career when I was finally through school at sixteen. I had quite a variety of interests, but I didn't really know where to start. I had a way of fixing things, and from an early age, possessed an understanding of how things were put together, how things worked. I even learned how to mend my own shoes, darn my own socks and patch clothes when I was just a wee bairn.

I'd resole or reheel my shoes on a cobbler's last, a small, heavy, three-sided steel anvil. We also used the last when we replaced missing studs from our football boots and sometimes as a doorstop, to keep the front door open on warm summer days. I'd once repaired the family vacuum cleaner, helped replace a couple of broken windows, took things apart and put them back together, sometimes making quick sketches as I worked. All this before I was ten years old. I loved mechanical things and later, in my teens, had helped restore a couple of motorbikes with my friend Billy and his older brother. An old BSA Bantam 175 and a Matchless 250.

I enjoyed solving mechanical puzzles, seeing which piece went where. But my very first remembrance of attempting to fix something was when I was six or seven. One day I overheard my mother telling dad that her small wristwatch wasn't working right. "It won't wind up properly," she said. So after she'd gone shopping, I thought I'd have a look and see if I could find out what was wrong. I'd surprise her by fixing it. Wouldn't I? I popped the back cover off with a small knife as I'd seen done before, and looked inside at all the beautiful, tiny wheels that usually rocked back and forth. Nothing was moving. I then noticed a long hair that was wrapped around the working parts. I gave it a little pull, and the long strand came right out. Great, I thought; that's the problem. That hair must have stopped everything from moving around. I clipped the back cover on again. Now it would wind easily, but still nothing seemed to happen; it wouldn't tick.

When she came home I told her, "I think I've fixed your watch mum. There was a hair wrapped around the little wheels inside the back."

"Oh no," she said, "that's the hairspring that keeps the watch going. Were did you put it"?

"I pulled it out and threw it in the fire."

That was the first and last time I attempted to repair a watch.

One morning in March, a week after my birthday, just to satisfy my curiosity, I decided to get the bus downtown, plod the streets and take a general overview of what kind of work was out there, waiting for me. I had some friends who worked at shops after school, and they were always flush with a bit of dough. So I was out to follow suit.

26

To Be or Not to Be a Butcher Boy

turned up at St. John's at 8 am. It was a bright, chilly, spring morning. I began to walk from stall to stall enquiring if they could use a lad like me for work on Saturdays and after school on weekdays. The greengrocer's response, as he elbowed a tall skinny boy, "We just took this lad on. You're a week late, sonny boy."

The fishmonger said, "We only hire girls here; they cut up the fish better than the boys." Wink, wink. Yes indeed. I could see the girls he was hiring. Wow! wink, wink, say no more! After just a short while walking around and asking here and there, a hand grabbed my shoulder from behind with the grip of a Scottish landlord, and as I turned to see if it were friend or foe, I came face to face with a curious little man, not much taller than my five-foot-five stature. He had a big beaming smile from ear to ear and a wild, happy way about him.

"Hey, young Wacker, are you looking for work?"

"Yes, Mister." I gathered from his blue-and-white striped apron and sawdust all over his boots that this jolly old fellow was a butcher.

"I need a lad for Saturdays and maybe a bit after school during the week. Interested?"

"Bloody right! Oops, sorry, sir."

"It's alright, son, just don't let the customers hear that or you'll be gone. OK?"

"OK."

"Jack Simpson's the name. But just call me Jack."

"I'm Peter, but me mates call me Digger."

"What? Why's that?"

"'Cause I dig it man, rock and roll? Dead right. How much are you paying like?"

"I'll start you at a quid for all day Saturday, and we'll see how you do. We have an hour for dinner at the pub. We start setting up at 7. Dinner's at 12, and you'll get half a crown for your nosh."

"Sounds the gear. What about after school?"

"I'll need you for two hours on Tuesday and Fridays to get set up for Saturday, that's our biggest day, as you can see," as we looked around at the madding crowd.

"Great, when do I start?"

"Right now, Pete, I mean Digger. Grab an apron and roll up your sleeves, we've got lots to do."

This was to be the first of five butcher shops that I would work in from fourteen to sixteen, all very different experiences. I was chuffed to bits to score a job with Jack; this was what I was looking for. This fitted the bill. In half an hour, I'd found something totally unexpected and exciting. For my job search, I'd dressed up presentably in a white shirt and tie. This was fortuitous, because all the butcher boys throughout the market wore shirts and ties, and their aprons; it was the expected dress code. I picked out the least dirty, worn-out, blue-and-white striped apron, tied up the long waist bands. The first order of the day from Jack was, "Put the kettle on, we're having tea."

"Yes, sir, captain," I replied, not knowing yet that this fellow, with the exaggerated limp, was a ship's butcher, and an old sea dog; kind-hearted and a bit rough round the edges. It wasn't an unusual expression to come out with "captain" or "matey" or some other nautical term where I come from.

Our town had been a departure and destination point for hundreds of years, and during the early ninetieth century, over half the town were sailor boys. One unfortunate black mark Liverpool had was that she was the main British seaport involved in the slave trade. We had many seafarers in our family. My granddad went off to sea at the age of thirteen; salt is in our blood. My butcher boss, Jack, had taken up his trade at sea as a teenager. He'd touched most of the notable ports around the world, travelled many times, in both directions, through the Suez and Panama canals and had lots of great stories that he often shared with me as we waited around for a customer to stop and buy a cut of meat. His limp was due to an injury suffered during some heavy seas on the Pacific side, the nearest port of call being Valparaiso, Chile. In hospital there, it was necessary to take his lower leg off to save his life, and they fitted him with a wooden leg from the knee down. His ship left a day after they'd dropped him off, and he spent some weeks in the Chilian hospital recovering, finally being brought home to Liverpool on a sister ship. He sailed for a couple of more years after that on shorter trips around Europe, the Mediterranean and Africa, then finally quit the sea, for good, to take a shore job.

Four other butcher stalls were scattered throughout the market aisles, each one with its lone butcher and one or two lads. Jack was a real motormouth. All day he was eating and talking, and he'd go through at least three pints of bitter, which he kept behind the screen at the back of our small congested retail outlet. I found his company educational, comical and his language consistent with his Liverpool upbringing, down to earth. After we'd set up the counter and laid out a nice display of produce, we sorted out what was to be cut up from the large slabs of meat, he'd teach me how to mark and divide a carcass. The various joints of lamb—legs, shoulders, chops, breast, etc.—and all the inside offal, which some people call "awful," the liver, heart, kidneys and sweetbreads, even the lungs, which we called lights. The lights were mainly bought by the older poor folk, who made soup out of them, and others cooked them up for their dogs.

I had a lot to learn, and it was all very interesting and new. It certainly wasn't a place for the squeamish, and you had to be quick to learn and also deft with a very sharp knife. There wasn't any time to be plodding along. It's a trade of speed and skill, high skill.

While dividing up a quarter-side of beef or a pork or lamb, I'd sometimes pretend I was a surgeon operating on somebody, removing the liver or kidneys, or amputating an arm or leg. As a kid, I'd watch the live surgery shows on telly and take down notes, and draw sketches of the appendectomies and joint repairs etc. I often thought I wanted to be a doctor, but that wasn't in the cards.

We'd have a laugh now and then, sharing our inside jokes as we served the customers. A leg of Jack meant a leg of lamb. (He'd often make up jokes about his lost limb.) Pigs trotters we'd label "tired feet." Once we displayed a whole pig's head with a banana in its mouth and a coconut on its head; the sign read, Fresh Caribbean Pork. Amusing behavior was all around us, and it made the toil of the day pass by quickly. Our counter would end up as a beautiful array of neatly displayed varieties of cuts: Argentine sirloin steaks, lamb or pork chops, bacon, sausages and minced meat. The rows of trays were bordered with parsley, tomatoes and discarded flowers from the nearby florest. We'd watch over the display and swab up the excess blood as it pooled on the lower end of the trays because they slanted down at the front.

"People will buy the meat if they see an attractive presentation with not much blood showing." Jack's words.

Throughout the day, we'd constantly replenish the sold product and keep things tickety-boo. If things were up to scratch, we could sit back on our chairs, sipping on a drink and enjoying a smoke. He'd have a brew in his big mug to pretend he was drinking tea, and I'd drink my tea or Coke, the slower pace allowing us to chat and exchange story after hysterical story. Our allotted areas in the market were pretty small for all the activities that needed to be done. To our left was a fishmonger, and to the right, a greengrocer's. Until summer arrived, the market was always cold, with no heat anywhere except at the baker's end. I'd wear two pairs of socks because of the freezing concrete floor. The marble counter for the display case on top of the refrigeration was always chilly, and it seemed our hands were always red and half numb. But we had the tea on the back burner all day, adding tea leaves and boiling water as the pot went down, the result being, a half-full pot of tea leaves and black super-strong tea, hardly drinkable. That's what kept us warm.

One of the largest objects that we had to dodge around, in our cramped area, was the huge butcher's block: a massive piece of laminated wood about a foot thick, stretching four feet across by six feet long. It showed the scars of years of heavy use and assault by cleaver, knife and wire brush. It could bare the weight of a whole hindquarter of beef with its stout oak legs and wide feet. The block was the center of the business; without it, nothing happens. Here was where we'd throw down a huge slab of beef, or a carcase of pork or lamb, attach the meat hooks—a large one for beef, and a medium hook on each hind leg of a pork or a lamb—lift the load together on the count of three and hoist it upwards, hooking it onto the overhead chrome steel rail. Before lifting the pig, its head would be taken off with a large handsaw while it rested on the block; we hadn't such things as electric band saws that are used in today's butchers shops. Up on the rail, the carcass of pork or lamb was sawn down the center of the vertebrae, from tail to neck, and divided into two sides (the reason for a hook in each leg), then lowered onto the block for dissecting. The various chops were also divided by the deliberate, careful aim of the heavy cleaver, hence the name chops.

At the end of each day, the big greasy, heavy block of wood required a good swilling down with hot soapy water, while we scrubbed like hell to remove all the remains of blood, pieces of meat, fat and bone fragments. Finally the block was swilled down again with scalding water, which had a tiny drop of bleach thrown in, until it was spotless. All metal objects—the cleavers, knives, saws, hooks and trays—were also cleaned and sterilized. Next, the sawdust on the floor was swept up and ditched and the floor hosed clean. The last task of the day was our favourite job, counting up the money.

Throughout its long past, the old market had been a haven from the cold elements for the occasional tramp or transient, and it still remained a place of generosity for needy folk. Jack and I would often give a free parcel to a poor old lady to take home. It was the spirit of the place. But there was a limit, and the well-heeled paid full whack. In fact, I remember watching Jack as he put his thumb on the edge of the scale to make the meat weigh a little more, and charge the wealthy-looking lady, dripping with jewelry, a bit extra.

"There's a couple of pints there, laddie." Wink, wink. As he shoved the extra coin into his pocket.

Cleaning up a butcher's shop, day after day, can be tediously dirty work, but it's all part of the graft. There's a system to follow, and half measures were frowned upon by respected butchers; everything had to shine, and if a butcher boy was slack, he was gone. History. All the remaining cut-up meat was transferred to clean trays to be refrigerated overnight, and any meat that was not to be kept was divvied up between me and Jack. We'd each end up taking a couple of bags home. We had our own friends and neighbors who would buy from us. Mrs. Brown bought this, and Mrs. Kelly got that and so on. We called it the spoils of war and made a few bob on the side for our trouble, and I especially kept it quiet at home, and barely breathed a word about extra cash to anyone. It all fell off a lorry.

Our stall was owned by a Greek that Jack had worked for since he'd left the sea. They didn't like each other too much, and so the old salt felt no guilt about helping himself to meat or money. To a degree, neither did I. We were both on the make, and we'd laugh about it. At the end of every Saturday, when all was done, it was time to collect my pay and a Sunday roast. For the first two weeks, he paid me a quid for all day Saturday and seven shillings and sixpence for each night after school. After that, I got one pound ten shillings for Saturday and ten bob for the weekdays. Sometimes I'd skip school to get to the market earlier to make extra dough. It would take me an hour on the busses to get there and an hour back home. I'd get home at 6 or 7 and be exhausted, have a bite, do my homework and pass out. I learned from an early age the meaning of long days and hard graft. For those two years before turning sixteen, I didn't have too many Saturdays to myself except for our two-week family holiday in summer. I only went a couple of times to see professional football games, Liverpool once and Everton once. I regret that I missed out on the footy a lot, and while most of my mates were out and about getting into this and that, I was learning the butcher's trade and making whatever money I could. Still, looking back at it, I enjoyed most of the work, and I always had Saturday night to chase skirt and Sunday to go fishing.

The front marble counter at our stall was in easy reach of passersby. A long wooden stop prevented the trays from falling onto the walkway. If we weren't watching, anyone could come along and take what they felt like. On one particularly busy day, when the dazed mulling crowd was larger than usual and the hustle bustle was all along the front of our stall, we were sitting back in our chairs and noticed this fellow sauntering by, reading his newspaper. He stopped for a moment next to a heaping pile of fresh chickens at the end of our counter and rested his newspaper on top. Then reaching underneath, he slid one chicken beneath his paper and carried on, pretending to read. We both saw this, and Jack whispered to me, "Watch this lad!" He reached for a leg of lamb from the rail, limped after the chicken snatcher and belted him right over his shoulder. Wallop! The man went to his knees, the chicken went one way, and the newspaper the other, while an old woman screamed and a man grabbed Jack by the arm. The place went mad, and in a few moments, two security guards had pushed their way through the throngs of onlookers, apprehended Jack and removed the lethal weapon from his grip, the leg of lamb (fortunately a fresh leg and not a frozen one). Holding onto the struggling robber, the guards dispersed the crowd and told Jack to wait around till the cops came, so he gladly sat back in his chair, behind the counter, poured himself a brew in his tea mug and lit up a smoke.

We laughed a little, and I could see Jack felt a bit exhilarated over the whole thing. So did I. It's always the gear to see a little action once in a while. Finally the police took statements from us both, along with other witnesses, and we were told that the culprit had a criminal history and was well-known to the local cops. Still, Jack was warned, in no uncertain terms, not to take the law into his own hands, or else. He agreed, like a schoolboy, nodding his head. As soon as the boys in blue were gone, we decided to call it a day and visit the pub on the corner to celebrate; any excuse for a drink, as they say. Jack became the toast of the market, and we both went home late and a bit inebriated, except he didn't get into trouble back home like I did.

As the months went by, he and I developed a finely choreographed routine. We kept the big key to the stall and the freezer in a secret spot, so whoever arrived first on Saturday morning could open up and get things rolling. It was usually me. Jack was getting tired of it all; he was getting on, and he really missed his years at sea. He'd bring old photos to work that he'd taken of his travels. In one picture, he was holding up a large shark he'd caught in the Red Sea; another was a shot of a football game on the docks with sailors from other ships that were waiting to unload cargo in Lagos Apapa, on the Ivory Coast in Africa. In these happy times, he was just a young, adventurous man, years before he lost his leg in Chile. I told him that I was also going to sea one day, with the Merchant Navy, when I was through with school, and would join my brother Geoff, who had also sailed around Africa. For an old salt, like him, life ashore was boring and too predictable, and he was really getting into the sauce. I had my worries about him being tipsy and working with the sharp blades, even though he was highly skilled. He'd even arrive at work on Saturday morning half tanked, and I'd sit him down, get him an egg and bacon sandwich from the café and nurse him till he sobered up.

One morning in the middle of summer, I was surprised to find old Jack had arrived early, and he and the Greek owner were arguing about the business going under. Jack was given his marching orders because of his mismanagement and the attack on the chicken thief two months earlier. As I approached the two of them in highly animated discourse, the owner turned and asked who I was. Jack said I was his helper, to which the Greek growled,

"Then he can fuck off too."

"Thanks," I replied. "Who the hell are you?" I'd never seen this nutcase before.

His response? "I own this fucking place. Now pack up and scarper."

Whoopee for me. This was the first time I was fired. I later found out that my old pal Jack was dipping into the till a lot more than I'd realized. He had a big gambling habit, and there must have been a pretty good load of debt he was carrying. After a few minutes, Jack gathered his personal stuff together, his knives and other objects of trade, told the Greek where to shove his shitty job, and the two of us took off down the street to the local café. He bought me some breakfast and gave me five shillings out of his own pocket for turning up.

27

Jack and Pete Ride Again

We knew all the butchers in the district, so Jack and I decided to do the rounds together and see if we could score a couple of jobs. Surely someone could take us on, we two shipmates—"The Captain and the Kid." Everyone at the market instantly became aware that Jack and Pete were stuffed; news always travelled quickly in that close community, and the word got round to help us out. One place we knew that had promise was one of the oldest stores in Liverpool where you could buy a slice of meat: the historical establishment of Brabin's Butcher Shop, on the corner of St. John's Market, was a bastion of tradition to the meat industry. With its big windows and archways, it was the vision of what an English butcher shop was supposed to be. They had six or so tradesmen butchers and a couple of lads. Its cellar, accessed only by a huge, heavy trapdoor in the middle of the floor which was big enough so you could carry a hefty chunk of meat over your shoulder down the dark stairs to the large walk-in freezer which contained a perennial mountain of chickens and hanging meat. Down in the bowels of that stinking hole, there remained a network of old broken, cemented-up drain and sewer pipes, conveniently used as a highway system for the rats that inhabited the square block. A subterranean larder of free food carelessly spilled by the market vendors on the stalls above.

Up on street level, across the adjacent alleyway, stood the other part of the Brabin business, the fishmonger, with its fabulous display of all the local fish brought in from the Atlantic Ocean and Irish and North Seas. It was an enormous array of shiny, bright-eyed swimmers—haddock, pollock, whiting, sole, plaice and cod, plus the dry salted cod from Newfoundland that was pressed flat and looked like tennis racquets. Conger eel, mackerel and kippered or pickled herring. Freshwater fish included trout and Scottish salmon and buckets of Spanish sardines, fresh-caught crab, scallops, shrimp and periwinkles from Northern Wales and the Wirral Peninsula and, of course, not forgetting the cockles and mussels alive, alive oh.

Here in the fish store were two old hands and one lad learning the slippery trade. Jack and I stepped through the front door to the wild reception of shouting and laughing. They'd heard about our morning start with Popagopolis the Greek and, like everyone else, thought it most humorous. Kenny, the tall, blond-haired, blue-eyed part-time entertainer, ran the joint. He was a real lad, a bit of a hard case, and famously, a very smart and tough boss, and a hell of a womanizer. His right-hand man, Short-arsed Terry, was partner in the store and a fellow band member in the club scene with the occasional gig. This Terry character was someone to look out for; we all knew him as a backstabber.

This magnetic place, Brabin's, had the radio playing all day long, and everyone would sing along with the popular tunes. It was the most ideal setting to work in. The tea was always on, just like at the last place, and the kitchen in the back had frying pans and ovens that came in handy for lunchtimes, where eggs, bacon and sausages was the usual, with fried bread. Mmm, bread, fried crispy brown in bacon fat or lard— the poor man's high-energy food. After inviting us for a cup of tea and some toast, Kenny offered old Jack a job in the fishmonger's side, but he had nothing for me at that time. I knew the odds were slim for both of us to score a number, so I was glad for my mate Jack. He began right away, rolled up his shirt sleeves and started into the fish, which he knew as well as meat. I lit up a smoke and hung around for a bit, watching as he filleted all shapes and sizes with the high skill of a surgeon.

Time was ticking, so I decided to wander back across the street to the market, a large box-like building that was being used while the old market was slowly being demolished and replaced by the modern shopping center that was to be called St. John's Precinct, a name I thought more suitable for a prison than a marketplace. One of the young greengrocer lads was a mate of mine; we'd hang around a bit together downtown after hours and had been to the Cavern Club lunch-hour specials a few times to see the bands.

Sid was an orphan and had grown up in a different part of town than me. He had a couple of older brothers and sisters and never knew he'd been adopted until he'd found out by accident when he was fifteen. His single mum had given him up as a tiny baby, so he thought his folks were truly his. I suppose the shock of finding out the real story had an impact on his view of life, and he began to rebel against everything and get into trouble at school and with the law. He was a couple of years older than me and was working steady all week at a grocer's stall while I was still going to school. Therefore, my pal Sid was in on all the market gen and mentioned the grumpy old butcher at the far end who had just fired a boy for some reason. I'd heard of this old guy named Henry who rubbed everyone the wrong way, and was warned about his miserable ways. Nobody I knew liked him. Henry was the stiff-necked curmudgeon who'd demanded extra security guards to watch things.

As reluctant as a chicken in a slaughterhouse, I walked down to Henry's stall, to check out the possible job opening, and his response, as he looked me up and down, was, "I heard all about you and your peg-leg boss getting sacked, but I'll try you out for the day, and see if you're worth keeping."

"I usually get a pound for Saturday, and I can also work after school," I said.

"A quid? Alright, but I don't need any help during the week."

He didn't understand that he was the one being tested, not me. I started work right away, and within a few minutes, it was lunchtime. I thought it kind of lucky: I was fired in the morning and hired at noon; that was quick.

The contrast between Jack and Henry was huge: one, the generous, patient mentor and pal, and the other, the hard, intolerant European with a strong accent and equally strong garlic breath. He spoke in a half whisper and half growl, like the familiar "Vee have vays of making you talk" kind of voices. I had no sooner put on an apron and rolled up my sleeves, when it was do zis and do zat.

He noticed that I had been trained well by Jack, and offered me more work for the next week, if I wanted it. I reluctantly accepted, and returned the following Saturday, only to quit after half a day. The circumstances were as follows.

Henry had gone off somewhere for ten minutes. He returned just as I had finished serving a customer and was sorting out the change in the till drawer. Henry went cuckoo. He picked up a short boning knife and put it to my neck, telling me clearly, in his angry voice, "Zat is my piano, unt I am the only one who plays vid it!"

This scared the hell out of me, and I told him that I was leaving immediately. It was obvious that he had no time to listen to my reasoning for sorting out the misplaced coins. I knew very well to keep my hands to myself with this fellow. He told me, in no uncertain terms, to get lost as I grabbed my coat and took off to get the market manager, who returned with me a few minutes later to give Henry hell. We began arguing back and forth, but all I wanted was my pay. Henry took a quid from the till, crumpled it up in his bloodied hand and threw it at me. Now the enraged manager told him that this wasn't the first time he'd crossed the line and he'd be proceeding with the termination of his lease. The old bugger just laughed and told him where to go too. As I left the scene with my dirty one-pound note in my pocket, I vowed that I'd see to him when he was least expecting it. Nobody was going to threaten me with a blade and get away with it.

I quickly exited the building and crossed the street to see Jack. After telling him what had just happened, he got jumping mad and was going to sort out the Jerry Bastard, as he always called him. I didn't want an old sailor with only one good leg fixing my problems. That night I had trouble getting to sleep. I lay there in my tumbled bed, haunted by that razor-sharp blade at my throat, and the insane look on that old bastard's face. He'd definitely shook me up, and he was going to pay, in spades.

28

Filthy Lucre and the Slide Down the Shute

Sid the greengrocer was becoming a good mate, and he would buy me the occasional pack of fags or a pint at the pub. We would go up the road for some good lunches at Yates' Wine Lodge, and I regarded him as a far better friend than some of my sly acquaintances I had back at school. As they say, you can usually count on one hand who your real friends are. Sid was one of them. We were both into lifting, and from an early age, we knew a bit about survival and knocking off. We'd pick our times and targets and eat our way around the market, distract the vendors and scoff back all the reachable food—easy pickings. One day we made an arrangement to meet at his stall late Wednesday morning, with a certain purpose in mind: to do a bigger job on the whole market.

In those times, it was an old English tradition that all stores would close for half a day on Wednesday and there'd be no shopping on Sunday. On that Wednesday, after Sid closed up the greengrocer's stall, we waited around the corner till his boss had gone home, then went back and hid in the stall till we heard the big iron gates of the market slam shut and the whole place was finally empty, except for the two security guards and their notorious dog back in the office. We realized we had only a small window of opportunity and began to slink around from stall to stall, checking the cash registers and the in-floor safes, where the dosh was kept. These small round safes had flat steel lids that locked with a padlock, flush to the floor. We knew that everyone was on the make in some way or other, so we also checked all the corners of interest for loot, and sure enough, when we had moved a till here and there we found a shuffled note and some coins. As we were gleaning the goods, we were also stuffing our faces with pastries, cheese, fruit, pickles and swigging back the milk. A little noise, once in a while in the distance, kept us aware of the guards and on our toes. After cruising the place for an hour or so, I suggested I leave a small token at Henry's butcher stall. Climbing over the short wall behind his well locked-up area, we bent his expensive till, and a few other things, out of shape. All his knives were, of course, locked away, but we nicked his nicely folded-up aprons and rubber smocks that he wore when hosing the place down.

Our time was up. Sid and I had finished our fun, and we each had a bag full of food and swag, and a couple of quid each in our pockets. We started towards the emergency exit. The heavy doors were the only way out after the main gates were locked. The exit doors led to a corridor and stairway down to the side street, and we understood that when we opened and dashed out, the alarms would go off. As we moved carefully along to that end of the market, we could hear the two guards talking and walking our way. Damn! We doubled back a couple of corners and climbed behind a dairy stand and waited, crossing our fingers. Fortunately for us, they were not walking the dog, which would have, no doubt, smelled us. We looked at each other and had to control ourselves from laughing then off we headed, quickly and silently, but when we got to the exit doors, we found them chained together with another huge padlock. We were stuffed. Now we were locked inside until the gates opened at 5:00 AM. We were two dumb fools hoping for a miracle.

After a stunned moment, we realized that the only way out was down the three-foot-wide garbage shoot, where all the vendors threw their slimy, filthy rubbish. It was a long stainless steel highway to hell that spilled the rotting mess into a huge square metal box down by the back of the building. But, it was the only choice left, and that was that.

Using the aprons and the rubber smocks we scored at Henry's, we each made an improvised toboggan, and Sid went first, carrying the bags on his lap. His exit was a bit noisy with an "Ouch! Fuck!" as he landed in the bin, which alerted the guards who were not far away. They shouted back, "Oy, who's over there?" At that moment, I launched myself over the rail and down the shoot, feet first. My exclamation, a little different from Sid's, was "Ahhh, Shit!" then a bang, as I landed into the greasy, stinking mess of vegetables, cardboard, tin cans and other crap. Sid was already out and over the high iron railings that surrounded the bins, and my adrenalin soon sent me over after him, into the back jigger. My god, what an escape that was! We left the two broken goody bags behind and legged it down the lane, covered from head to foot with rubbish; the back of my head was slicked with this dirty, greasy mess that smelt like rotten cheese. I could have died in that box just breathing the air. It was dead grotty, to say the least. Up the alley a few yards was the back door of an old pub we'd been to a couple of times. It wasn't our usual local, but the open door was very convenient. We needed a good cleanup. In the gents, we pulled the old, well-used towel off the wall and mopped ourselves down. I had my head in the sink, washing off the mess with a large block of soap, when in walked a geezer eager to pay a visit. His remark was, "What's all this then?"

"I fell over in the back lane and got this mess all over me 'ed."

"Won't be the first time," he laughed and closed the closet door. After we were cleaned up a bit, possessing a slight odour but looking fairly presentable, we decided to enjoy a pint and count the few bob we'd found, a couple of quid each, which wasn't much to write home about, but the adventure was worth the risk. It was a great laugh, to say the least.

Sid and I shared only a brief friendship before he took off to London to see the sights and moved in with his mates who were apparently having a wild time down there. There was loads of work in

London at the time, and plenty of action with the clubs and birds, and lots of Northern lads were heading there. Nobody at the market ever guessed who had done the pilfering of food and the mopping up of loose change, but there was the ongoing joke about Henry's buggered-up stall and his relentless bellyaching about his stolen aprons. Eventually he left the market for good. When anyone spoke of him, it was always, Poor Henry, the Jerry Bastard

29

A Real Butcher Shop Cutup

A special weekend was set aside for the annual cleanup of all the stalls and shops. I was still out of work, and I knew it was going to be a busy time at the market, so, on a Saturday, crossing my fingers, I took the morning bus downtown, arriving before 7 at Brabin's Butcher Shop. I stood there waiting in the doorway, leaning against the window, having a smoke, when I was met by Kenny, Terry and my old mate Jack as they turned the corner together.

"What are you doing here, Pete?" Kenny asked.

"It's the big cleanup weekend, and I thought you could use some extra help for two days?"

"Dead right, young Wacker. You can pitch in for a couple of days, if you want?"

"How much?" I rubbed my fingers together.

"Three quid for two long days, twelve-hour days. OK?"

"Cheers, Ken. I'm in."

He wasn't kidding. Not only was it a very busy Saturday with loads of customers and the usual running of the butchers and the fishmongers, we were also moving nonstop on the cleaning side. For those two days, there was the atmosphere of a collective army, tidying up everywhere, sweeping, scrubbing, hosing and mopping down with gallons of bleach and pine disinfectant. The windows and glass counters were shined up with whitewash and newspaper, which was the sure-fire way of cleaning glass at that time. The overhead chrome steel rails, where we hung the big quarter sides of beef down to the legs of lamb, were also cleaned and shined. The main reasoning behind all this scrub-a-dub time was the yearly inspection by the City Health Department, and the issuing of the annual license. Throngs of customers dodged the brooms, mops, pails and hoses all day Saturday, but on the quiet Sunday, things were a lot smoother. At quitting time Saturday night, the lads were all wrapping their Sunday roasts, and I also took home a nice beef joint for the family, but didn't get to enjoy it this time. I'd be working late on Sunday, but I made up for that at the shop, when Terry and I cooked up a pile of steaks for the gang. I was fitting in very well with the place, and Kenny asked me to demonstrate a few of the butchering skills Jack had taught me.

"Here, Pete," he said, as we walked over to some hanging meat. "Throw that lamb on the block and give me two leg and two shoulder joints. Take off the breasts and make up the loin and shoulder chops."

I knew, first off, not to throw a whole lamb carcass onto a block before splitting it down the middle first. So I lowered it a bit first, by adding two more hooks to the two already holding it up from the hind legs. It was hooked between the Achilles tendon and the bone onto the overhead rail. With the open front of the carcass facing me, I started sawing and chopping from the middle of the tailbone right through the vertebrae to the neck, and swung the two halves apart. Now I could deal with each side on the block. After a bit of guidance and help from a couple of the other men, I finally got through it and arranged the selection of various cuts on trays for display in the window.

"That's a good start, lad, and you've still got all your fingers? Ha!"

As I was finishing and scraping the block clean, I turned to see old Jack, standing in the doorway adjoining the fishery side of the business, dressed in his waterproof apron and Wellington boots, a mug of tea in hand, a fag in his mouth, a long knife in the other hand and wearing a pirate's hat he'd fashioned from a *Liverpool Echo*.

"Aha, me hearty. Cut out his gizzard!" he growled.

Sunday finally tapered to an end. I'd got stuck in to prove to Ken that I was a dependable lad, in case a part-time job came up. When 7:00 PM came around, he called me into the back room and presented me with five new crisp one-pound notes, two quid more than I expected, as a bonus for working like a machine for two days.

"You're on for next Saturday, if you want, Pete. Jack wasn't kidding when he said you were keen. Now wrap yourself a bag and get home."

"Thanks, Ken. I've had a great time here with the lads. Look for you next week. Cheers!"

And I was off to catch my bus home. Upstairs, after I'd finished my Player's ciggie, I dozed off, and woke up half an hour past my stop, got the return bus back from Lee Park, and dragged myself home. I was totally knackered and too tired to stay up. I told my dad I'd made two pounds for the weekend, and, as per usual, he reached out his hand, and I gave him half—a one-pound note.

"Good lad, keep it up."

"And look here, mum, another bag of meat," as I handed her a load of goodies and one more Sunday roast.

"Thanks, son, that's great, see you in the morning."

I took a cup of tea upstairs, flopped on the bed, reached into my pocket and pulled out four one-pound notes, and knew I was back in the money again. The next day was a bank holiday, so I could sleep in and have a good day off from miserable school, maybe even take my rod to Calderstones Park and go fishing with my mate Billy. In the morning, I woke up, still fully clothed except for my boots, and followed my nose to the kitchen where everyone was getting tucked into sausages, bacon, eggs, tea and toast.

"Thanks, Pete, here you go, breakfast at the Hilton." I was chuffed to be bringing home the bacon again. Really made up.

30

A Winning Ticket on the Nags

I was becoming a pretty good handicapper on the gee-gees, and sometimes my dad would go through the forms with me, using his little blue book from the previous year's races to judge the promising performance of the current races. It's an interesting science of logistics.

My dad always had an affinity with the equine world, the sport of kings, and although he had a strong religious lean, his excitement for sports hadn't been extinguished. Football and horseracing were some of his favorite passions, and I think he placed a small bet here and there but never revealed that to any in the family. He had the occasional bit of fun with the gee-gees, and that was it. We'd sit with a cup of tea and look inside his horse-racing formbook, comparing horses to horses, jockeys with jockeys, track conditions, trainers and questionable odds.

One of his brief tutorials would go something like this: "Look here lad, it will be raining tomorrow at Epsom Downs, and this horse here," as he points, "Bobby's Boy, stands a good chance of showing up in the top two, along with Sandpiper, who also likes to burst in the rain; they're what we call Mudders. And look here at these two on the forth race; they're stablemates, Copper Penny and Try Me Out—same bloodline, same stable and same trainer. Except, even on training, Copper Penny always lets the other one lead and runs along side at half a length back; it's a habit these two have. There are all kinds of things to look out for: weight, weather, companion horses, jockeys the horses like as a mount (or dislike), their favourite tracks and their health. If a horse takes a tumble in its last race and it isn't rested and fit, it's a problem. If a jockey gets ill or slightly injured, avoid him, till he's back to A1."

Boy, it was great to share this other side of my dad. It was a break from the hard-nosed father that wouldn't allow us many indulgences, such as me learning to play a guitar, 'cause rock and roll was the Devil's music. Still, he was now dealing with four teenage boys who were full of piss and vinegar and who were out to find our world, our way.

At the market, I was surrounded with horse punters—the neophytes and the seasoned gamblers—and after just a short while, I became the bookie runner. I was usually asked by the boss to go around to our mates, stall to stall, collecting the bets, writing down the names, times and stakes of the day, such as a Yanky double on these two, a bet on the nose here and a place bet there. Then I'd walk a block down the street to the bookies next to the pub, where I'd place all the bets and return the slips to the hungry gamblers back at the market. A lot of us would go to the pub for a bite of lunch and watch a race or two on the telly while we scoffed back our steak and kidney pies or egg and bacon sandwiches. If you were lucky and scored a win, place or show, you could just go next door and collect your winnings. It was all very convenient. I was doing quite well with the nags, and some of the older men would even ask me for a tip on a race, which was a novelty for me. It has to be said, there's nothing quite as exciting as watching your horse coming from behind, on the outside or against the inside rail, and hanging onto the lead by a neck or a length to win at the post. Especially when you have money on the filly to win. I'd won on some good horses and, as they say, "fed a few."

The ace day for me occurred in the spring of '65, when I placed a bet, a number of bets, on the biggest race of the year in England, the Grand National. It was a Saturday morning, March 27, and lots of lads at the market were high with excitement about the big race at Aintree track, just outside of Liverpool. This grueling horse race went two long laps and included thirty hurdles to jump, some famous ones, like Becher's Brook, the notorious water jump, and the Canal Turn, a place where a few horses were injured, at the sharp turn, and some horses died. It's probably the most watched horse race in the world, with millions of wide-eyed punters glued to their telly sets for the ten-minute scramble to get to the finish line. The name of the winning horse on the very first National, in 1839, was Lottery, a great name for the betting game.

The Queen Mother and Princess Margaret were in attendance, and the whole country was alive with anticipation.

When I got home from school the night before the National, my dad was already sitting in the front room going over the last few pages of the newspaper, which included a big spread of photos of the horses, jockeys and the handicaps. Forty-seven horses would compete over a four-and-a-half mile course. Dad gave me a big smile as I sat down beside him to look over the forms. Both he and I knew we'd both be placing bets without talking about it.

"There's the horse to watch," he said as he underlined Jay Trump with a pencil. "It's a Yanky horse, and there's only one reason he's running here. It's not to place or show; that horse is here to win. And look at the odds, sixty-six to one (the odds would be later moved to one hundred to six as the race started). I think Tommy Smith will bring him in." He continued, "And his trainer is the great Fred Winter. There's a tight field of good mounts here, but my shilling would be on Jay, or maybe Freddie?"

A shilling? I thought. Dad will be putting out a bit more than a bob on that nose, and so was I.

The next day at Brabin's, the radio was turned up high for the live broadcast. Not a piece of meat was being cut, not a thing was being wrapped, and even the customers inside leaned on the counters, gazing into midair, as the call came over the airwaves: "....and they're off!"

"Here they go!" someone shouted out, as we all waved our betting stubs in the air. "Go Freddie!" "Go Jay Trump!" "Go April Rose!" "Come on Mr. Jones"—go this, go that.

Between the fishmonger's next door and our place, the dozen men in bloody aprons must have put bets on half the field of jumping gee-gees. The place was noisy with excitement, people were thumping their feet, howling and banging on the tables, as we visualized the thundering hooves galloping past us and around the familiar jumps.

"And here they are," continued the broadcaster, "approaching Beecher's Brook for the first time...." And on and on it went, as we all began jumping around the shop whistling and screaming for our horses: "Go, Baby, Go."

Man, did we go crazy! Lots of horses didn't finish the race, and many didn't even clear the first few jumps. Out of a starting field of forty-seven, only fourteen finished the grueling course, and when my horse came in, I and a couple of other lads went wild!

A handful of us had just made some really good winnings. A short while later, we closed the shop for an hour, and it was "steaks all 'round" from Kenny, and a few glasses of brew to celebrate, donated by Harry, our old codger, who was the one who most trusted my handicapping tips, and had made a packet like I did.

"What a race!" We all shouted as we raised our mugs of brew. Our good ol' Yanky horse, Jay Trump, showed his colours and held off Freddie, the Scottish horse, by nearly a length, to win.

Yes, my quid, and not my shilling, was on Jay Trump to win. I also put money on Freddie, Rainbow Battle and a couple of others. I'd laid out the equivalent of a week's wages on one race, and felt not only very keen, but also excitedly nervous about stretching my luck, and my dosh so far. That one race paid me five months' wages at the bookies, close to eighty quid, rolled up in a tight bundle, stuffed in my pocket. I'd got the first, second and fourth positions—Jay Trump, the American Wonder Horse! (In the National, you can make money on the fourth place, unlike most races.) I kept the story to myself, and only hinted to my brothers that I'd made "a couple o' bob." When I got home, Dad said it was "a great race," and I replied "You were right about Trump." He jingled the coins in his pocket to show me he'd done well—but maybe not as well as me?

Most of my winnings went into my post office savings account, with the other money I'd scored from here and there. It was growing nicely, and I had thoughts of buying a motorbike or a scooter, but that never came about. Other expenses got in the way.

Over the next few months, the money I'd won began to burn a hole in my pocket, so I put out a few quid on a tailor-made three-piece suit sewn by my friendly Jewish tailor, Louis Schintz on London Road. I also scored some nice shirts and fancy shoes to keep up with the dress code of the day. Winkle-pickers and chisel-toes were "with it, man" in the mod trend. In the summer, mam and dad were surprised to find an unopened bottle of Harvey's Bristol Cream on their bedroom dresser, with a little card, "Happy Birthday, Dad."

Whenever Lady Luck smiled on me, I enjoyed showing a little generosity here and there. Later that year, Billy and I went to Scotland for two weeks; his dad paid for our B and B, and I covered Billy's drinking bill. I should say, "The nags paid for his drinks."

31

Horseplay in the House of Meat

All of these butcher shops had an ever-present, dominant macho environment—constant ramblings on about women, sports, toughness, cars and money, much like anywhere else where men work without the presence of women. In those days, before a bit more social awareness stepped in, there was no holding back with ignorant attitudes. Aggressive behaviour was prevalent amongst the young bucks at the market, and lads had to take it and give it back if they wanted to get along. Most of the time, there were silly jokes pulled on you or smart remarks that had to be countered, but with an overseeing monitoring by the older crowd. When too much annoying behaviour happened, someone usually stepped in. At Brabin's Butcher Shop, Kenny allowed a little horseplay once in a while, as long as customers weren't in the shop and nobody was getting hurt, and he would even participate in some crazy moves himself, such as doing a song-and-dance routine with Terry, his sidekick in their part-time entertainment act.

I mentioned earlier that singing Terry was not a person to be trusted; he also had a mean streak. I couldn't understand why Ken tolerated him till I found out they were distant cousins. Once in a while, Terry would start picking on young James, a timid boy, a bit older than me, who'd been there for a year. We'd call him Jim, as we regarded the name James to be a bit presumptuous for our surroundings, but privately he preferred James. I always thought he was in the wrong job and had a mummy's boy way about him, coming from the posh side of town.

One Saturday, when Terry and James had been in conflict all day, things came to a head when we were cleaning up after the shop closed. Out of the blue, Terry pushed a handful of chopped calf's liver down the back of James's neck, which caused a bit of amusement to some, but not to all. He was not only left bloodied and uncomfortable with the slimy mess dripping down to his backside, but he also felt so humiliated and angry that he ran into the back kitchen and began shouting and throwing things around, which sent the shop into a state of unease. This brought out one side of Kenny I hadn't seen yet.

"What kind of stupid fucking games are you up to, Terry lah? For God's sake, you've been on his case all week. What's the score?"

"It's just a fucking joke, Ken. Anyway, that wanker's been pissing me off since he got here, so what?"

"Well I'm telling you, leave the kid alone. That's so what! Look at that noise now!" As he points to the howling noise coming from the back, "Enough's enough. Go and apologize. Now!"

Terry walked into the back and was greeted with, "Go fuck yourself, maniac," as James was stripped down to his undies, wiping the bloody mess from his back and legs. "You're a piece of shit! Piss off!"

Kenny told everyone to get back at it and get over it, and we continued the cleanup in a more subdued manner, while he went in and told James to clean himself up and go home.

I found out later from Jim that Kenny had told him to pick his moment and get even with Terry when no customers were around. "You've got to take it and give it back, if you plan on staying around here." Wise words from the big guy. Terry, the short-arsed bully, got his due rewards one day, when they were all putting their coats on to go home. He found, to his shagrin, that his coat pockets, including the inside pocket, were full of stinking bits of fish. It was in the middle of the week, and I wasn't there that day, but I heard James had gone home early, complaining of a flu coming on. I imagine that was the moment when they both declared a truce and called it evens: a dollop of chopped liver for a few pockets full of fish.

We all had our share of tricks pulled on us, and mine was to befall me one week before Christmas Day. A few minutes to closing time, I was sent downstairs to the dirty old cellar's walk-in freezer to find a fifteen-pound turkey for a customer. The freezer was about fifteen feet long by eight feet wide and was piled high with all sorts of rock-hard frozen meat—large slabs of beef, pork, lamb, etc, plus the Christmas birds.

To get to the turkeys, I had to climb over a hill of chickens and get to the back to find the right-sized turkey. Two dim lights came on automatically as the door opened, as is the usual case with all walk-in freezers. On the inside of the door was a large plunger with a big wooden knob to push and release the door if it slammed shut on you. This plunger was connected to the outside latch that had a metal bracket where a padlock was used to lock up the freezer at the end of the day. We secured the shop like Fort Knox every night, including the main freezer, the cellar door in the floor, the front and back doors and a steel gate across the alleyway between us and the fish shop.

While I was searching through the pile of frozen birds, the door slammed shut and the automatic lights went out. I scrambled over the hill and pushed hard on the plunger, to no avail.

"Open the door!" I shouted at the top of my lungs. Nothing! Kick, kick at the release lever and again, nothing. It wouldn't budge, the door was jammed closed.

"Open the door someone! Hey, Kenny! I'm locked in the freezer, open the fuckin' door!" Thoughts were flying through my head: it was the end of the day, and someone had locked up the freezer for the night and forgotten about me, and I was going to freeze to death in this stinking box.

I felt a serious panic when I heard the heavy trapdoor slam closed at the top of the stairs. Reaching around in the unlit antechamber of hell for an object that could make a loud bang on the door, I found a leg of lamb on a hook.

"Hey, anyone, I'm down here, get me out!"

What's with this? I thought. They must know I haven't gone home yet. My coat was still on the hook. Where the hell is everyone? And just as I began swinging the leg of mutton hard, like a caveman's club against the door—Boom! Boom! Boom!—it swung open, and there, howling and laughing, stood the whole crew of conniving scallywags,

"You bunch of bastards," I shouted.

They continued to laugh and scream like a pack of hyenas at my reaction to the nerve-racking ordeal. Terry, who was holding up the hook that he'd pushed into the locking hole where the padlock usually went, passed me a bottle of beer at a good arm's length, not wishing to get too close to my rage. It was so intensely cold in there, in what had felt like an eternity, that I had to run my hands under warm water for a while to get the feeling back. Deep deep cold must be one of the worst ways to die. We sat around upstairs for a while and fried up some sausages to eat with our beer, and reminisced about all the stunts we'd pulled on each other over the year. As a peace token, Terry and Ken drove me home.

32

'Alf a Crown a Pound

We had one day left to sell all these frozen birds downstairs, and we played around with a couple of ideas. Sometimes at the butcher's shop, I'd doodle away with a black crayon that we used to add up the prices of purchases on brown butcher's paper.

The sheets of paper were first used to wrap up the meat, and then a final sheet of newspaper was used on the outside of the parcel. I would take a couple of blank sheets into the back, during my tea break, and draw away as everyone was in conversation. Sometimes sketching caricatures of the guys or cartoons. But also a landscape or seascape, my usual doodling subject. I had a fondness for "ye olde English writing" and would play with my words, so after a couple of weekends at the place, Kenny asked me to write up the prices of the day's meat on the large front window, as all the shops would do. The method was to use whitewash, mixed up in a small pail, and a thin brush to decorate the windows with not only words and prices, but a picture or two.

Whitewash is powdered lime, commonly used to paint the backyard walls of our houses, not only to brighten them up and make them more presentable, but also to act as a deterrent to insects and vermin. At the shop, we'd mix up a small batch with water to produced a smooth, white paint that dried quickly on the window and was easily rubbed off later with a rag. Someimes when the shop was closed, and the windows weren't cleaned, the passing kids would rub off a letter here and there to add some humour to the words.

"Here's the prices, Pete. Put your artistic skills to use on the front window and add a little picture or two," Kenny said as he handed me a sheet with all the various prices of the day: leg o' lamb, half a crown a pound; pork chops, one and six a pound; minced meat, one and three a pound; fresh chicken, two bob a pound and so on.

We were still dealing with pounds, shillings and pence, otherwise known as L.S.D.: the L, with the two stripes across, was a pound; the S, the shilling and the D, the Greek symbol for a penny. The various coins and notes had nicknames. Anyone in Britain would know that a quid was a pound. The coin equivalent was the sovereign gold coin or twenty shillings. An unusual coin was the guinea, another gold coin worth twenty-one shillings, which was initially introduced in 1663. A bob was a shilling, a florin was two shillings, half a shilling was a six-pence, which we called a tanner, that equaled six big copper pennies. Half a tanner was a thrupenny bit, a brass coin with twelve sides. After the penny was a half-penny, pronounced ha'pny; and even half of that again was the farthing. This quarter of a penny, a small copper coin with a robin redbreast on the obverse side, was discontinued in 1961 because nothing could really be bought for that small amount any-more, except a couple of sweets.

The combination of these coins and bills would again have their own names and abbreviations. Half-way between a penny and ten shil-lings was five shillings, officially known as a crown, or five bob. Half of that was two shillings and sixpence, simply called half a crown. Nobody went to the trouble of saying shillings or pence all the time, so it would be two and six, and we all knew what that meant. The most used nicknames for currency abounded throughout Britain: "Give the lad a tanner [sixpence] for some sweets, he can't get much with a couple of coppers [two pennies]." This kind of jargon went on until the awful introduction of the decimal monitory system on February 15, 1971.

Getting back to my artistic work at the butcher shop: after I'd made a quick draft on paper, I set out to test my typographical skills on the big clean shop window. After writing the prices, I'd fill in around the edges with pictures: a pig driving a convertible car with a word bubble, "Catch me if you can. Pork chops, one and nine a pound." Another time, I drew a pair of lovely legs with high heels and a miniskirt next to two legs of lamb: "You think you've got nice legs? Check out our Welsh lamb."

Not only did I do the window, but I also got recruited to stand out-side the shop door on Saturdays and shout out the prices: "Roll up, roll up. Look 'ere, legs o' lamb, half a crown a pound. Cheap at half the price!" That was a bit of banter I called out to the titillated audience of Saturday shoppers. An attempt at bringing in the customers was to offer one free chicken, twice a day, to the lucky person in the crowd that gathered. The method, after I called out a few prices of our special deals, was for me to turn my back to the mob and throw a wrapped-up bird through the air, over my head. It was a bit hilarious to see the throng of adults diving for the frozen prize. My performance became the ticket to call the eager crowd into the shop for the half-hour specials on the rest of the produce. "There's only fifty chickens left, folks. Better get them now or miss out on your Christmas dinner." We actually had over two hundred left downstairs, and more were on the way.

Near closing time one night, a truck pulled up out front, and we were all asked to stay on and unload a special delivery: a hundred turkeys, five hundred chickens and fifty sad-looking ducks, wrapped in plastic bags, not looking very appetizing. We formed a line through the shop and down the cellar stairs to the walk-in freezer, passing the birds one by one, until there were two large mounds of turkeys at the back, and chickens to one side. After all that unloading, we arranged a couple of tables to clean up and doctor the ducks. We set up some buckets of water, one to wash the birds, and the next to rinse them off. We unwrapped them, cleaned them up, dried them well in fresh towels, dusted them lightly with white flour and finally repacked them in new plastic bags, which had a nice large A on the front, indicating that these once-ugly ducklings, class 'C' quackers, were now beautiful fresh 'Grade A' produce. The highest quality, at the highest price, and we all made a few bob for our cosmetic work. Funny thing, an old couple came back the next week and remarked on what a fantastic duck dinner they'd had. They wanted to buy another one, but Kenny gave them one for nothing, and they became loyal customers from then on.

33

Cougar Had a Little Lamb

The mid-sixties were a time of sexual liberation, and we all had our very own experiences. Some happened in the wild world of the butcher's shop.

The back kitchen of the butcher's was wallpapered to the ceiling with dozens of pinups. The place was a macho bad-boy environment, with constant behavior that would turn granny in her grave. Whenever a nice-looking lady passed by the window or came in to buy something, it seemed that all time stood still, until she walked out of sight, and then, of course, the place would fill up with sighs and comments, while the distracted lonely hearts club got back to cutting up meat and not their fingers. Distraction can be a dangerous thing while working with a very sharp instrument.

The term "cougar," used for an older woman on the prowl for a younger man, didn't exist at the time (and reportedly it originated in Canada), but it is an apt expression for my next story.

A curious thing started happening to me at Brabin's. Yours truly had captured the attention of a beautiful middle-aged lady who would come into the store Saturday after Saturday. All the lads kept on at me to see how far this would go. They were having a great time at my expense, as per usual. I was a tad bewildered; after all, she was the one hitting on me all the time, and not going after the older, more mature men. It was my first cougar encounter, and actually, I was pretty chuffed about it, 'cause, without a shadow of a doubt, she was drop-dead gorgeous and very well-off.

Mrs. Cynthia Taylor was about thirty-five years old or so, very distinguished, politely spoken and had a million-dollar smile. It was interesting that she had the same last name of another famous goddess of the day, Liz Taylor. So when she was not around, we referred to her as Liz. We were all crazy about her, and it became a little embarrassing when each time she walked into the shop, her bubbly speech was, "May I please have Peter serve me?"

Kenny would smile at her and wink at me as I stopped whatever I was doing and approached the counter with my usual "Yes, Ma'am, how can I help you?" A question that sent smiles and sniggers throughout the shop.

"Good morning, Peter. That's a lovely tie you're wearing today," etc. She was always full of compliments, whether it was the beautiful chops or steaks in the window. Whereas, we were all thinking of the lovely legs of lamb, the beautiful rump roast and the chicken breasts.

The babe was always dressed to kill, and she knew it—high heels, miniskirt, fishnet stockings, beautiful long jet-black hair that trailed down her figure like a bottle of Coke.

We all fantasized that she was possibly a movie star or a high-fashion model. As they say, "She's got the power, you got the need." After buying a variety of expensive cuts, enough for a small banquet, she'd often need me to give her a hand carrying the heavy bags around the corner or up the block to "her ladyship's car." She and I would head out of the shop, and as I'd look back, I'd see the bunch of lunatic butchers cooing and pulling funny faces and of course making the usual lewd hand gestures. It was hard for me to keep a straight face, and our lovely Cynthia was aware of everything.

Her car was a beautiful new, dark blue Humber, plush and shiny. She'd pop open the boot that was usually jammed with her Saturday morning shopping. She sure knew how to spend it. Where did all that dough come from? It was always a curiosity to me. Probably her hubby ran a bank; maybe he'd robbed one? She certainly sported a couple of large rocks on her fingers.

"Oh you're such a helpful lad, Peter, here you go," as she'd give me a tip for my services, usually a half crown. "Have a nice day, ducky".

Ducky? It always annoyed me when she said that.

"See you next week, sweetheart. You always cheer me up. I love your silly sense of humour," as she drove off in her shiny car.

My comrades in arms, back at the shop, finally cornered me one day and told me that I didn't have the nerve to ask her for a ride in her car.

So I committed to ask her the very next week. When the magic moment finally arrived—after I'd rehearsed my lines all week long, even in the bathtub—I popped the question in a sort of stumbling, awkward way, while I was wrapping up her order.

"Mrs. Taylor?" I said.

"Cynthia, Peter! Mrs Taylor is far too formal. Yes?"

"Cynthia," I continued, "that's a fab' looking car you have there."

All knives stopped cutting. All eyes stared straight at me. All voices stopped talking, and all ears tuned out the radio and tuned in to the question.

"Does it perform well on the highway? And er does it go pretty fast like an E-Type Jag'?" I was remembering the time when my mate George and I had taken a ride on the wild side, down the East Lanc's Road in a stolen car the previous year.

"Peter, if what your saying is, you'd like to have a ride in my car sometime, I'd love to take you for a spin, Ducky."

Throughout the silent shop, jaws dropped. Plunk! Plunk! Plunk!

"How about a spin through the tunnel and back, it doesn't take that long." (She was referring to the Mersey Tunnel, of course, that connects Liverpool to the Wirral Peninsula.) "Maybe on your lunch break?"

"Today?"

"No, not today, love. Let's do it next week. How would that be? Is that OK?"

"Perfect, next week sounds the gear."

"Oh, I suppose I could spare him for an hour or so, Cynthia," Kenny interjected.

"Thanks again," I finalized, as she exited the store with only one bag to carry and not her usual four.

"Bye, boys," she called as she stepped out onto the sidewalk and tippy-toed across the busy crosswalk in her high heels. After she'd left, one of the guys in the back called out, "Thanks again, Cynthia, ooh ooh." Followed by the expected, "Can I climb the ladder up your nylons, Cynthia?" Then the usual stuff and nonsense started up.

Her reply sent me into a state of stunned excitement.

"There you go, you idiots. I asked her, didn't I? And we're going for a ride, next week. And you bunch of wankers all thought I was too chicken, eh? Well now you know."

"Well done, Pete lad. She might make a man out you yet," someone called out, and then started up with "Baby you can drive my car, guess I'm gonna be a star," and the rest joined in, including me: "Baby you can drive my car, and maybe I'll love you. Beep beep, beep beep, yeh." One of our favourite Beatles tunes.

They carried on laughing and yelping, and Kenny and his vaudeville sidekick Terry began dancing around in a waltz-like mode, embracing and grabbing each other's arses and calling out, "Ooh, Peter ducky, ooh, Cynthia baby, ooh yeh, yeh, more baby more, don't stop."

It's always a sight to see how eight young, and some old, men can turn into a troupe of mad monkeys. There was never a dull moment in this nut house they called a butcher shop.

Then someone called out, "Peter, put the bloody kettle on."

At afternoon tea break, the lads were full of more jest and suggestions. I began to feel very vulnerable, and the dark clouds of doubt descended over me. I felt like the sardine who'd made a dinner date with the tiger shark, and by the end of the day, I began to wonder if I was making a fool of myself and heading into deeper water than I could handle. I thought for a minute that this might be a trick. After all, Kenny had been the one to egg me on, and he seemed to know her pretty well, so maybe they were just having a chuckle at my expense. But then again, maybe she had her eye on me after all. My imagination began to race again.

Was she going to drive us down a country road and pounce on me? Was she really leading me down the garden path? Yes that's it, I think I've been set up, or maybe not, bloody 'ell! She was a woman of the world, and I was an excited fifteen-year-old.

As the week went by, I told a couple of my schoolmates, and they just said that I was full of bullshit and expressed total skepticism. At home, my eldest brother, Fred, shared a few ideas with me, just in case she became a bit friendly, so to speak. And all three of my older brothers offered to come along to help out.

"Ha!"

On the big day, I got dressed up in my above-average butcher's gear. A nice shirt and tie with shiny shoes was the dress code of the day. I slapped on some of Fred's Old Spice aftershave, even though I was miles away from growing a beard and still sporting a face full of bum fluff.

On the bus to town, I sat upstairs and lit a smoke, and the old fellow sitting next to me, looked me over and remarked,

"Are you off to work then, lad?"

"Off to work alright, mate. I've got a big day ahead of me. I'm working at the butcher's, at St. John's Market."

"You smell like you're off to the dance hall."

"Dead right, Whack, I'll be dancing tonight alright."

As I took a deep drag from my cigarette, the way Humphrey Bogart does in the movies, I added, "Maybe I'll be dancing all night, you never know."

We had a bit of a laugh and then changed the conversation to the day's football match, Liverpool verses Spurs.

My stop arrived.

"Have a great day, lad, enjoy the dancing tonight, wink, wink."

"Thanks, ol' fellah, I think I will, tarrah," and I hurtled downstairs and jumped off.

The day was early and fresh. It had rained hard all night. The old cobblestone streets were clean and shiny, and the sun was coming up, nice and bright. I felt on top of the world.

When I turned up at the shop, the lads wondered why I was so spruced up. I reminded them of Cynthia's offer of a car ride at lunchtime.

"Oh yeh, Pete's eloping with Liz today, to Gretna Green."

Terry called out, "You don't need a blacksmith, Pete, butchers can marry people as well," as he shook a chicken upside down, making its wings flap and announced, "With this wing, I thee wed." Laughs all round. After a short while, things settled down, and mugs of tea were passed around with the accompanying plateful of toast and marmalade.

The morning dragged on, and finally 12:30 came around, but no sign of my hot little Princess Cynthia in high heels. Kenny came over and whispered in my ear that he could only allow me a half hour today for my break "'cause the place was getting busy." I looked back silently with eyes that said, "Are you for real?" But before I could respond, it was, "Just kidding lad. But I don't think she's turning up, if you know what I mean like?"

My head and heart were now resolved to the inevitable. I hung my bloody apron on a hook, dusted the sawdust from my pants and shoes and headed out of the door to buy a sad little lunch for myself at the pub. My appetite for the day leaned towards steak and kidney pie, chips and gravy, and a pint of bitter. Your typical "healthy" English meal.

A couple of the lads joined me as I legged it across the street, and just as we were turning the corner to the ale house, lo and behold, who should pull up right outside our joint but the bunny in the blue car.

"See you later boys," I said, as I belted it back across the lights. She saw me and, with that great big smile of hers, waved wildly as I approached. A skip and a jump and I was at the car door.

"Sorry, ducky dear, am I late? Have you finished your lunch break?"

"No, Cynthia, I was just starting." And I thought, you can call me ducky all day long if you want. Quack, Quack!

"I'll drive us first," she said, "and then you can take over on a quiet road if you want."

"Sounds great!"

"I've got something special in mind for you, Peter, a surprise."

"Something special. What's that?" I choked.

"You'll see, put your parachute on, we're off."

And she gunned it as we crossed in front of head-on traffic, horns blasting at us, and headed for the tunnel entrance. She paid the toll, and we were now plowing through the busy, midday traffic of lorries, semis and speeding motorbikes, all moving in unison to the Birkenhead side of the River Mersey.

The Queensway Tunnel, opened in 1934 by King George V, was always an adventurous ride for us inner-city kids heading out of the city on our summer holidays. But on this particular day, the destination was a "something special" place. Whoa! Steady boy, whoa!

As she drove her comfortable gliding car through the tunnel, the bright orange sodium lights along the walls flew past in a hypnotic dance. She offered me a cigarette. I did what they do in the movies: I put two of her Players ciggies in my mouth and lit the two together, then passed her one.

She was a dangerous crazy driver, but it was thrilling to watch her behind the wheel, shifting through the gears in her short black miniskirt, red high heels, red wooly coat and red-hot lipstick. She looked fabulous.

"I'll let you take over the driving on a quieter street in a minute, as we get a little closer to my place," she said. My place? I thought. Thank you, God, for answering my prayers, Amen.

Sure enough, after a while we pulled over on a lovely quiet country road, and switched seats. I gave it a couple of revs on the pedal and slid it into first gear, nice and easy, without crunching the clutch once. I put the blue machine all the way through the gears, from top to bottom, through hill and dale. I felt like a million quid.

"Where did you learn to drive so well, Peter?"

"My mate George taught me a bit, and I taught myself the rest."

As I shuffled it into third to climb a hill, she jokingly suggested that she'd like to hire me as her personal chauffeur. "We could drive to London for the day sometime."

My response, "Of course, certainly, Ma'am." We laughed over that, and as we'd finished our first ciggies, she lit up two more and gently placed one in my mouth. This lady was a chain-smoker. The close proximity of her hand smelled of lavender and smoke combined, a fragrance I remembered from another time in a night club when I danced with a tall Dutch girl named Sonia. Smoke and lavender. Amazing how a confusing mix of scents can recall a memory!

We changed seats again, and within a half mile, she turned into a spotless new driveway, and pulled up at her spiffy house.

"Is this your place? It's fabulous. It's the gear, love." She laughed at my Liverpool slang.

"Remember, Cynthia, I can't stay too long, I've got to get back to the shop, and I haven't had any nosh yet."

"No worries, love, we won't be long."

I climbed out of the car in a flush of excitement. Then she tooted the horn, beep, beep, and I saw this big middle-aged fellow waving and banging on the window inside the house.

"Who's that?" I asked, surprised.

"Oh, that's Jeremy, my lovely hubby. I've told him all about you."

"Oh yeh?" The front door opened and out came this big guy with a wide mustache, smoking a pipe and sporting a Welsh National rugby shirt.

Great, I thought to myself, let's go for a drive in a hot car with a hot bird and meet her flipping husband, isn't that just Great!

The big fellow shook my hand with his grizzly bear paw, slaps me on the back like he's belting the dust from a rug, and with his strong deep Welsh accent comes out with…"Hello, Peter lad, I see you've made a big impression on my lovely Cynthia here. She's told me all sorts about you. Feel like a brew, boyo?"

"And a sandwich please, Jeremy dear," she adds, "we're both famished."

God Almighty in heaven! Is this how the other half lives? The missus running around all day, shopping, picking up young lads, bringing them home and having hubby make sandwiches for everyone? This was more than odd, to say the least. I'd never rubbed shoulders with these kind of people before, but I had to admit, they were somewhat interesting, a breath of fresh air and a bit cuckoo and happy to please. I was beginning to like this surprise.

"OK, a couple of sarnies and a pint it is then. Say no more, say no more," as he rubbed his hands together with the excited glee of a priest in a confession box.

"Yes please, a sandwich sounds great. Can I help?" They both laughed and threw their arms around each other, exchanging one big long smooch. "Just relax lad, you're our guest," as he pretends to tip his top hat.

There's one hell of a lucky guy, I thought to myself, what a life he's got—the life of Riley. He looks like he's retired already, and he's only half the age of my dad.

The day had chilled off, and so I offered to help out by starting the coal fire. I rolled up my sleeves and brought in a bucket load of nice-sized, shiny black Welsh coal from the backyard coal shed.

Ah, yes, coal, the British fuel that warms the heart as it does the hearth. The black piece of fossil that my mother put in a sink of cold water to stiffen up the lettuce leaves for the salad. Smoky coal that stinks of sulfur, and fills your chimney with soot; the black dust that makes a sweep's handshake lucky and whose kiss to a new bride brings the promise of great fortune. Coal, God's gift to Wales.

"I'll show you how we light a coal fire back at our house," I said. "Got any old newspapers?" I ruffled up the first piece, put it on the grate, then folded the next sheet of paper into a large triangle and rolled and flattened it into a long one-inch-wide strip, folded it in half to form a ninety-degree V shape, then turned and folded, turned and folded, till it becomes an origami-like concertina. This exercise of making kindling from newspaper was just an acquired skill for those who have no trees, and a bundle of wood chips cost you money at the chandler's. I made six of these art and craft fire starters in a couple of minutes, laid them like a raft, across the loose piece and carefully placed a few nice chunks of coal in a close pyramid on top and lit the bottom paper. Bingo, in five minutes the coal was blazing away, and we were sitting around the living room scoffing sandwiches and knocking back the brew. A cozy place to spend a lunch hour.

"Come on then, Peter lad, let's get back before your boss finds another butcher boy," was Jeremy's last call as we threw our coats on and took off, heading back through the smoky old tunnel to Liverpool. Breaking speed limits, we arrived and parked right outside the shop.

I was an hour late and a bit on edge as we entered the store. Everybody just stopped whatever they were doing and gathered around to hear about my wild adventure in Birkenhead. Kenny shook hands with Jeremy and nodded his head at Cynthia with a polite, "Hello again, Mrs. Taylor, how did your date go with Peter?"

With this statement, everybody burst out laughing. All except me and Cynthia, who went into great detail about how well I'd driven her car, and Jeremy interjected and told all ears how pleased he was to meet such a young gentleman as me.

To be publicly complimented was a new thing for me. Where did all this come from? It was another embarrassing moment, to say the least.

Kenny took me aside later and forgave my late return, reassuring me that these were special adventures we must always remember and cherish as we get older.

"You only live once, lad, then they put you in a cold box. Get all you can, and drop dead with a smile on your face." The Epistle according to St. Kenneth.

All night I was tossing and turning and hardly slept a wink. It was, "Cynthia! Oh, Cynthia." She was Ace.

34

The Wavertree Shop

During those two years of working at butcher shops, as I'd mentioned before, I found there wasn't one person, from the boss to the tea lad, who wasn't on the make. If we weren't robbing meat, we'd be dipping into the till. Some of us were very hungry and desperate young louts, with no regard for the consequences of our behaviour.

At one shop on Wavertree Road, I was put to work with an eighteen-year-old nutcase, Joe Tracer. He'd be the one training me in some more butchering skills. A couple of years older, he was well-versed with the ins and outs of the trade, but he was big trouble, in more ways than one. There was no limit of what he wouldn't do for a laugh, and he roped gullible me into some of his craziness. We'd get up to mischief all right. On Saturday mornings, we'd hide down the back jigger, and hurl uncooked meatballs at the large billboards across the street, spattering freshly ground-up beef all over the picture of the girl shampooing her hair or the fellow with a cigarette in his mouth. We'd also aim at the buses passing by, and scream laughing as the startled riders looked back in shock to see where these meatball missiles smashing against the windows were coming from. Occasionally we'd sneak out the back of the shop, after packaging up parcels of meat for our own customers, and hide them along the backyard wall till everyone had gone home. Then we'd cruise down the jigger, collect them and be off to sell the meat. We did this week after week, and my pockets were feeling no pain. But enough was enough, and the novelty of this carrying on was wearing off. Here I was working alongside a crazy guy who'd already done time in the juvey house, stabbed a guy at school, been stabbed himself on his arm and thought nothing of having sex with his sister-in-law on the day his brother married her. Just one more head the ball' I found myself working alongside. While we were having tea breaks, he'd brag to everyone about his mad nights out, chucking half bricks through shop windows and stealing cars.

One Saturday morning, as we were all in the back sorting stuff out, and no customers were around, Joey started an argument, picked up a thin boning knife and began to threaten another young butcher boy, Dave, who was minding his own business. But although our featherweight Joey boy, the mad hatter, was rough and threatening, the other guy, Dave, the welterweight, was way tougher and stronger. They grabbed at each other's arms, and Dave, with the quickness of a cat, twisted the knife from Joe's hand, then smashed his own cup of tea against the wall and cut Joe across the face with it. The boss, who was in the front of the shop when this happened, ran to the back and dealt with the commotion. After we'd separated the two brawlers, the ambulance was called, and the boss's wife, who calmly ushered the customers out of the shop, accompanied the injured fool to the hospital. As he was being bundled up and sent off, we were all questioned by the police about what we saw. It was simple: Joe went bananas, and the other fellow just defended himself. And that's the way it was. Self-defense was witnessed by all, and Joe stepped back through the revolving door and went inside the local clink to cool off. This time not to juvey, he was going to the big house.

Part Four

Foot Loose and Fancy Free

35

Tommy Was Gone

In our school, blacks, whites and browns never had a problem mixing; we all played together on the various teams: football, rugby, cricket, basketball, swimming and gymnastics. Rarely would we call one another names, only in moments of conflict, and anger. We'd all argue and fight amongst each other, but we'd also fight together against other schools or district teams. For a short while, I belonged to one of our district gangs, called the Childwall Valley. We probably had a standing team of about sixty lads, ages thirteen to seventeen. Only once did I get into a large rumble of about forty boys a side at Sefton Park. Most of the time, we had about ten to twenty out for some menace and exercise, teenage boys looking for the wrong kind of action.

On one unfortunate night in autumn, a bunch of us out for a laugh, up by the Abbey Church, in the old side of Childwall, decided to scale a huge stone wall and raid the orchard. It was full of ripe apples, pears and gooseberry bushes.

This stone wall was pretty high, nine or ten feet, and a couple of feet thick. At the top, it narrowed to a point capped with the usual concrete and broken glass. Somebody must have made a phone call, because after we climbed around the trees like a bunch of wild monkeys, throwing fruit at each other, the cops arrived in a couple of Black Marias, which we called paddy wagons, with their little bells ringing

Opposite: Lord Street, downtown Liverpool, Christmas, 1962

and blue lights flashing, dingalingaling.

We scarpered across to the other side of the old Victorian orchard and vaulted the lower wall, avoiding the broken glass as best we could, and hurtled down a steep embankment. The majority of us doubled back a half mile across some fields that led to a railway line and tunnel at the bottom of a hill. Most of us were fleet of foot and got away quickly; others, who were useless escape artists, were nabbed by the rozzers, and a few boys cut their hands on the walls. I was quick and nimble and kept up with the front-runners without a problem.

At school, my good buddy Paul Dale and I competed every year against each other for a spot in the first three places at track and field— the hundred-yard dash, the two-twenty, the hurdles. We also did well in long-distance and cross-country races. I usually played right wing or inside right at football, and winger or scrum half on the rugby team. At gymnastics, my mate Joey Price and I did really well until he broke his neck landing on the wooden floor after doing a backward somersault from the top of a pommel horse. It was the final movement of a gymnastics performance in front of the school on Parent's Night. We were both chosen to do the same vault at the same moment from pommels ten feet apart, stacked with other gymnasts laying across each other, four high. It was to be the grand finale. I thought I heard his neck crack as I sailed backwards through the air and landed on my feet. We did some performances in bare feet; no plimsoll shoes were used. Joey was out of action for more than a year and returned to P.E. but with less gusto.

So, with the physical education we got at school, most of us were fit as fiddles, and running away from cumbersome English Bobbies, wearing tall dunce hats, was easily done. After all, they were unarmed except for a truncheon, or billy club, and a whistle for calling other coppers to assist on a chase. This was high-tech for the police department in the British sixties: a club, a helmet, a whistle and a pair of cuffs—the tools of trade for the British lawman.

As we shambled down the railway tracks, our group headed north while the rest split up like scattered sheep, some going through the tunnel and a few along the nearby streets. Considering around twenty of us started out, only two were picked up. Not bad odds for a bunch of amateurs. About ten remained together as the evening progressed, and we divvied up any money we had and sent our two biggest lads into the off-license side of a pub to buy a few pint bottles of beer. I remember all the pubs were very relaxed about serving you a brew, even if they thought you were well under the legal age of eighteen. There was no such thing as ID, especially photo ID; only a little red driver's license book that one would carry if you'd done the test. None of us had driver's licenses, we'd drive cars or motorbikes without them; we didn't really care. So, therefore, ID was an unknown entity.

Into the pub went Derrick Cole and Ollie Taylor to buy the drinks; they were both seventeen and could easily have passed for twenty. Colie and Ollie were the cocks of our gang, a term used for the best fighters. The boxing champion of our boys' club, Colie was a tall, very tough black lad whose folks came to Liverpool from Jamaica—our Cassius Clay, our Mohammed Ali. Ollie came from Cardiff, Wales, and had just been in our district a couple of years. He was a freckled-faced red-headed Celt, with a strong Welsh accent. With shoulders as wide as a door and a head like a coconut, he'd take a punch and smile back. As they say, "No brain, No pain!"

These two lads squared off the first week Ollie moved onto our road. They met on the street, exchanged a few comments towards each other, and a large crowd gathered as they sorted each other out. What a great barny that was! When they'd had enough cuts and bruises, they shook hands and declared a truce. They became the best of mates and were always in and out of trouble together. If they couldn't find a scrap elsewhere, they'd fight each other for exercise.

Some of our team members carried a pair of skintight leather gloves with buckles across the wrist that we'd wear in an encounter with another team. These gloves saved your skin and also sent a visual message of intimidation. When our two lads emerged from the pub's side door carrying two large bags of brew, we all noticed something was up. Colie started giving the two-finger salute to a bunch of guys sitting just inside by the window where a big crowd was making a hell of a noise. It was a rugby team obviously out for a good time and a few drinks after a game. They were a youth team from Wales, just across the border from us and were visiting for a cup challenge. A couple of the Welsh lads ran outside and challenged Colie for telling them to "Piss off back to your sheep-shagging country." (Now, here's a word to the wise: Don't ever tell a half-drunken rugby team where to go; it doesn't work.)

They all looked at least eighteen years old, a big tough team, while our crowd ranged from fourteen to seventeen, and most were under-nourished ragamuffins, loud-mouthed striplings with attitude. The street rules stood as this, Never back down or show fear, even when the odds were badly against you. There was one other thing our gang also knew: if it was a one-on-one to settle things, Colie could pretty well take on anybody. He was very fast and hard, our champ. He danced on air and possessed lightning fists. As Cassius Clay would say, "Float like a butterfly, sting like a bee."

Most of us were average scrappers, but some loved to fight; they couldn't get enough of it. I personally hated the whole scene but was swept up into a vortex of continual trouble, day after day, week after week.

The offer from the Welsh boys was taken, and the fight was on. Colie, being the scrapper that he was, quickly handed the bag of beer over to one of us. He had his black leather gloves on already and was gliding around the street like a ballet dancer, calling out to the two Welshmen that he'd "take the two of yous together." As he jumped around, mocking them, one of the boys called out, in no uncertain terms, how he was going to knock his "nigger block" off, and as the

words were still pouring out of his stupid mouth, a hard straight right ·
to the head sent him down onto his arse, to a great cheer from us
crowd.

It was always live entertainment to watch or participate in one
of these street rumbles. Words were always shouted or squealed out,
and the stupidest moves were made. The awkward fighters flayed and
swung their arms and fists into the wind, hoping to land a lucky one,
the experienced scrappers remained very cool and calculated, picking
off their opponents skillfully and calmly with relish.

Before you could count to ten, the team had emptied out, and we
all became enveloped in a warlike roar of madness and shouting. A few
boys paired off to fight. Some bottles were thrown, and broken ones
wielded around here and there.

In a matter of moments, a large brawny bulldog grabbed me by the
coat and in his broad Welsh accent, slurred out something that sounded like, "Llan de fuckin' shite, boyo." My immediate instincts, because
we were so close, face to face, was to deliver a Liverpool Kiss, otherwise
known as a head-butt right to his nose. I heard his nose crack, and at
the same moment, he returned a heavy fist to the side of my head that
nearly sent me into next week. We exchanged a few more punches and
kicks before being pulled apart by some middle-aged men, because, by
this time, the whole pub was out in the street, and a few of the adults
were separating the young brawlers one at a time.

My ear, nose, mouth and leg were bloody and hurt, and my opponent was madly jumping around growling and holding onto his bloody
nose, raging that I'd done serious damage to his face. His mates held
him back as he tried to get another piece of me, and I felt lucky to be
standing, but not for long. As I leaned over a parked car to catch my
breath and mop my mouth, out of nowhere, I got a hard boot to the
guts and went down on my knees on the roadside.

I'll always remember what I witnessed next. In a moment of horror, I saw my mate Tommy, just ten feet away, get hit over the head

with a heavy fencepost. It was a three-foot bludgeon of wood pulled off a nearby fence. The attack was so violent the wood broke in half over his skull, and Tommy dropped dead right in front of me, on the dirty street. A pool of dark crimson blood formed a big circle around his head, almost like a halo. An old man tried to stop the bleeding with a rag, but to no avail. I couldn't believe my eyes! Tommy was gone!

In stunned silence, we stood around looking down at him and each other, some spitting blood and others vomiting. The perpetrator, who'd swung the fence post was now being held on the ground by a couple of guys who'd been putting a halt to the chaos, and he was shouting his curses to some and apologies to others. As the police arrived, a fat woman approached the "stick-wielding lout" and swung her handbag, belting him square across the face. "I knew that boy, you bastard," she screamed. A couple of policemen ushered her away, and the rest of us were lined up, our hands on our heads, facing the wall of an old graveyard opposite the pub. Not all the boys were arrested, some scarpered, but the few of us that were grabbed ended up in the back of a couple of paddy wagons and sent downtown to face the music. Music composed with the notation of ignorance, the rhythm of poverty, the timbre of racism, performed by the street orchestra of class distinction and neglect.

Tommy was one of those memorable lads. He and I were just casual friends. I'd heard he was a hell of a guitar player, but never had the chance to hear him. His older brother and one of mine were acquainted, and we'd first met a couple of years earlier on a wild night near Lee Park, when a handful of us entered a bakery, climbed to the roof and began throwing slices of bread down into the passing traffic.

Tommy's dad kept racing pigeons and maintained a handful of champion micks, as we called them, and some prized homers. One night he asked Tommy and me to carry four pigeons he'd sold to a fellow club member down the road. He had a pigeon loft on his roof, accessed only by a ladder. After quietly ascending and entering, we were gently handed two beautiful pigeons each, to carefully put inside our sweaters, and instructed to walk calmly to the other fellow's place down the road, a place everyone knew—the guy with the stinking mickie pen and the complaining neighbours. The birds were very relaxed as they were held tightly and safely under our coats and sweaters. They cooed all the way there, and we were rewarded with a couple of bob each for their safe delivery.

36

Fashionable Rebels, Jacking the Jag

The end of the school week meant that most of us lads would dress up in our swanky gear and head out. There were clubs downtown with names like the Sink, where your membership name and number was on a tiny tag, glued to the back of a sink stopper on a chain, as well as lots of other well-established joints. At the Cavern, on Mathew Street, I'd first seen the Beatles and Gerry and the Pacemakers, Billy J. Kramer, the Mersey Beats, the Searchers, the Swinging Blue Jeans and others. Little Stevie Wonder made a guest appearance in '66 and was lead on stage as he howled away on his harmonica doing his big early hit "Fingertips." We went to a lot of lunchtime sessions, and even went back at night, our ears were ringing with all that volume.

The Cavern used to be an underground storage cellar in the middle of town, with only one entrance that led down a set of stairs, past the cloakroom, and to the stage on the right and the dancing and snack bar to the left. It was a smelly, dark and dank gathering place for all the youngsters who'd drink Coca-Cola, dance the stomp, twist, jive and generally stand in the one spot, nodding their heads to the rhythm of the Mersey Beat bands. Yeh! All us cool cats leaning against the dirty walls, looking the part, with ciggies hanging out of our young gobs. Groovy man!

Other well-attended places like the Grafton, the Rotunder and Locarno were always busy. If a big show was in town, a bigger venue was needed like the Empire Theatre. In March 1963, Billy and his brother Derek and I saw the Four Lads up on the Empire stage, on the same billing with Chris Montez singing about a guy called "Les Dance," and Tommy Roe singing about an Australian girl called "Sheila." The girls were all screaming and crying. It was a fab night, man! I got a sore throat shouting my head off.

There were also dozens of halls and weekend dances to choose from and never a shortage of bands to hear, with new ones starting up every day in someone's back room or basement. Every lad in the town thought he could be another John, Paul, George or Ringo. The city was mad with British rock and roll, R and B, Motown, trad jazz, mod jazz, Yanky rock, the lot.

And we were "dedicated followers of fashion," even if the sub-zero streets were like sheets of glass, and blistering cold; we never really dressed properly for the elements, no wooly long johns or thick socks. Instead, we were all decked out with shirt and tie, suit, shiny shoes and our heavy dark overcoats—the dress code according to the mod fashion. The mods usually rode the scooters and the rockers the motorbikes. I enjoyed the big power over the mods' flashy, multi-mirrored Italian lawnmowers, even though I dressed like a mod. We even sported dead short, penitentiary-like haircuts with a part shaved in on the left side, just like the black R and B Motown lads from the us whose music we all danced to.

From the earlier days of zoot-suiters in the States, to Teddy boys and their duck-tail hairstyles and crepe-soled shoes, times moved on to the mods and rockers. All these trends were a rite of passage for the young and restless and a complete joke and annoyance for much of the older generation.

Before the Beatle mop-tops and mod hairstyles hit the scene in the early to mid-sixties, we lads sported the quiff hairstyle, and after going for a swim and a hot shower at Margaret Street swimming baths, we would all line up at the Brylcream machine, which was attached to the wall outside the changing rooms. For a penny in the slot, you could get a good dab, but we'd sometimes keep watch while one of us gave the box a good boot at the bottom, as someone pushed the dispenser button all the way in. The result, more times than not, was a large dollop of the hair grease into a waiting hand, which we all shared, for our hair-style needs. We'd slick it back and rub it in, and stand in front of a shop window sharing someone's comb. "Kookie, Kookie, Lend Me Your Comb," and we'd do our heads up like Elvis, Buddy Holly or Conway Twitty and the rest of our rock-star idols, including our very own homegrown British superstar, Cliff Richard.

In the fifties, our dad would send the four of us, once a month, to a barber's shop down Breck Road. Maybe he had made a deal with the barber for sending us all together. Knowing my dad, he probably got four haircuts for the price of two, and he'd check us out when we got home to make sure he got his money's worth. He'd tell Fred, who was in charge of the visit, "Don't forget to tell him—short back and sides." And we'd return home with our army haircuts.

The short hair was helpful in some ways, and we never had a problem with lice as some families did. Not one nit was ever found in our house, and at school once or twice a year, we'd all line up for head inspections by a district nurse. No matter which nurse arrived to look at all those heads, we always called them "Nitty Nora, the Hair Explorer."

The Brilly, as we called the hair gel, did a fine job of turning a bunch of kids into famous singers and musicians as we paced our steps on the street, like Hank Marvin and the Shadows. We were all going to be rock and rollers, 'cept none of us possessed an instrument of any kind, well, maybe a gob organ or a beat-up bongo drum.

As we got into our mid-teens, when Friday and Saturday night came around, we would meet up, and the first thing on the agenda was to score a couple of brews at a pub somewhere, then head downtown to a dance or wherever the birds hung out.

One particular night, two of us boys decided to go in another direction. My mate George knew a fair bit about hot-wiring cars. His older brother Derek, who was in the clink on a six-month stretch for robbery, had trained him well from an early age. In fact it got to the point were Georgie boy began carrying a tiny tool kit with him in the deep inside pocket of his overcoat, ready for a score—pliers, screwdrivers and bits and pieces.

That summer we nicked a beautiful maroon E-type Jag' and took it for a spin down the highway. We'd spotted the sleek hot car parked behind a row of shops on Penny Lane, and, while I "kept kye ", my mechanical mate had her ticking over in a few minutes. He got behind the wheel, and we were off. George was quite a driver for a sixteen-year-old, and from what I was told, he'd driven everything from tractors to sports cars since he was twelve. After a few miles, cutting down side streets and back lanes, we finally got to East Lancashire Road. It was already dark, but traffic was light. Now it was my turn, and once I'd bounced it from first into second gear, I knew I could handle this machine. I'd had a few goes before, driving your average English family vehicles, your Morris Minors, Prefects, Hillmans and such, and my clutching was pretty smooth. Big G had never seen me behind the wheel before, and he was fairly impressed. It was "the gear lah." After a few moments booting it, and bringing her up to a reasonable speed on a straight stretch, both of us screaming and yelling at the top of our lungs, it suddenly started raining cats and dogs. We fiddled around with the switches and got the wipers going. They'd swung back and forth a few times before I suddenly realized that we were rapidly approaching a roundabout. I skidded as I tried to make the left turn and ended up in the middle of the island, loosing the right front wheel as we hit the curb. The bouncing car cut a deep furrow across the lovely smooth grass and flowerbed, deep enough to plant a nice row of Irish spuds. As we jerked to a halt, there was an enormous bang, and a cloud of smoke and steam rose from the engine. During the crash, I cut my knee and George bust a couple of fingers on his right hand when he'd grabbed the dash. Nobody wore seatbelts in those days.

Although we were shook up and hurt, we got the hell out of there like jack rabbits being chased by farmer Giles. My two thumbs began to swell up painfully like two bananas due to me hanging onto the wheel so tightly as we hit the curb, and George's hand was turning black and blue. He was a bit of a hard case and insisted on us going for a pint to "dull the pain a bit." We came across a warm inviting pub not too far away from the back roads, knocked back a couple of pints of bitter, cadged some Aspirins off the barman, bid the place good night and laughed our stupid heads off all the way home. It took us forever to get back. Having spent all our dosh at the pub, we had nothing left to catch the bus. We'd even tried pushing every refund button on every public telephone on the way for some loose cash; all to no avail. The bright red Dr. Who boxes were already damaged and looted. Then finally a friendly trucker pulled over after we'd tried for ages to hitch a ride and took us part-way home. The rest of the way was on shank's pony. It was very late, and we were very tired when we got there. George stopped off at his doctor's office, and woke him up to have his hand checked. The doctor lived next door to his surgery. An excuse of falling down some stairs satisfied the unquestioning physician.

The next morning I told my mother I felt a flu coming on and was allowed to stay home from school while everyone went to work, and I rested up from my hard night.

37

Devil's Music at the Boys' Club

The Salvation Army had just opened up a new boys' club a couple of blocks around the corner, which had become a popular place to meet friends and have some fun and recreation after school. They had various programs of interest for us teenaged boys with lots of energy and not much direction, such as boxing, PE, running, woodwork, board games, chess club, books to borrow and other things to keep the kids off the streets. For the first time since the new district of Childwall Valley was built up, we kids finally had a center to get our ya-yas out.

Shortly after it opened, a couple of American guys, probably in their thirties, who wanted to teach us English lads the fine art of baseball, turned up out of the blue. We'd seen the tobacco chewing, 'throw a tantrum game' on telly and the movies, but none of us had ever played this Yanky game, only its English equivalent, rounders, which had similar rules. But there wasn't any problem catching on, and with our cricket background, we sure knew how to smack a ball.

The two odd men appeared a bit soft, and it became obvious to everyone that they liked the company of young boys a bit too much; they would hand out a few ciggies when out in the playing field and had offered to give some younger lads a ride in their car. They handed out a few baseballs and a left-handed mitt, which we found unusual because we caught the hard cricket ball, a heavy wooden ball wrapped in a skin of red leather, with our bare hands. So why would we put the glove on the left, when most of us were right-handed? None of us had personally engaged in the game before, and because it was a Yanky game, we didn't take it too seriously. We thought the Yankees went hysterical over the smallest things. It was all Disneyland, Elvis and rich people with flashy cars.

Undoubtedly a lot of us were raised with a certain disdainful feeling for the Americans, except, of course, for their music and movies. I'd often heard the older generation complaining about the tough times in the war, when the "Yanks always arrived a bit late," just like the First World War, and when the GIs did arrive, the saying then became, "They're overpaid, oversexed and over here." This was not an uncommon complaint about the swaggering overfed Americans who gave out token sticks of chewing gum to kids, and offered nylon stockings to the young ladies for a favour. In Britain we were rationed till the mid-fifties, and I remember going to bed hungry many times.

After a short while, the two odd balls, who kept trolling our boys' club, stopped showing up. We'd all backed away, dismissing and laughing them out of town.

One other big attraction at the boys' club was the modern music lessons. Sergeant Major Esther Sweeney was in charge of the music, and on the second night, I turned up for the music class; she handed out six well-used, six-stringed acoustic guitars. I scored one, and we were told we could even take them home for practice. Other lads who had their own guitars could bring them along and join in the lessons. We beginners sat in a half circle, and watched intently to these instructions: "Here's an E, and a B7th and an A. Copy them down in your exercise books, and practice every day. Learn these three chords, and we'll be all on our way." This was the sweet guidance from the not-bad-looking, mid-twenties sugar lump, in the Lord's uniform.

"Yes, Sergeant Major!" We all sang out, as our tender young fingertips fumbled along the fretboards while we were looking back at the blackboard and figuring out the first to sixth string on the correct fret from the nut. Drang! Twang! Prang! Bang!—as one lad hammered too hard, and bust his G string. Whoops!

"Easy now boys, just strum along with me, nice and gentle now." Our angel's tender words.

"Get that thing out of this 'ouse! You're gonna learn rock and roll on that! It's Devil's music," was dad's reaction as I walked happily into the house with an old guitar.

"But dad, we're gonna learn the church choruses and stuff for Christmas and things like that."

"No you're not. Anyway, churches should only have pianos and organs playing the Lord's music. Take it back!"

"But dad..."

"Enough!"

I turned on my heels, and was back at the boys' club in ten minutes with the curvy music box, just as the place was closing up.

"Sorry, but me dad won't let it in the house. He hates modern music."

"What?" she said. "We'll be learning all the choruses for church. I'll come over and talk to your dad. Wait here, we'll go together." And shortly thereafter, as quick as a quaver, we were back at our house, and she was telling my dad to let me take the guitar lessons for all the right reasons. I stood there, fingers crossed behind my back, dreaming of getting some Beatles tunes down pat.

"Hello, Sergeant Major, what are you doing here? I've told him already, none of that nonsense in this house. That's it." He pointed to the guitar case.

"There's no way you could..." she started.

"No, there's no way at all. Thank you, Sister. Good night." And that was that.

So, after that, every night when I visited the boys' club, she'd still let me learn guitar with the rest of the kids, but I couldn't take the axe home. The old fellow didn't need to know.

This entertainer spirit was always in me, and I was often disappointed and frustrated with my dad's strict and intolerant ways. But I wasn't going to let that hold me back. I secretly made my own guitar.

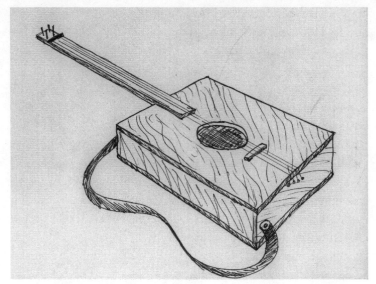

My guitar

It was an oblong wooden box with a neck with no frets, more like a square violin; the strings were four different break-test fishing lines tightened at the end with wood screws that I'd drilled holes for at school, and it had a plywood face-board with a round hole. I connected an old belt to each end, as a guitar strap to sling over my shoulder. When I finally got a few bob in my pocket, I went to a music shop in town and bought four real steel strings, E B G D and began strumming along to the tunes. Four strings out of six was better than none. When the old fellow was out of the house, I'd stand in front of the mirror in my room, and let it rip. "She loves you, yeh, yeh, yeh," "If you knew Peggy Sue," and on and on. My brothers knew I had the square guitar and had a good laugh over it. I kept it hidden under my bed.

Back at the club I was learning my sixth chord, and my fingertips were toughening up. The Sergeant Major even asked me what was the first song I'd like to learn, and she'd help me through it.

"Well, the best song out there, right now," I said, "is 'My Girl' by the Temptations. It's a fab song, and it goes like…"

"Like this?" she said, and began with a flawless intro to the hottest Motown tune on the charts. Man, was she a fabulous player or what? The whole club stopped everything they were doing and got into the tune. We all sang that cool song word for word, straight through. Some of us watched her chords, trying to catch on, like a veritable "cats choir on a hot tin roof," à la "twang twang."

"That's one of my favourite songs too," she said. "I love Motown and Little Stevie Wonder and all those bands."

Esther Sweeney was a wonderful teacher and a good friend to all in that music class. She allowed us the freedom to jam along, make up notes and invent chords and sounds without embarrassment, just so we could relax and be confident with our creativity, and become one with the magical instrument. It was a refreshing change from the regimentation we all had at school.

Yes, we also had our years of school music lessons, usually boring stuff dished out from the education system. We also learned how to write and transpose music and recognize various classical pieces and their composers and time frames. But even in our form school, we had no such thing as a school band; there wasn't any money for that. As wee kids, we'd all learned how to play the recorder, and then forgot it. Those lessons were helpful, and in all English schools, the recorder was the standard place to start.

Without exaggeration, all the kids in Liverpool were totally enveloped with the Mersey Beat and Motown, but our music teachers were from the old school, and most would mock what we liked. They had no understanding or appreciation of modern music.

All except for another young woman we had for a short while, Miss Downs. She filled in for the old battle-ax who was away on holidays.

So, instead of us writing down scales and exercises and listening to the old hen screech away in her pretend operatic voice, while tinkling on the ivories, we had this young, good-looking teacher running the show and giving us the gen on how modern music came around, from the Roaring Twenties to Elvis and the local music scene. One day she surprised us when she brought a Beatles EP to class, and played it, allowing some of us to get out of our chairs and dance to the tunes.

Pat Fitzgerald and I were always dancing in the hallways, and at the school Christmas party, we had won first prize for the twisting competition, a chocolate bar each. Wow! This dancing in the classroom caused a bit of a ruckus in the hallway, as other kids and some teachers poked their heads in the door to see what the score was.

"Musical appreciation!" was her reply, when the headmaster inquired about the loud commotion booming down the hall and told the crowd to disperse.

"I see! Musical appreciation? A little lower please, Miss, er?"

"Downs, sir. Miss Downs."

"Yes, well, please!" And he motioned with his hand to turn down an invisible volume knob, then walked away, shaking his head in disbelief.

One fine day, I was greatly surprised when my brother Geoff, the sailor, gave me a handmade Czechoslovakian guitar. Our rugged lad was home at last from his latest adventure at sea. Sometimes he'd be gone for months or just short trips to America, but he'd always bring me a gift: a bongo drum or an African hat, a carton of cigarettes or some other souvenir from afar.

He'd won the old scratched-up guitar in a card game, from a friend on board, and it was my first real guitar. This nylon string dealie had a very wide neck, and I found it difficult getting my fingers to stretch across the frets. The guy who made it must have had digits like a spider. But despite its awkward feel, it made a descent sound after I changed the tattered strings. This well-travelled guitar replaced the square Bo Diddly battered box with fishing line that I had been hammering away on. Having learned enough from Esther Sweeney to get me started, I could get my fingers around six proper strings and at fifteen I was now old enough to insist on keeping it. My bedroom now rang with rhythm.

38

My Magic Fishing Box

In the summer, I'd sometimes go through the railway tunnel to a large field with a lightly wooded area and fish in the local fishing hole, Jacko's Pond. Jacko's was a great place for a young kid to spend a few hours of adventure in the world of make-believe. There was a couple of rafts lashed together with scrap wood and planks, that you could barely stand or balance on, and push across to Treasure Island, a small island in the middle of the pond. A bunch of us kids would play at pirates.

Back in the winter of early '63, it was one of the coldest times in a century, and the ice hung in thick sheets on the inside of our bedroom windows due to all that condensation. We'd force the windows open and throw the sheets of ice down into the street below. During that brutal winter, the ice was also very thick on Jacko's Pond, at least four or five inches. A few of us decided to try out some ice fishing for the first time, so we hammered a couple of holes in a few places, sent down a few hooks baited with a tiny pieces of cheese and pulled out tiny roach and perch, one after the other, then returned them to the pond. (This would be good practice for my later times in the Yukon, Northern Canada, with my ice-fishing adventures in 1972.)

A young man who lived on our block of flats, who was mad about freshwater and sea fishing, introduced me to the great sport, even lending me an old rod and reel a few times. I eventually made my own gear from different pieces of broken rods and a rusty reel that another fellow down the road gave me. With a little time spent whittling away with my penknife, the mismatched odd bits soon began to fit together, and with some twine and varnish, the end result was a very passable three-piece fish-catching masterpiece of ingenuity: my very first eleven-foot fishing rod, which I treasured for a few months until the annoying day arrived when it was knocked off.

One of my favourite places to fish was at Calderstone's Park, where I'd caught a prize fish, a two-pound crusian carp, a great size, when the British record was only about six pounds. After carefully weighing the gorgeous fish, bronzy like an overgrown goldfish, I returned it to the lake.

On the day my rod was taken, I was at Calderstone's and had left it at the lakeside while I took a quick visit to the public toilets. All morning there had been a lad, strange and lonely looking, hanging around the edge of the small lake. He'd bummed a smoke from me and kept asking everybody stupid questions about the different techniques and ideas about bait, float and weight, things that average anglers knew backwards, and then he was gone like a ghost. It was obvious to myself and the other anglers along the grassy reeds that the curious boy with the motor-mouth was the thieving sod who snatched my prized possession and legged it. This wasn't like stealing a pack of fags, and it delivered some personal insight for me. Now I was on the receiving end of a theft. This experience of violation took away my happiness and peace of mind. My blood boiled as I rode my bike home. I cruised that park on and off for weeks, looking out for my rod but never saw it again. If I'd found that lad, there would have been hell to pay.

That night, my dad told me I was fortunate in some way. My tackle/lunch box with the upholstered flip-top seat, my woodworking class masterpiece, had not been stolen. Also left alone was the holding net, or keep net as we called it, where we'd store all the small fish captured throughout the day, submerged to keep them alive, then released back into the water later, to be caught again by one of the thousands of recreational fishermen who lived in the city limits. So, that was the first and last time I ever made a rod from scratch; after that, I bought them from sports fishing or second-hand junk shops.

My fishing box

This magic tackle box I'd made was my dream come true, and I was now totally absorbed with my fishing passion, and was borrowing library books to study the myriad techniques and skills of freshwater and sea fishing. I was also persuaded by a friend to join the Liverpool Anglers' Club. This was to become my fortunate escape from teaching Sunday school to little kids at the Salvation Army. My father gave me permission to fish on Sundays instead, with the prerequisite that I brought fish home for the family dinner, which, simply put, I did religiously. I prayed fervently over many a baited hook.

I especially enjoyed the times when our club would pile on board the double-decker at Lime Street Station for those excursions to Anglesey, North Wales, at the seaside or the Shropshire Union Canal. I began to gather great experience and mastery at the art of angling, and mucked in with some of the old geezers from the club, who passed on all kinds of secret skills and wily tips they'd garnered over their years in the fine art of sports fishing. But also on the rare occasion, as I would experience with my trips to Scotland and North Wales, there were moments where bringing edible fish home trumped the code of ethics for that noble pastime. I'm not alluding to the great Northern Canadian method of poaching the lakes with a stick of dynamite in an empty Coke bottle, no, just the use of an extra hook or two. In some cases, the use of multiple hooks on one line was allowed by the British fisheries. One example was the old-fashioned paternoster, a weight with two horizontal lines each carrying a hook, a sure-fire method for bottom fishing at sea. Sometimes it caught flatties, two at a time—fluke, Dover sole, plaice or dab, all pan fryers.

I'd first been introduced to this legal method of multiple-hook fishing when I was fourteen on a summer holiday with my folks, down in the southern end of England, at the glorious seaside town of Torquay, Devon. The charter boats packed with groups of visitors would chug out to sea and provide each person with a hand-line, rolled around a small spool. The long line had a weight at the end and a number of very large and colourful feathered hooks, spaced out just up the line. The captain would cut the engine of the old craft way out in the briny, letting her gently drift on the slack tide, and when he'd spot a large school of high-speed mackerel passing below, on his electronic fish-finder, he'd shout out, "OK, folks, start jigging, they're under us."

Down would go the lines, and within seconds, people would start howling and whooping as the fighting fish snapped at the flies, tugging in desperation to release themselves and rejoin their dark blue-striped shoal brethren with their shimmering, silver underbellies, as they escaped, darting and dancing in perfect unison, off into the deep. Some novices brought in three fish at a time; they were so plentiful, and the deckhands had their hands full, busily unhooking fish and tossing them into a large wooden box mid-ship, marking all of our charter cards, "you got four fish, you got three…" Clouds of screaming seagulls circled and dove into the bubbling sea froth as the fish were gutted and their entrails tossed over the stern. An epicurean delight for the sharp-eyed winged scavengers.

Back at the dock, you were given the option to bag your mackerel or leave them to be smoked and picked up at the dock in two days, which my folks and I decided to do. So, a couple of days after I'd hooked my half a dozen, we were treated to smoked mackerel for breakfast at the B and B. We had a big one each, which filled up our plates, and the rest were devoured by the innkeeper and his family.

Mum and dad in Torquay, Devon, 1964

39

The Attack Dog

The innkeeper who owned the Torquay B and B was a bit of an odd duck, and his main passion in life was training police dogs. His name was Desmond, a name I could never forget because my mum called him Desi Arnaz, like Lucy's husband on telly. He also had that jet-black greased-back hairdo, and was always flirting with the female visitors at his "Top of the Hill" B and B. An ex-copper, he fancied himself a lady's man.

One morning when we were sitting around after breakfast, Desi offered to take me out to a world-famous kennel that trained all kinds of service dogs: police dogs, search and rescue dogs, blind-assisting dogs and show competition dogs. The kennel, just a few miles away, hired Desi as a home-trainer for police dogs, and he'd take them on for a few months and return them after they'd learned a few obedience skills. I agreed to go along for the interesting experience, and within an hour, we were at the kennel and looking at a couple of options of bringing a dog back with us. One was a black Lab, and the other, an Alsatian, about eight months old. We ended up driving back with the Alsatian, which Desi wanted to train in tracking and apprehending a running suspect. Guess who was going to be the suspect? This fair-sized dog had already done a bit of training, and had a good nose for finding the scent; all that was needed was a little more time with the apprehension moves. After figuring out how well she could perform, Desi asked if I could wear this big brace that fitted over my arm so the dog could grab it when she lunged at me. The only important thing was to be careful to shove the plastic false arm in the dog's face when she got close.

"It's OK, Pete, I've done this before with other dogs, and all you do is turn towards her as she gets closer to you and just hold out that arm, and she'll grab it till I call her off. And she'll be on a leash anyway." The rope was about twenty feet long, so the plan didn't seem too bad.

But I still needed to do some thinking about this as I'd become a bit leery of big dogs over time.

Back on Cadmus Street, a pile of us small kids had witnessed our favourite little dog, Trigger, who lived at number 2, next to Everton Road, get mauled and killed on the street and dragged around by a huge black Alsatian from the next street over. I heard the monster was later picked up and destroyed, and the neglectful owner got a half-brick through his window.

And one time when I was on my way home up Hartsbourne Avenue with two armfuls of groceries, I began wondering why a crowd of people on the other side of the road were all looking silently across at me. No one was walking on my side of the street. As I continued past a shop doorway, a large Alsatian approached me, growling and baring it teeth. I just stood still, frozen like a statue, with my arms wrapped around the big bags and avoided eye contact. Then as I turned slowly away to cross the street, it lunged at me and bit into the side of my coat by my ribs, and it was only then that some people ran across and scared it away. It was a guard dog that had jumped over the fence from a nearby building site and was on the loose, but after the cops came, it was caught and taken away. I examined my side, and I had a good-sized bruise where the beast had left his mark through my coat and heavy sweater.

So I had good reason not to be in a hurry about Desi's brilliant idea, but I gave it a bit more thought, and decided that I could do it at the end of the day.

With the excited dog in the back of the car in a crate, we took off to a field nearby that was surrounded by a small thicket. I went up towards the trees with the big false arm strapped over my real one and hid while Desi gave her a sniff of a rag I'd been carrying.

There they were, heading over the field below me, and the black restless brute was on the end of the long rope dragging him like a powerful sled dog after my scent. When they were no more than a hundred yards away, Desi dropped the leash, and the big bastard took off like a rocket in my direction. Bloody 'ell! I thought, as I turned and scarpered up the rise of the hill and clambered up into the first tree with some low-lying branches. Up I went, like a chimp escaping a leopard, and when the big snarling beast arrived, all Desi could say was, "Pete, you could have just stuck your arm out."

"Are you kidding?" I replied as the crazed wild-eyed animal gnashed it's teeth at me. "Forget it man! I'm not doing this! Why did you let go of the fucking rope?" He just shrugged his shoulders, and put the dog into the crate in the back of the car, and no more was said as we drove back to his place.

So it was all over even before we got to see if the dog could do it's job. No more training attack dogs for me. I'd become fondly attached to my arms and legs. And I'd become less and less tolerant of the threats that surrounded my vulnerable world: from attack dogs to the war-damaged teachers at school.

40

Stranded on Hilbre Island

By now I'd gathered some fishing experiences, so with my beautifully handcrafted fishing box, I was eager to try my hand at all the aquatic species that dared swim within striking range of my line.

Across the River Mersey from Liverpool, on the far side of the Wirral Peninsula, lies the small seaside town of West Kirby, an old getaway for the city crowds seeking clean, sunny beaches at the wide mouth of the River Dee. A good place for digging up cockles to take home. Just out from the shore, across the golden Irish Sea sand, are three islets, Hilbre Island, and two smaller rocky sisters, Middle Eye and Little Eye. The largest island has a lighthouse, a caretaker's cottage and is still, to this day, a bird and wildlife sanctuary. An island with history, dating back beyond the Doomday Book and the Romans. A secluded place where hermit monks followed their vows and lived on flatfish and seaweed, a millennium ago.

At the southern end of Hilbre lies a cozy little cave, its entrance opening onto the surrounding golden beach and rugged rocks. It was here that my mate Billy and I had intended to stay for a day's fishing and camping adventure, then head home, but it turned out to be a bit more than what we counted on. We'd left Liverpool that morning by bus and train and arrived at West Kirby, assuming we wouldn't have too much problem legging it across the hard sand on an outward-going tide, but we'd arrived a bit early and hadn't checked the tide tables. You had to be very careful to get your timing right, or you could be in for a bit of a dash, a splash or maybe a drowning. So now we had to wait while the cold sea slowly tipped itself out of the wide-mouthed chilly bathtub. "Time and tide wait for no man."

While waiting for the sea change, we split an order of fish and chips at the local Chinese fish and chippy. The Chinese folk always made the best fish and chips, and we knocked back the light lunch with a small bottle of Coke each. Besides our usual fishing gear and rods, we had our sleeping bags and carried a wax-paper bag full of fish guts, which I'd scored at the market a few days before. The bag of frozen bait had been as hard as rock when we'd left home, but now the bag was beginning to drip blood and stink to high heaven. We didn't realize till we'd got to West Kirkby that the beaches had a bountiful supply of big juicy cockles, prime bait for the ground fish. So bringing this messy bag of fish guts was as unnecessary as a ditch digger wearing a bowtie and tails. The hours passed at an agonizingly slow pace, then people started wading through the troughs of the retreating tide.

"Here we go," Bill said. "That's us then." And off we trudged in our wellies, across the corrugated beach, to our island escape. My mother had told me of times past, when her dad and her younger brothers had gone to Hilbre to catch fish, and how they'd used a couple of dozen safety pins as hooks to catch the flatfish, proper hooks being a rare commodity during the lean years, and they spaced the hooks a yard apart on what was called a beach line. This paradise island location and method of fishing was something I'd wanted to try. So during the week before our adventure, I'd spliced together my version of a beach line with hooks attached to some heavy monofilament, "a yard apart" as I'd been told by folk with beach line experience. But along with that unsportsmanlike rig, we brought our regular sea-casting rods to fish in the usual manner. We had to be careful with our negotiation of the tide and running rivulets, and watch out for areas of very soft sand that acted almost like quicksand. You could sink up to your knees, submerging your wellies in the heavy muddy sand, as the suction tried to claim your footwear.

As we walked, we began to understand and read the higher, harder sand, and stick to it. Finally, on the beachfront of Hilbre, we let out with a "whoopee" and laid our fishing boxes and camping gear down near the cave entrance, just above the high-tide line.

We'd heard about this convenient cave from a friend who'd been there a few times in the past, and true enough, this cave opened up into an accommodating shelter, complete with a large folded tarpaulin placed to the side as you entered, left there by the last fisherman who sought shelter from the elements. The tarp could be hung across the entrance by its eyes on big rusty nails driven into the cracks of the rock. This cavern had a small hole in the far-off ceiling, allowing you to light a campfire out of the weather. The smoke could escape through the hole and, from outside on the grassy hill, coil up into the wind and disappear. We could only find a few wind-broken bushes and tree branches along the hillside that were damp, but with a bit of persuasion, and some paper we'd brought along for wrapping up our catch, the branches were soon blazing, and our wee frying pan jumping and sizzling with sausages on our Primus stove. This was camping at its best. Fried sausages, fried bread and a pint of beer between the two of us beside a toasty fire.

But before we could settle into relaxing and exploring the island, we had to set out the beach line as far as possible before the tide came rushing in through the wide-open channel that separated England from Wales. This River Dee had such a wide estuary that the incoming sea surged across the sand, carrying piles of frothy seaweed and flotsam and jetsam—discarded rubbish from passing ships, pleasure boats and landlubber litterbugs. In contrast, the River Mersey, on the other side of the Wirral, had a narrow entrance, and its bottle-neck prevented the river emptying out too much, leaving the shipping lanes with enough depth for ocean-bound vessels to easily navigate.

In one large haversack, I'd packed the beach line, about forty feet of heavy fishing line. The hooks had small pieces of Sellotape on the points to prevent them from snagging up into a ball of raveled hooks and line we called a "bird's nest." Last out of the bag were two steel rods that I'd scored from metalwork class. The two-feet long rods secured the ends of the line in the sand, and to make sure we could find them later, a small red plastic float, the size of a tennis ball, was tied off on one rod. We'd spot this marker first, bobbing around, even before the tide was fully out. And sure enough, after the sun had gone down, the sea was black, and the sky cloudy, we spotted our little red ball with the use of my trusty bicycle torch, way out there in a couple of feet of running tide, signaling, "Here I am, pick me up, there's fish!" We huddled around our campfire a bit longer, had a smoke, then guessed the tide was low enough to venture out and feel for the line. We made sure the water was below the tops of our boots, as we'd had to dry out our socks once already. Then—fantastic! Out of a dozen hooks, we'd scored eight fish, mostly good-sized flatties: sole, plaice or flounder and one small whiting. They splashed and jumped as they came to the surface, and we disgorged them from the hooks and threw them in the bag.

We were your usual teenagers, always hungry, so back in the cave camp, we fired up the Primus cookstove again, fried a couple of fresh fish and devoured them immediately, along with the last of our bread and margarine.

After an uncomfortable night in our sleeping bags, we poked our heads out of the shelter and realized we'd overslept and missed out opportunity to leave. The tide was coming in again! Now we'd have to wait another half a day to get back to West Kirkby and the train home. And we were nearly out of food. We had a piece of cheese and two apples, and the only water we knew of was at the caretaker's cottage up the hill. So off we went, along the cliff edges, the rocky beach, toward his cottage. The sun was barely up, and the heavy overnight rain had slowed.

While we were scrambling up a rocky face, practicing our skills climbing, we came across a couple of seagulls' nests, with eggs in each one. These beautiful seaweed-patterned eggs were worth a try to hungry boys. The coastal communities of the isles of Britain had relished the arrival of these shelled delicacies for centuries. All manner of seabirds—gulls and terns of all types and sizes, gannets, puffins, cormorants, you name it—were laying eggs by the millions at this time every year along the craggy wind-swept cliffs of Great Britain. So we grabbed a couple each, much to the chagrin and diving protests of the lesser black-backed gulls, and scrambled back to our hideaway. In one respect, we were lucky: when we cracked the eggs into the frying pan, they weren't addled and spoilt. Two fried eggs each was enough; not only did they taste and smell a bit fishy, but were rubbery and unappetizing. Yuk, we didn't take more than a couple of bites. Now we were convinced that a knock on the door at the cocky watchman's house was it. As we rounded the corner of the island to his cottage, there he was stood, with an old couple, having a smoke and a chat.

"Morning, boys," was his loud greeting, as we dragged our sorry selves to his cottage door. "Did you sleep over in the cave then? You know there's no overnight camping here anymore? It's a wildlife sanctuary, and they've stopped all that." He continued with a big drag on his smoke.

"Sorry, sir, didn't know that. We thought it's OK to camp out, like. We were told it was all right, by a friend of ours, who comes here all the time. Is there any chance we can get some water for a cuppa? We'll be getting back to the mainland when the tide's out."

"Water? No problem, lads, there's the tap," pointing to the tap on the side wall. "In fact, I don't suppose you'd like a little breaky, would you? We're about to have a bite."

The old couple gazed with amusement at our disheveled appearance.

"Bacon butty sound alright?" he offered.

"Yes please, sir," we chorused, happy at such an unexpected invitation.

If there's anything that will cheer the hearts of two English lads, half wet, cold and tired, after a restless night in a windy cave, it's the offer of a large mug of tea and a thick bacon sandwich, smothered in HP Sauce. The gift of the gods.

We had an interesting visit, and found out that the old couple were biologists who'd spent a few days on the island doing research and counting the nests and eggs of the various seabirds. Bill and I both looked at each other with the same thought running through our heads: Keep our gobs shut.

"Hey, Tim," I said to the cheerful caretaker, as we were leaving to get ready for the off, "any chance we can cadge a couple of fags off yeh for our trip home?"

"No problem, Pete. Here take a handful, as he reached into his pocket and pulled out a pile of hand-rolled ciggies. "I roll dozens of 'em all day long; it's cheaper than 'tailor made.'

"Tah, lah! Cheers," we said, as Billy and I divided them and stashed them in our dry, coat pockets.

Dodging the ripples and ridges of the out-going tide once more, we were soon back on the mainland and waiting at the railway station. The couple of fish we'd kept to take home were filleted and wrapped up in bags. Now we thought we'd do a bit of fund-raising before the train arrived. From Penny Lane to Woolton Village, when we were sagging school, we'd sing and dance on the street and score quite a few bob for our usual needs, food and smokes. We both knew a lot of the old tunes: "If You Knew Susie, Like I Know Susie," "Show Me the Way to Go Home," "I've Got a Lovely Bunch of Coconuts," "If You Were the Only Girl in the World" and so on. So a little jig here and a song and a joke there, the next thing we knew, we'd scored a few bob, enough for a bag of fish and chips, with a bottle of Coke each, for the train trip home.

Back in the Pool, we had a few tales to tell our mates at school and at the local boys' club.

41

Wee Lizzie

During the summer of '65, my mate Billy Watloe and I took off on a two-week trip to Bonny Scotland to do what we most liked to do, chase the girls, have a few drinks, catch some fish and generally partake in the angel-cake from heaven, unsupervised, mad fun. In the spring, we'd made plans, saved enough play money, and Bill's dad had offered to pay for our stay at a B and B in Dalmellington, Ayrshire, a quiet inland village. It was all arranged, and I was chuffed; I'd never been to Scotland, and was raring to go. So, on a warm sunny morning at the end of July, we took the charabang from Lime Street to Glasgow, changed buses for the town of Ayr and finally jumped on the rickety old country double-decker to Dalmellington.

The small town was quaint, with rolling hills, winding roads and a crystal-clear stream that bubbled and meandered its way right through. Our B and B was operated by an equally bubbly old lady, who the whole village, even down to the wee bairns, affectionately called Wee Lizzie. She stood about four-foot-ten, and was as round as she was high. Always wearing an apron and continually busy around the house with her cooking and cleaning, she'd bump you out of the way like a rolling barrel if you stood in the wrong place at the wrong time. Never one to mince her words, she had a strong opinion about everything and everyone in the "wee toon," and she was never wrong. After all, most little old ladies less than five feet tall, with arms like Popeye the Sailorman, are seldom mistaken about anything, and, of course, Lizzie's character judgments of the neighbours and shopkeepers were impeccable. The old girl had lost her husband a few years earlier and had started the B and B not only for a little money, but also for need of company. It seemed, without exception, that all the meals she made for us were greasy, and considering that, I can easily see how her husband had died like he did, from a massive heart attack while carrying in a bucket of coal from the backyard.

As soon as we arrived, she took us outside for a view of the street, and told us: "...and keep away from that crowd across the street; that hoose over there with the broken window upstairs. They're a bunch of heathens, they are. I've never seen them go to kirk once since they've moved in; and the big lad? Well he's a Borstal boy; that should tell you something."

"Naughty boy, eh?" I said.

"Naughty?" she replied. "I think he's a bit more than naughty." Little did I realize that, a few months down the road, I'd be doing a few weekends at the Woolton Youth Correctional Center, which was like nursery school compared to doing a stretch in Borstal.

We went back inside and were about to start unpacking. "And you see," she again pointed out the parlour window from behind her curtains, "just look there at those two down the road, hanging out the window like two bloody stray cats looking for a mouse. Now that's trouble to keep clear of too. Trouble, if I ever saw it!" Our eyes were drawn to two young nice-looking ladies, leaning out of the upper window a few houses down the way, both smoking cigarettes and shouting across the street to the postman making his rounds.

"So what's the problem with them Lizzie?" I asked, like an innocent choirboy.

"They're a pair, those two. The older one's married to a lorry driver, and he's never 'ome, and the young one there doing all the shouting, she's her sister, who's been here for months and does nothing, doesn't even have a job, just hangs out the window all day, talking to every pair of trousers that walks by. They're a bloody disgrace, the pair of 'em. And the hubby? Yeh'll never see him around till he turns up in the middle of the night in his bloody great big noisy lorry and wakes up the whole street. This here wee toon has gone to the dogs, with all these bloody Glasgow crowd moving up here."

"Ah well, Liz, we're here now to give yeh a wee bit of company, and we'll behave ourselves like good Liverpool lads do, and we'll watch out for that crowd. I can smell trouble a mile away." I responded with a slight wink at Bill, as she walked into the kitchen to rustle up some sandwiches for two hungry boys.

Later on upstairs, Billy chuckled, "We'll behave ourselves, Lizzie?" as we unpacked our bags in our tiny room with one old double bed that we'd have to share for two weeks. Lizzie only had one spare room that she rented out at her world-class B and B. The house was tiny, and you couldn't swing a cat in our room, but we only intended to be there for meals and a place to crash after we'd had our fun oot and aboot. We soon developed our routine of meals, tiptoeing in and out at all hours, concealing booze in our bags and listening, with great patience, to all of her gripes and complaints.

Morning reveille came at 7 AM when she'd kick open the bedroom door and walk in with a tray of tea and ginger biscuits, "Here yeh go, boys, sit up. 'This is the day the Lord hath made.' Breakfast in ten minutes."

Oh boy! we mockingly thought, as we knew after two days what would be waiting for us on the kitchen table. And sure enough, there it was, all dished out in gastronomic splendor, our breakfast. I knew what greasy food was, but this took the blue ribbon.

Like a condemned pagan's last meal, there it lay: bacon, sausages, two fried eggs, a piece of fried black pudding, known as blood sausage, a fried tomato cut in half, two thick slices of fried white bread and a couple of homemade potato pancakes, all swimming in a deep pool of grease. And to crown off her pièce de résistance, a small glass beside each plate containing one measured ounce of cheap Scotch. And, not forgetting a big mug of strong tea with a little milk and too much sugar. Wow! We couldn't wait to scoff all this back and run to the lavo' and loose it. As we arrived at the breakfast table, half-awake and hungover from the night before, we'd lean on our chairs, gazing down at the "caveman's delight." Lizzie would come out with something that sounded like, "Ahch! Sto' yer greetin', sit doon the noo and eat those totty scons…and knock back yer wee dram, OK?"

The days passed, and we began to discover the wee hamlet of interesting people with their wonderful broad Scottish accents. We also realized that our landlady wasn't the only one with a penchant for gossip. The humour of it all was to see how everyone, without exception, had their own take on everyone else, and no better place to catch up on local news than in the pub at nighttime after tea. A veritable Scottish "Coronation Street."

We'd also heard from Liz, herself, that the best fishermen in the village were her own four sons; and this was the general consensus everywhere, by everyone, to the extent that each story featured a bigger fish than the previous. We couldn't wait to meet these angling juggernauts. After a couple of nights attending the darts tournament at the local drinking hole, we were introduced to her youngest lad, Harry, the "ace fisher of the glen."

"Hello lads, I'm Harry, Wee Lizzie's favourite son and best troot fisherman this side of Aberdeen, ha." Which was pretty well the whole East-West stretch of Scotland. The bartender, affectionately known as Curly, with hardly a whisker on his big round head, leaned over the bar, and with a wide smile, which revealed half his front teeth were missing, interjected, "Aye boys, you'll nah find a better man who thinks like a fish, swims like a fish, acts like a fish, can catch any fish, and…"

A voice from a corner calls out, "Smells like a fish!" to a groaning applause from the drinking audience.

"How about taking us out fishing, Harry? Is there a lake nearby to score a few trout?" I asked.

"Oh aye, lads, there's some wee lochs and rivers to play the fish, but tomorrow I'll come by me mam's and take you up the hill for a lesson on tickling troot, and I think Saturday morning me and Thomas, my big brother, will be taking you two to our favourite place to do some real fishing. In the meantime, I'm going home to tickle the missus."

His head tilted and his eyebrows lifted. "Bye, lads." We laughed a bit, and when he'd gone, Curly, while pouring a drink, remarked, "He just got married a wee while ago." Wink.

We entered the kitchen, at 7 AM, after our tea and bikky, in great trepidation of finding two floating breakfasts, but to our delight, we sat down in front of two large bowls of good ol' Scottish porridge, and a third bowl at the end, half devoured already by our visiting escort, Harry. Lizzie followed this with two poached eggs on burned white toast, and we were off to see what this "tickling fish" was all about. After walking upriver for fifteen minutes, we stopped at a low area with large flat stones all along the river's edge.

"Crouch down, boys, and quietly follow me." Harry slowly took off his coat, rolled up his sleeves, lay down quiet as a cat along the biggest stone and lowered his arm ever so slowly into the cold water, right next to the rock. It was an overcast day, as were most of the days up there in the village, and everything was dead silent.

"There you are, my little beauty," he whispered, and flung his hand out of the babbling brook, throwing a small trout over his shoulder onto the grass.

"Woo hoo," we shouted, "look at that!"

"Shut up, lads, there's more here." Then after a few minutes, another fish.

I've got to try this, I thought. "Can I have a go?"

"What you've got to do," he explained, "is put your arm deep under the rock, at the bottom end, and slowly bring it forward from behind the fish 'cause they're facing upstream. And then you'll feel the gentle movement of their tail going back and forth, as they are taking a break going upriver. You can tickle their bellies very gently and then quickly grab them, and in the same motion, sling them up and out, over yer head."

"Right," I said, as I lowered my hand in.

My god, the water was like Arctic ice, and I thought my arm was going to fall off, it was so cold. I tried to feel for a fish. You could see the small, nine-inch trout dashing back and forth. But try as I did, no luck! Not a fin or a tail, nothing but a frozen arm.

"You're next, Billy." Harry lay back on the grass and lit up a smoke.

"Bloody 'ell, it's freezin'." Billy gave it a shot but likewise, nothing.

"It takes a while to get the hang of it. I've been doing it since I was knee-high to a jackrabbit, but let's get going now. I've got to get my car fixed, or we won't be going anywhere on Saturday."

"What kind of car do you have, Harry?" asked Billy, my mechanical genius friend.

"An old Vauxhall Victor I found last year when I was working in Newcastle."

"So what's the score with it, like?"

"It won't start well, and then it floods. I don't want to take it too far in case it buggers up and I'm stuck."

"We'll check it out for yeh. We just restored two motorbikes back in the spring."

"Oh yeh? You can fix engines, can yeh? Well, you're welcome to try, boys."

We got to his backyard, and there parked on the grass next to the coal shed sat an old wreck in its death throws, covered in muck and coal dust. We proceeded with our inspection under the bonnet.

"Tell you what, Harry," I said. "You treat us to a pub lunch and a couple of pints, and we'll have this running like a Rolls in one hour. Do you have some tools? A few spanners and screwdrivers?"

"It's a deal. Two pub lunches and two pints."

"Two pints each," I pointed out.

"OK, two each, if that thing runs like a Rolls in an hour. Done."

Our jackets off and sleeves rolled up, we went at it. The first thing we noticed was the large accumulation of corrosion all over his battery terminals and loose connections on two plugs. They were pulled off and cleaned in minutes. So with those things out of the way, the car was pretty well fixed of its starting problems, but we continued on with a cleanup and the resetting of all the spark plugs and tightened a wire here or there. Within the space of half an hour, the car was running like a top.

"There you go, mate, how's that engine sound now?"

"My God, boys, it's running as smooth as a baby's arse. What was it?"

"Ah, Harry, if we told you our secrets, we'd be out of business. It was something only two experts like us could fix. Now how about that lunch?"

"You're two tough salesmen, I can tell. You could probably sell a fridge to an Eskimo."

"Maybe we could sell a Bible to a whorehouse?" Billy added.

"That's funny, laddy, but don't you let me mam hear you talking like that, or you'll be camping out on the road. There's no joking about the good book like that at her place."

I stepped in. "Oh aye, we know that, Harry, we're very polite around your mam, we're always respectful. She's a good Christian lady, is your mam. Billy, you'd better be careful with your fuckin' gob, alright, our kid?"

"Is that right now? I'm more careful than you are. You're the one with the fuckin' gob."

"That's enough of that, lads, let's get something to eat."

Bill and I sometimes crossed swords but never came to serious blows. We'd actually got to know each other after a fight at school when we were about thirteen. There must have been half a dozen fights in the schoolyard that day, when all the boys were sorting each other out. We were coerced into fighting for no other reason than troublemakers egging us on. It was that way sometimes. We actually talked it over first, and I found no reason to fight this stranger who I thought was a nice-enough guy, and he thought the same. The conversation went something like this.

Billy asked me, "If you get me down, would you kick me in the head?"

"I'll be kicking your fuckin' face in alright," was my reply. Even though I detested fighting. To make an impression and get ready for the task in hand, one had to show how hard you were before you actually proved it, and the rambling gob-shite was usually the first offensive displayed to a challenger. It was mostly bullshit trying to baffle brains.

"ok then." he replied, "if I get the better of you, I'm going to kick your stupid head in!"

This was at morning break, and we arranged to meet at the end of the day at the bike sheds, where hundreds of the kids' bikes were chained up. After we'd taken our coats off and looked each other in the eye, I knew this was one more unnecessary tangle I didn't need. One rule I always remember growing up on our old street was, "There are no rules in the scrapping game." And now, in this new district, where some posh types lived, I felt I'd be able to take on some of the best. But, from the old slums to the new ghettos, there were still some very tough boys in this locale, and I had been quickly made aware of the fact.

Billy approached and began to ask me a question, and while the words were still coming out of his mouth, I let loose with a couple of quick punches, plus a heavy boot to his leg and a lucky head-butt to the side of his face. I'd seen it too many times before. When a lad got within range and asked a stupid question to distract you, it was usually quickly followed with a surprising onslaught of strikes, and street smarts dictated don't let anyone close in. After the first moment, I was a bit surprised to see that, despite dishing out a few decent hits, he started coming back, rushing in with his head down like a rugby tackle and pushed me back over a couple of bikes. I fell over on top of one, the pedal jabbing me in the back and knocking the wind out of me. Fortunately, he also stumbled on top of a bike and hurt his arm, at the same moment he hit me squarely on the nose. We were pulled up by the crowd and pushed together again to keep the scrap going. I could see he was as reluctant as I was to carry on, and I shouted, "Do you give in, Billy? Had enough?"

"Fuck off!" was his reply as he held his arm in pain.

"I'll fuckin' work you if you don't give in!" I repeated, as he turned his back to me.

"OK! That's enough," I called out, as the mad crowd of kids shouted for more: "Kick his head in. Put the welly in. Take him! He's yours!"

"He's had enough, arsehole!" was my reply to the loudmouthed Riley who had set off the whole thing. My adrenalin ran high, and my anger burned toward everyone who wanted more blood. I swung my boot at the instigator and sent him howling to the concrete, with a sore leg.

"You're a bastard snake, Riley. Keep away from me." And I stomped on his leg once more. "I'll kick your head in, yeh fuckin' rat."

I felt compelled to go over and ask Billy how he was. I could see his arm was bad, but his mates pushed me off and told me where to go, so I gathered myself together, wiped my bloody nose, spit and cleaned my dirty hands, unlocked my parked bike and took off down the hill.

I felt sick as I rode along the road, but I still had a feeling of achievement as one does when facing up to a challenge. The next morning in school, I spotted him, and as one who's always believed in fairness, I went over, offered a handshake and said, "No hard feelings, Bill. Fair fight? No hard feelings?"

His reply, "You're lucky, mate, I hurt my arm. OK! Fair fight." We shook hands and, in just a short while, became the best of mates.

We had a lot in common: girls, fishing, smoking, robbing stuff, fixing motor bikes, drinking his parents' booze, listening to the Mersey Beat on Radio Caroline and watching out for each other. Really good mates. And now here we were, in Scotland, free as two escaped lions from the zoo.

After Harry had treated us to a pub lunch and a couple of pints, it was back to Lizzie's to get cleaned up for a night on the town. Lizzie found comfort each day in two important things: watching the telly and knocking back a mickey of cheap scotch. A mickey a day kept her doctor away. Not a day went by when you wouldn't find one more empty twelve-ounce bottle standing at the kitchen sink. Out the back door, by the rubbish bin, boxes and boxes of empties leaned against the wall. I asked her if it wouldn't be cheaper to buy larger bottles, but only drink them half-way down? Her idea was to use the smaller ones 'cause she'd know her daily allowance was up. And, like I said, there wasn't a breakfast that wasn't accompanied with a shot of Scotch for everyone.

After our evening meal, we caught the local bus to Bluebell, the next town, where a local fundraising dance was being held. The money was going towards a youth club or something, and the place was crawling with young kids to the elderly. It was an amusing moment for us, not being accustomed to such a wide spectrum of ages under the same roof, all mixing in and dancing to every kind of music from the wartime favorites to the Kinks. Alcohol was not allowed, just bottles of pop or tea. So, due to the restrictions and the lay of the land, one could see, from within the seated crowds encircling the hall, a little bottle appear now and then, passed under the tables and tipped out into the tea cups or glasses, a wee dram here and a wee tot there, everywhere a wee wee. As the evening rolled along, the younger crowd, as expected, would slide out of the back door, quickly pass around the bottles of beer and return in a more boisterous manner, shouting and howling along with the blur-ring music, which emanated from the over-burdened, crackly speakers.

It was the Scottish equivalent of a mad night at a Mississippi barn dance. In the Pool where Bill and I came from, one was expected to dress up a bit if you were going out to the dance; but these hicks weren't out to impress anybody, and working gear was the usual garb. The music was crap, the girls were plain, and the only judy worth looking at was surrounded with half a dozen panting boys. The whole atmosphere was alien to us city boys, so we caught the first passing bus home and found Wee Lizzie passed out in her chair, with the telly turned up loud.

"Let's get her to bed," I said. So the two of us carried the old girl, her arms over our shoulders, off to her bedroom, took off her slippers, wooly socks and cardigan and rolled her as gently as possible, trying not to wake her, though she kept on murmuring to herself. Finally, when she was nicely tucked in, and as we tiptoed out, we heard her croaky little voice, "Thanks, boys, I really enjoyed that."

42

Feshin' for the "Wee Troot"

A couple of days later, we were to be treated to the most surreal moment of fishing we could never have anticipated. On Friday night, we were at Lizzie's, and Harry arrived with his oldest brother, Thomas, in tow. After a beer in the kitchen, while the old girl was busy watching a game show on telly, we got the lowdown on our promised fishing trip the following morning.

Harry was the spokesman. "It's an early start, lads, we'll be here around 5, so be ready to shove off right away."

"What gear do we bring? We've got our fly rods, and I bought some good-looking flies before we came," I mentioned.

"Don't bring anything; we've got all the stuff. What flies have yeh got? Do you have any Alexander Gold?"

"What's that?"

"It's the one we use this time of year, as the gnats are getting bigger." And turning towards his mum, he called out, "And don't forget, bring loads of sandwiches, and a flask of tea with bikkies." And then to us across the table, "We'll bring a couple of brew."

I grabbed my prized tackle box, found the small container of my carefully kept fly collection that displayed the wide range of handmade hairy, furry and feathered miniature appetizing lures.

"Let's see what we have here now," says Thomas.

"Look at the size of that, Harry. Bloody 'ell. Do you fish for marlin or swordfish back in the River Mersey, Pete?" as he holds up my largest piece.

"That's for Atlantic salmon. I thought I could use it up here if they're on the river run?"

"River run? There's no' many salmon-spawning rivers around here, lad. That's further north. We'll be looking for the wee troot. Nice shiny, panfryers. You'll see tomorrow. Oh, look at that, then. Hey mam…"

"I know, I know," returned the old girl's half-awake, croaky voice from the front. "Lots of sarnies and bikkies. I should know by now. Fifty years of sarnies and bikkies."

"Love yeh, mammy. There'll be fresh fish in the pan tomorrow for yeh, and I'll get you some smokes and a wee bottle for all your trouble."

"Ach, away wi' yeh!" was her last remark as her sons closed the kitchen door and headed home.

Morning arrived and we were awakened by the delicious smell of bacon frying in the pan, and a growly call from our short, fat boss,

"Git yersel's going. Yer'll be late, yer lazy buggers."

We were up and downstairs in a flash, splashed some cold water over our faces, scoffed back the greasy breakfast, put on our weather-proof coats and wellies, grabbed a big duffle bag loaded to the brim with food for an army, and before you could shout "Robby Burns," headlights appeared out front, illuminating the sheets of rain pour-ing from the heavens. We'd just had a decent week of semi-overcast weather, and the very day we need sun for our magical fishing with the legends of the glen, the windows of heaven opened, and the curse of a chilly Scottish storm arrived. Thanks, Lord, I thought, you must hate anglers.

We were off, and the car soon filled up with blue smoke, as the four of us lit ciggies. Then we began tearing down tiny lanes and bumpy country roads, heading off to what was supposed to be the loch, or lake, that nobody was to know about, our sworn secret.

Only a moment had gone by when Billy called out, "Harry, we need to pull over sometime soon. I gotta take a dump."

"You'll have to hold on to it lad, till we get to the petrol station in the edge of town."

"How far's that?" came a subdued reply, as Bill was taking shallow breaths.

"A coupla' minutes and we'll get some petrol, and they'll let you use the shithouse."

"Ooh, Let's 'urry up then! Please!"

The rest of us were laughing at Billy's dilemma when he came out with, "Alright, yous, I've had the trots since we got here, and been fed all that greasy stuff your mum feeds us."

The car came to a screeching halt, and Harry quickly turned off the engine.

"Are you telling me my mam can't cook? Do you think we're all big and strong in our house because our mam can't cook?"

I stepped in to rescue my motor-mouth friend.

"Your mam's cooking is just great, lads." I turned to Bill, "It's the beer up here that you're not used to. The food's great, right?" I elbowed my mate in the ribs.

"Sorry, Harry, the food's fine. Pete's right, it's probably the brew, maybe I got served a green one somewhere. Let's get to the shithouse please?"

Just a couple more turns down the road before we swung into the Esso station, and Billy was out of the car and limped his way around the back to the oothoose. The station wasn't open yet, and it was still a bit dark, but he was lucky enough to find the toilet was unlocked. It was apparently always left open for any needy traveler, especially late night drunks on their way home from the local pub. It was a regular drop-in center, with a distinct air about it.

After he'd mailed his letter, he was back in the car to find us all holding our breath in deadly silence, staring into oblivion, waiting for his comment.

He started, "What a bloody hole. There was such a stink in that place. And there was this shilling that was stuck to the floor, right next to your feet as you sit down."

"You didn't sit down, did yer?" I put in, with a startled look.

"No way, mate. I always do the hover."

"Yes, I always do the helicopter in a public shithouse," Thomas whispered.

Harry explained, "That shilling's been stuck with glue on that shithouse floor for years, and some say, the weird git that owns the place has a peephole next to the mirror, where he spies on people trying to pick it up. His private little peep show. Ha."

"Well he'll have to glue a new bob down there now, won't he."

"What?"

"Yes, I poked it off with me penknife. Look at that."

"Yeh dirty bastard," I said. "That's filthy, that!"

"A bob's a bob mate, and it's free. I'll just clean it up a bit, and it'll buy me a pint."

"Well don't you be handlin' any of the 'pieces' till you've scrubbed your hands, yeh dirty bugger." Harry called out from the front. (A piece being the Scottish word for sandwich.)

The sun finally broke through the clouds, and the rain abated when we turned into the driveway of an old farm, and pulled up at the gate. A toot of the horn alerted a lad about our age who came running out of the old farmhouse, opened the gate and held out his hand, wherein Harry placed a bright shiny florin (two shillings).

"They're away," The lad said. "Don't forget to close the next gate behind you, please, Harry."

"I always do, Willy. Thanks." We proceeded as the first gate swung closed behind us.

"How much was that, for opening a gate?" Billy asked.

"There's a small fee for entering the Laird's land," was the reply. "It's two bob each way now. It used to be two pennies when our dad first brought us up here, forty years ago."

"And that Willy boy, who's he?"

"He was born here. His dad used to be the groundsman, till he died a while ago and the Laird took the boy into the household."

"That's too bad. How did his dad die?"

"The tractor flipped over on top of him, as he was going up a steep hill, crushed him."

Just a few more yards, and as we crested the hill, we were presented with a beautiful vision of a lake way below us, blanketed with a thick fog, revealing what appeared to be a small castle, or fortress, sitting right across on the other side—an ancient vision, and eerily foreboding in its bleak solitude.

"My God! Look at that, will yeh. Welcome to Camelot," I said.

"Welcome to Loch Doon," announced Harry, as we passed through the second gate.

"The first time we came here, I was barely walking. Our dad brought us here to catch dinner."

"How did that castle get there?" I asked.

"Well, that's what she looks like sometimes, eh, Harry?" Thomas spoke. "It looks like it's floating in the middle of the lake, sure enough, but it's really on the bank on the far side. I think it was moved off a wee island, across to the shore, in the thirties, when they flooded the valley for the power plant. But when that fog comes up, it looks like it just walked back into the water all on its own. Amazing!"

"Beautiful!" Harry agreed. "Just beautiful!"

Pulling up near the edge of the lake, we started emptying the bags of gear from the boot of the car.

"Where's the fishing rods and the rest?" I called out.

"Ha, there's none of that fancy sports-fishing stuff on this trip, lads. Get those old bags over here, and that short pole. We're here to catch fish, not play around."

As I poured four small mugs of tea, and after thoroughly washing his hands in the lake, Bill unwrapped some sandwiches. We watched with amusement as the old boys started unraveling a spool of thick fishing line off an old wooden reel.

Next they pulled out what appeared to be a small foot-long block of wood, like a carved wooden boat with a brass rail that ran along one side.

"That floating boat has been in our family for over a hundred years."

As the line was unraveled, artificial flies were tied on every eighteen inches or so, for about fifty feet, and ending with twenty feet of clear line. A swivel at one end of the line was attached to the boat, while the last twenty feet of bare line was tied to the tip of the pole. We were laughing as the two brothers set things up.

Their reaction? "You'll be laughing alright, just you watch."

They both stood at the water's edge with the line stretched out between them, Thomas holding the short rod and Harry the wooden boat. They spoke quietly to each other and synchronized the casting of the floating block. With a one, two, three, Harry flung out the block and his brother followed with his rod. The block flew through the air and landed with a heavy splash.

As the water settled and calmed, Thomas walked slowly along the shore, giving little pulls and jerks to the line as he went, which caused the big float to drift further out on an angle, because of the sliding rail on its side, in a wedge-like motion. "Come on, sun, come out," was the beckoning prayer. Thomas tugged and heaved slowly at the taut line. The block was retrieved and thrown a couple of more times before his prayers were answered, and the sun broke through as we were sitting on the bank and a couple of fish rose to the irresistible Alexander Golds glittering on the surface. Smash, splash as the finned predators struck with decisive hits at their artificial breakfast treats. "Here we go boys, they're on."

We cheered, but were immediately told to "Shut the hell up! They're here. Shhh!"

Thomas walked up the bank, pulling the line out as his brother unhooked the small trout, one by one, and flung them up to Bill sitting on the grass; he put them happily into the canvas bag. The process was repeated a couple of more times, each throw bringing in two or three fish.

It was now our turn. Bill threw first, then me, and with a little direction from the pros, we started getting some results. All in all, as we moved along the water's edge, a hundred yards to the left and right, taking a couple of smoke breaks plus eating up all the food, we'd scored over fifty small fish, all good panfryers.

Throughout the process, it was easy to understand that we had more hits when the sun peered out from behind the clouds. On one throw alone, we hooked six fish. This was the way of bringing home dinner; it was nothing at all to do with the fine art of gentlemen's angling. No, this was poaching at its very best. The morning was over, and we were packed and off back to the gate, where the young fellow met us one more time and asked, "How was the fishing, gentlemen?"

"Terrible," Thomas replied. "Bloody terrible. We hardly got a sausage. Here, lad," as he handed him another couple of bob. "Mum's the word?"

"Aye, mum's the word." As the boy kissed the two pieces of silver coin in his hand and shoved them in his pocket. "When are you back?"

"In a month or so. Cheers." We drove off.

"Not a sausage, hey, Tom?" I said.

"That's right lad, not a sausage, just two big bags full of lovely fish. Ha! This has been our best day in ages, hey, Harry?"

"A blooming wonderful day. These lads must be good luck. What d'yer say?"

"They sure was that. I think we all deserve a beer all 'round. Get them out, boys. In that brown bag back there."

Bill popped the jinks off with his penknife, and we all made a cheer.

"Here's to the Wee Troot," I called out.

"The Wee Troot!" we all shouted.

I was so damn thirsty, I chugged mine back in a few gulps and asked if I could go for a second.

"Bloody hell, lad." Harry said between gulps, while driving quickly down the narrow lanes. "You're supposed to savour it boy. That's good Scottish brew you're drinking, not weak English piss."

"OK, I can wait." I replied, feeling that bad tempers obviously ran in the family. But sure enough, as Thomas the light-hearted mediator finished his beer, he told me to open some more, and we continued home in a tired kind of silence, gazing at the lovely countryside and counting the miles back to Dalmellington.

Lizzie was hanging out the washing when we pulled down the lane to her back yard and parked.

"Fish for tea?" she asked.

"Oh aye, mam, some nice ones."

We humped the bags of fish passed the old coal shed and into the kitchen, where we pulled out a few fish at a time and gutted them in the sink, rinsed them off and put them in the metal tray at the bottom of the old fridge.

"We're taking a few for ourselves, and we'll leave the rest for you and the others."

The others being the rest of the tribe who lived across town. They had quite the clan, and sharing was expected. Dinner was fabulous. Lizzie simply fried up the fish with a touch of butter, salt and pepper, till the skin was nice and crispy brown. We lads had two trout each with mashed spuds and peas, and we ate till we were stuffed. It was the best meal of the trip, washed down with a large mug of tea.

43

A Mad Night at the Ayr Fair and a Beatle Tale

Billy and I were determined to get to the fairgrounds in the town of Ayr before our holiday was through, so after a quick clean-up and a change of clothes, we were off on the fat old, double-decker bus to see the sights. A couple of nice-looking girls were sitting up front, so we sat opposite, and they quickly asked if we could spare a couple o' ciggies, which immediately started up a conversation. Everyone cadged smokes from each other; it was a way of breaking the ice. They were heading to the fairgrounds to meet up with friends, and as we got to town, we bid them adieu and leaped off at the first pub, appropriately named The Pipes and Thistle.

In the northern latitudes of England and Scotland, the summer sun doesn't go down early, and twilight lingers till eleven or later. We decided to have a few pints before cruising the fairgrounds, as they were open past midnight. No sooner had we walked into the corner pub when we were greeted with a shout from the window table where two fellows from the same street as Lizzie's were sitting and drinking.

"Hey, you two Liverpool lads. Get over here," the big boy summoned. "What are yous doing here?"

"We've come to check out the skirt at the fairgrounds. We hear it's the place to find all the action."

"You heard right lads." The drunken boy carried on, "There's usually loads of lassies at the twurly wurly, whatever the hell they call that spinny thing?"

"The twister," added the other lad.

What's your names again? Pete and Micky, wasn't it?"

"It's Pete and Billy. And you guys are, let me guess, Tom and Jerry, right?" I shot back.

"Ha, that's funny. Yeh, hic! Alan and Jimmy, that's us," slurred the big fellow, as he nearly fell off his chair, reaching over to shake our hands.

"Sit down, yous two, I'm buying yeh both a pint," was the Scotsman's remark.

Delighted at the jolly fellow's offer, I responded, "Nice! That's what I like to hear. What's the score here like? Is it your birthday?"

"Nah!" He reached into his pocket and pulled out a bent envelope. "Here's a letter here," as he waves it like a flag, for all to see, "offering me a scholarship to a university in London. I scored all my GCEs with the highest marks in the whole of western Scotland, and now I'm off to become an engineer. So here we are, celebrating."

"Pint of bitter please, Alan."

"Me too, Al me pal," adds Billy.

"An engineer? What kind? One that drives a train, like? Ha."

The future engineer responded, "Ha, you're a funny card for sure, Billy boy. No, I'll be designing anything from bridges to rockets. The world's my oyster right now, and tonight's my night. Damn the torpedoes. Four pints and four wee chasers over here please, lassie."

The lovely buxom waitress sauntered up to the table with a smile and said, "Sorry! You and your mate are cut off. The barman says you've had enough for one day. Yous should be jumpin' the bus, and gittin' yersels hame."

Al turned in his chair, like a defiant schoolboy, only to be met by the stern raised-eyebrow glare of the large man with his arms crossed, standing tall behind the bar.

I said, "I think she's right, Al, but we'll gladly have ours and try and catch up with yous two."

"All right then, two and two for these mates of mine." He pointed at us and passed her a ten-bob note.

"Keep the change, baby," purred our inebriated engineer, like an Elvis Presley impersonator, staring unabashedly with his glazed eyes at the perfect wiggly bum in the tight miniskirt.

"Get stuffed!" was the only response he got from her. We hid our faces in our pint glasses, pretending to drink, and tried our best to not laugh out loud at his embarrassment.

"I give her tips all day, and all I get is, 'Get stuffed'?" as he holds up his two hands in the air, like an Italian with a flat tire. "What's with that?"

After sitting like a statue all this time, our silent friend, Jimmy, finally puts one in. "For God's sake, man, leave the bird alone, will yeh? She's been putting up wi' your crap all day, now shut the fuck up."

We all sipped in silence, while following her movement, goo-goo-eyed, as she wobbled like Daffy Duck back and forth. Finally, she cleared our table of all the empties, just in time, as Billy and I were still gasping for relief from thirst. Shortly, we were delivered four more gifted drinks and the plates of fish and chips we'd ordered. Back at the bar, our waitress turned up the volume on the television just as the new and wildly popular Batman show came on.

"Dadadadada Batman!" As the show started, the inebriated choir joined in, "Dadadadada Batman!"

The pub developed a comedic atmosphere and a total abandonment of self-restraint, as our famous, comic-book characters, Batman and Robin, swung into action to take on the bad guys.

"Bang!" "Biff!" "Zap!" We all shouted in unison, as the big words flashed across the screen and the two super-heroes beat up the villains; then we all booed and hissed as the Joker tried his best to blow up Gotham City with his silly, sinister weapons. The pub was turning ballistic. This was beginning to be a good start to our night on the town.

"Cheers, boys!" as we raised our glasses and shouted, "To Bonny Scotland."

"Bonny Scotland" was the call back from around the room as the merry crowd got noisier and wilder. Another pint and a shot, and Billy and yours truly were feeling no pain and thoroughly enjoying the free entertainment.

"Here's to Scotland the Brave," I called out, to which an old fellow on the next table remarked, "What the hell are two Liverpool Sassenachs doing toasting our country?"

"Ah go fuck yoursel', yeh old bastard. What's wrong with him toasting Scotland?" shouted Al.

"Yeh!" I interjected. "Shut yer gob mate. Some of my ancestors came from Aberdeen, so you can fuck off with your Sassenach shit."

"Aberdeen?" sprang another voice. "I'm fay Aberdeen, which part of toon are yeh fay?"

"I'm not from Aberdeen," I continued, "my great-grandparents were from 'The Northern Lights of old Aberdeen.' I'm from Liverpool, the land of the Beatles, the capital city of rock and roll."

"Alright!" called the bartender, listening in to all the shouting across the room, "if you're from the Pool, you're welcome here, boys. I've got really nice rellies down in Liverpool, and they've seen the Beatles."

"Me too, mate, twice. And I saw George and John at George's house."

"Bloody 'ell!" said the barmaid, crossing her arms and shoving her loveliness up a little bit.

"Dead right I did, up on Macket's Lane."

"How did you do that?"

"A couple of years ago, one of me mates was in the schoolyard, selling a couple of autographed photographs of the Beatles to some of the girls. So we all gathered around and asked where he got them?"

'I got them last night off George; he's me cousin.'

'Your cousin?' we all asked. 'Guess where we're all going tonight?'

So about six of us got on our bikes and went straight there, a couple of miles up the road when school finished, and we got lucky. We all stood inside the gate, while Danny knocked on the door, and there comes George, with his hair all over the place and his slippers on. George Harrison!"

"Go on then," The lassie said.

"George comes out with, 'What's all this like?'"

"Dan said, 'I've brought some mates over for some autographed photos. Have you got any for us?'

'Here you go,' and he reached around the door, grabbed a few and passed them to his cousin. (There must have been a box of them just sitting there ready for the fans.)

'Here, lad, pass them around.'"

"Well I tell yeh, as soon as we all saw George answer the door, we all started shouting, 'George, Georgie, George!' Then just as we're about to leave, the living room curtains pulled back, and we saw John Lennon, waving at us and pulling faces. Now we all started shouting 'John! John!' Then he started waving us off and telling us to leave, but we kept on shouting, so then he raised both his hands and gave us the two finger salute."

"You mean he told you all to fuck off?"

"Yes, exactly that," I said laughing.

"Well, what pictures did you get?" the waitress asked.

"There was loads, and after we swapped a few around, I ended up with four single and four group shots, most were autographed."

"Have you got any with you?" she continued.

"Nah! Are you kidding? I flogged them all the next day in school for five bob each. The girls all snapped them up like that." and I snapped my fingers.

The bartender walked over and put his hand on my shoulder, looked at Bill and asked. "Is he lying, son?"

"No, he's not, it all happened, just like that. I saw him at school selling the photos to the girls."

"You silly bugger, selling them? For what?"

"Five bob each," I replied.

"Five fuckin' bob? I'd give you five quid each for a single, and ten for a group shot. Bloody hell!"

"Well I needed the dough. and made a couple of quid, and I thought I'd get more sometime later, but that never happened. We all thought the Beatles would be a flash in the pan anyway."

"So?" I looked sideways at the drunken curmudgeon on the next table, as he looked up at the strapping bartender and said, "Five quid? Five quid for what? I wouldn't give the sweat off my left ball for ten of those pictures. There a bunch of jumped up Sassenachs."

"You and your fucking Sassenachs. You know what you are, Nick? A worn-out old sod. That's what you are. Don't you know the Beatles are the biggest name in rock and roll right now, bigger than Elvis, Cliff Richard, Buddy Holly, even bigger than Frank Sinatra." The whole place shut right up. And we all looked over at the beer-slinger who had named the one person who made everyone shake their heads and cringe.

"Frank Sinatra?" moaned Alan. "Bloody Frank Sinatra? Get stuffed, man, he was the biggest wanker that ever scrubbed a stage. He was a Mafia playboy that wouldn't last five minutes in a club over 'ere."

The curmudgeon added his endorsement to the young man's comment. "Yeh, and that Cliff Pritchard, he's a queer, and that bloody Elvis is just another spoiled Yank."

Somebody in the crowd, egging him on, shouted, "And what about Buddy Holly, Nick?"

"Bubbly who? He's fuck all, him." Turning his head to someone else across the table, "Who, the fuck's this Bully Wolly?"

"He's another Yanky rock and roll star, but he's dead now."

The old crazy man stood to his feet and shouted out, "There all queers with long hair, and I don't like their shithouse music, so they can all get stuffed."

Us four lads were nearly pissing our pants laughing, as the old man was unceremoniously grabbed by the scruff of the neck and thrown out the front door. Down the front steps.

"There you go, Nick, you stupid bugger," shouted the bartender. "Go home and sleep it off, and don't come back till you can behave yoursel'. You're just a pain in the arse."

We all piled up by the windows and watched as the old bastard tripped and weaved his way down the road. Billy and I looked at each other, with tears in our eyes; we hadn't laughed so hard, or had such an entertaining night since the last New Year's Eve in Liverpool. And, as he sometimes did, Billy took a smoke out of his pocket, broke it in half and put half a fag up each nostril, crossed his eyes and began doing his Hunchback of Notre Dame impersonation, Charles Laughton style, around the tables. Now it was us four lads who were told to leave.

The sun had gone down when we gave our farewells to our plastered Scottish friends and headed towards the noise.

We arrived at the carnival after 11 PM, and the place was really rocking. The loudest, best music place was the twister, the girl-magnet Alan had told us about. It was one of those rides where four sat in a row and the overhead bar came down and locked you in your seat. The music playing was all the latest pop hits, and as assured, the place was full of fun-seeking lads and lassies. This particular ride circled up and down in a dizzy spin, and we were not only a bit maddened by the crowds and excitement, we also realized it was a place to be careful to keep ones stomach contents down, rather than up.

As we stood watching the ride, two nice-looking girls approached us and began saying something in their broad Scottish accents, over the din. We could hardly understand a word. We took their actions to mean that they were inviting us to get on the ride together. So we happily climbed into the seats with them. As the ride began to move forward, lifting us higher and higher, a bunch of guys gathered down at the bottom and started shouting up at us and the girls. They were becoming very animated about something. Apparently we were riding with the girlfriends of two of the lads. Looks like we'd abducted their lassies. We looked at the girls, with humorous curiosity, but they just burst out laughing.

Oh, oh, trouble! Yes, they were their girlfriends all right. Now what? As the wild ride slowed to a stop, and the safety bar swung up, we both vaulted over the side rail to the ground, and legged it as fast as we could towards the nearby brick wall that surrounded the end of the fairground. Just yards behind us was a bunch of angry Scottish lads, shouting "Sassonachs!" Bill and I had already had a very long day, but we legged it as fast as we could and just made it to the wall and climbed over, only to find bits of glass in the cement top. We got a couple of nicks, and the back of my brand-new suit coat was now ripped in half, up to my neck. We escaped, but that was it, we were finished for the day. Knackered.

We made it back to the town just in time for the last bus. The double-decker was free to all the stragglers, mostly drunks. There must have been twice the number of passengers as was legally allowed. The seats were full of people sitting on the laps of others, and the bus stank of booze, smoke and BO.

Normally speaking, smoking was restricted to upstairs, but on this bus, the downstairs was also enveloped in a blue haze. The red double-decker crawled along agonizingly slow, from corner to corner, village to village. It was a boisterous ride home, consisting of shouting, laughing, swearing, snoring and singing. We finally got off in the middle of our wee toon, Dalmellington, after an hour of having other drunks fall on our laps, and some lying flat out in the aisle. We wove our way up the back lane and into the back door, crept upstairs and to bed.

Every morning, Lizzie would wake us up with a cup of tea and biscuits, but the day after the drinking binge in Ayr, she woke us up by lifting the bed sheets and hurling a cup of cold water over our legs. That was her gentle way of saying "Serves you right." There was nah a gentle thing aboot our Wee Lizzie. She was tough as a badger and possessed the grip of a blacksmith. Och aye!

44

Two Lovely Lassies

A couple of days before heading back to Liverpool, we decided to pay a visit to the two ladies who lived across the street. Lizzie had spotted us a couple of times saying hello and waving over at them as we came home from oot an' aboot, and she'd given us a piece of her mind. Warning us again to keep our distance. But this second to last evening, we wanted a quick adventure with the hopes that our inquisitive landlady wouldn't notice us through her side window where she always sat knitting and sipping while scanning the street like a pudgy private eye. Maybe her radar wouldn't catch us slipping across to the "House of the Rising Sun." Earlier in the day, we'd bought a small bottle of sherry at the off-license, guessing that this would cover our entrance fee as unexpected visitors. So after dinner, as the street grew dim, we pretended to head out to the local pub. Our stomachs were stuffed with meat and potato pie as we exited the back door, circled through the lane and up the foggy street to the target.

A light knock, and the door swung open to the welcoming call from the young, bouncy bird, "Hey, Viv', we've got two visitors."

The lovely lassie at the door was dressed in skintight red jeans with

226 *LIVERPOOL LAD*

a floppy mohair sweater that perfectly accentuated her generous figure, one that would make grown men cry. She was a real darling, and
she knew it; even with the dozen curlers stuck all over her jet-black
hair, she had the goods.

"Hello, love, my name's Peter."

"And I'm Billy."

"I'm Jill."

Popping her head over the banister at the top of the stairs, the
other lassie appeared. A young-looking thirty-year-old jolly housewife,
she continued to brush her long blond hair, her mouth jammed with
hair clips, while she summoned us upstairs to the top floor. We immediately kicked our shoes off, even though we were told not to bother,
and galloped like two Olympian athletes, two steps at a time to meet
our host, Vivien.

"We've noticed you two for a few days now," I said, "and wanted to
say hello properly before we left town. We thought you might want to
join us in a farewell tot?" I held up the gift of Cream Sherry.

"Ha! A wee tot, you say? You've picked up the lingo since you've
been here, haven't you? Wee tot! How long have you been up here
now? You're starting to sound like two young Scots lads, but I know
yous are from the Pool, eh? I had a boyfriend from there once, before
I got married."

"It'll be two weeks tomorrow," I answered.

"Two weeks and you've just managed to get over here from Wee
Lizzie's prison? Did she warn yous two about us girlies here? Or was it
the friendly postman said something?"

"Or the milkman?" Jill added.

"Oh no, nobody's said nowt about yous girls," I said. "Anyway,
what would old Liz have to warn us about?" I inquired, like the canary
asking the cat.

Viv walked into the kitchen and reached into the cupboard for
some glasses. She turned around, leaned on the counter, stuck one foot

on the chair like Annie Okley getting ready for trouble and growled.

"Lizzie has never stopped talking about us since we moved in months ago, I've heard it from everyone, but she's never had the manners to come over here hersel' and meet us personally. She's an old gossipy bitch, that one. So, as far as I'm concerned, she can get stuffed and keep her nosey arse off my doorstep. But we're glad you boys came over to say hello. Here, you can pour." She placed the four glasses on the table in a neat little row.

"Make mine a small one. I'm not partial to sherry, I'm a beer and whiskey girl, me."

I poured the drinks, and we retired to the living room. The telly was on, and we all sat as close to the fire as possible. The house was a bit cold, and I was asked to bring in some coal, so I grabbed the bucket and skipped down the stairs to the yard. I was back in two minutes with a nice bucket of coal and noticed Billy had already moseyed over to sit on the wide stuffed armchair with young Jill, so I reckoned that left me with the older woman, Vivien. I placed a few hefty blocks of coal on the dwindling fire, and within minutes, we were warming the cockles and feeling quite toasty. The mickey of sherry didn't last too long, and our hostess with the mostess displayed great generosity and brought in a large bottle of Scotch and two pint bottles of beer.

"Do you fancy a cheese butty with your drinks, boys?" asked the leading lady.

"Love a butty, Viv, can I help?" I asked.

"Woo! We have a chef in our midst, Jill. He makes sandwiches. Can you cook too Peter?"

"Can I? I've been cooking at home since I was a little lad." I winked at Billy.

"You mean, since you were a wee bairn, don't you?" We all laughed.

"Yeh, a wee bairn, and I've been a butcher boy for the last two years at the market. And every Saturday, I cook all the roasts and meatballs and pies. I love cooking, it's great!"

"Meatballs?" called out Jill. "We're good with meatballs, aren't we Viv? That's our specialty, spaghetti and meatballs. We love all that European food, and red wine, an' all."

Billy and I knew we were having our legs pulled a bit by these two mischievous, fun-loving gals, but we also knew that they knew we knew they knew we knew. Our kind of girls.

While Bill and Jill were climbing up the hill on the couch, Viv and I, the mature people in the crowd, were now in the kitchen: me buttering a whole loaf of bread, while the blond, with her hair in a knot, was slicing up the cheese, tomatoes and a piece of ham she'd found in the fridge.

"Pour us a beer will you, Peter love. I always do better in the kitchen with a small dwink."

"A small dwink, eh? Two beers it is, coming up, lovely," I said. "How about a wee dwam of the best?" as I returned from the front room with the Scotch.

"Oh aye, you read me mind."

"I always like a chaser with a brew," I whispered.

"Me too, pour me a double," she winked. "No reason to hold the bottle twice, as me dad used to say. Ha." (It looked like she came from a drinking family.)

"Hey, bring that bottle back here when you've finished," Billy called from the front room. "Yeh we want to keep up with yous two lovebirds in the kitchen."

Lovebirds? I thought. Could this be my lucky night?

"Looks like you're the two lovebirds in this house," said Vivien, as she peeped around the doorway, finding the two front-runners, arms wrapped around each other, cozied up to the fire face to face, giggling.

Vivien went on, "Me? I'm a respectable married woman, didn't you know?"

"Yes, we all know that, Vivien. Ha!" called back Jill. "Married to an arsehole."

I kept my mouth shut and just listened and buttered bread, as their shared complaints about her husband continued.

"I know your married, Viv, but what's that got to do with anything? We're only over here for a friendly visit."

"It's alright, Peter, it's just that I married the wrong man, that's all. I should have married Phil from Liverpool. He would have been the best husband ever, but!"

"But what?" I responded, as Bill and Jill were now standing in the kitchen doorway listening. We were all ears.

"You don't need to know any more boys, it's history now. I'm just lumbered with this Dickhead of a husband, and that's my problem."

I leaned back against the counter with my double in one hand and a buttering knife in the other, and spoke sincerely. A perfect stance for a serious question. "Vivien love, can I just ask you one thing?" She knew this was coming. "Why didn't you marry this Phil guy from Liverpool? What happened?"

Jill leaned back against lucky Billy, looked her sister straight in the eye and said, "Go on then. I don't mind hearing it for the hundredth time. Tell him, it's good to get it out. Come 'ed, Viv'." A deep breath and a slug of Scotch and...

"When I met Phil, my whole world lit up with this, this magic. That's what it was, pure magic. I knew he'd left someone, somewhere, but I didn't want to know anything because he made me feel, for the first time in my life, loved. Then after we were going out for a while, he says he had another girlfriend back home and just found out that he got her pregnant, and he said he had to do the right thing, and so he married her."

I put everything down and put my arm gently around her shoulder. "It's alright, Viv', you don't have to tell us any more, it's your private story. I shouldn't have asked anything."

She smiled at me and leaned on the kitchen counter and continued "Otherwise I know he would have married me. So everything went wrong, and I lost him. But that's not the end of the world, I'm going to get out of here and get a divorce. This Richard, I call him Dickhead, is only here part-time, when he's back with his bleeding lorry from London. He drives long-distance. And he knows it's curtains for us. I'm so stupid. He's the last person on earth for me, but me and Jill, we've got things figured out, and thank God, there's no kids."

"That doesn't sound too good to me, Viv, I hope you can sort things out love?"

"Oh she will, Peter," Jill put in. "It won't be long now."

"Yeh, thank Christ for that," Vivien concluded. "Let's put the telly back on; there must be something to have a laugh about. What night is it?"

"Friday!" we all said. "There's probably a horror movie on," Jill said.

"Great," I said. "There's nothing like getting scared on Friday night." We all piled into the front room with a large plate of sarnies and some drinks, the two lovebirds sat in the same spot, while Vivien asked me to join her on the couch.

"I might get scared," she said. "And don't worry lads, Dickhead doesn't get home till tomorrow."

That's reassuring, I thought. She might need a little cuddle or two. You never know. A song came to mind, "Wishin' and hopin' and thinkin' and prayin'…"

Still I felt a little bit nervous, thinking, if Dickhead got home early, walked in the house, saw me cuddled up with his missus on the sofa, eating his bread and cheese, knocking back his brew and watching his telly, he might not be a happy camper. It might be an "out the window and down the drainpipe scene" from the movies. Then I thought, just relax and enjoy the moment. If he comes in angry, me and Bill will knock his block off, pack our bags and catch the next bus back home.

With not much to look at on the telly, we just sat around, kept the fire going and talked about general things. The main subject that kept coming up was their mistake of moving to this small village from the bustling town of Glasgow. They complained of boredom and the lack of stimulation from the local Beverley Hillbillies, but did allude to the little fun offered by our friendly postman, who'd stop in for a cuppa and a wee chat, and from what I could guess, was possibly a bit more than that, by the way these two lassies rolled their eyes.

"Aye, if it wasn't for Joe popping in to say hello, we'd be going bonkers here in this hole of a place," Vivien sighed. "Aye, he saved us from going stark ravin' mad, he did. And you lads, you've cheered us up just great, coming over here to visit. I wish you could have come over sooner, hey Jill? And now they're leaving, what a bad bit of luck that was, eh?"

"Yeh, it's been great having you over," was Jill's sad reply.

"That's alright. We haven't left yet," I said. "The night's still young. Let's put some music on. Do you get Radio Caroline here?"

"Yeh, let's have a dance," said Viv. "It's been ages since I've let loose."

I tuned in the channel and up came a clear signal with, of all things, the top twenty. We always picked up the signal for Caroline better at night. They were playing the last few numbers, and of course, they were fabulous hits, so we shoved the chairs back and paired off, moving and grooving to the tunes. Then after a couple of minutes, we changed partners and got nice and close on the slow songs. This was more like it, we were all enjoying ourselves and dimming the lights helped. A couple of more drinks, and we began singing along with the radio and acting up. Billy looked like he and Jill were getting places. But me and Viv stopped when she tripped over the carpet and belted herself on the edge of the table, causing her to knock the radio off and call out, "That's it for me tonight. I'm off to bed. I'm plastered, and my bloody shoulder hurts."

"Jill, love, you put things away, will yeh? Night-night lads, I'm sorry it's all come to an end, but it was fun while it lasted, and I'm just too tired to keep going. Maybe we'll see you again before you go home?" Jill looked as disappointed as we lads were.

"Night, girls, we'll see yeh soon, we hope. Maybe in our dreams?" And out the door we went, pissed off that we couldn't have stayed longer.

"Bloody hell, man!" Billy said as we sulked our way down the hill to the back road that led to Lizzie's.

"Boy, I should just sneak back and see if Jill still wants to carry on. Boy was she hot or what?"

"Yeh, they were both steaming hot birds, man. That Vivien was driving me nuts, and she was all over me in the kitchen too. You can go back if you want, but I've had enough, I'm knackered. Go and try your luck."

Billy checked his watch. "Listen man, it's after two o'clock."

"If you get caught, you'll probably piss off her sister," I said.

"No, I'm going to see if Jill's still up. I don't carry these French letters around in me pocket for nothing," as he waved a wrapped Durex condom in the air. "Catch up with yeh," he said, as he disappeared around the dark corner.

I carried on up the lane and snuck in the back door, making my way upstairs to bed. Before I turned in, I looked across the dimly lit street down to the house I wished I was still at. I couldn't see any sign of Bill, and all was dark. Within five minutes he was back.

"Any luck?" I asked as he stumbled around the room pulling his gear off, "Nothing, mate, nothing."

The next morning, as we were lazing around in the living room after breakfast, we heard the sound of squealing brakes, out on the road.

"That'll be him back," Liz said, as we all stuck our faces to the window. "Looks like Dickhead's home," I said.

"What was that?" Lizzie scowled, not appreciating bad words under her roof.

"Looks like Thickhead's home," I said quickly correcting things.

"Thickhead? Yes," she added, " you're right there, thick as a brick on my auld oot hoos." That's as far as we went, and not long after, we were packed, and on our way.

Billy and I cadged a mickey of Scotch from Liz for the trip home and had a good laugh over a few things, as the bus stormed its way back to Merry ol' Liverpool. A trip any fifteen-year-old mates should take. Cheers. Here's to Bonny Scotland.

Part Five

Crime and Redemption

45

Teachers, the Good, the Bad and the Ugly

Woodwork class was one of my favourite places at the Comp'. Don't get me wrong; interesting things were constantly happening all the time among us kids, but the lessons were uninteresting and uninspiring. And obvious to most of us; the teachers were not only usually half psycho and vindictive, but also bereft of any kind of skill to make the process of learning rewarding or satisfying. Our lot was a pile of damaged goods with teaching certificates. Everyone blamed the war for their personality hang-ups, and to give them credit, they had a very big case. War does screw up your head. Not many of my memories of my later school days were very happy. So this could be one of the reasons I excelled at being the class clown and daredevil, retaliating and creating havoc, for which I paid dearly with corporal punishment. The girls in the class thought it very brave to stand up or speak back to the teachers. Upon receiving the cane, we few rebels would usually show off when hit, by trying our best to be stoic thus proving to the onlookers what brave young men we were. We were good actors.

One history teacher was a prime example. On one occasion, he spotted some of us copying each other's answers in a small test, and gave us an ultimatum.

Opposite: Dr. Who Spaceship

"OK, you, you, you and you, stand up. How come I find the same brilliant answers to the same questions on all your sheets? Did you all, by chance study this chapter together? Do you share a study club? Or are you all just lazy, useless, good-for-nothing copycats. Do you foolishly think I can't catch a whiff of cheating when I smell it. You've made a big mistake, my young deceiving subjects."

We stood up, looked straight ahead, listening to the torrent of sarcasm he'd just come out with, daring not to smirk, grin or glance sideways at each other. This big burly fellow could wield the rattan cane with the best.

"I'll give you four cheats a choice. For your punishment, you may choose from two of the best." He bent his cane in a threatening curve. "One on each hand or five hundred lines. 'I shall not cheat during history exams.' Make your choice."

"But sir!" one started, as all eyes turned left.

"Yes? What was that?"

"Nothing, sir."

My mate Rod Sykes and I asked for the cane. We hated lines, and were used to a whack from time to time. The other two boys asked for lines. The surprising response from our weird teacher, being obviously a well-versed student of Niccolo Machiavelli, was this.

"OK, you two cowards," pointing at the other two with his cane, "come forward." So, to their great astonishment and dismay, the ones hoping for written lines stepped from their desks, to the front.

Now, the oratorical giant, who ate dictionaries for breakfast, pronounced, "With expedience, I'd like to unequivocally demonstrate to this classroom my revulsion toward spineless cowards. Hands out!"

The whole class just sat in silent shock at what was happening. The two boys, who thought they'd spend an hour after school doing lines, were now on the receiving end of two hits each, two very painful swipes from the cane.

"But sir." The red-faced boy started again.

"Yes, Collins? Speak up, boy!"

But glancing back at the sea of gob-smacked faces, there was not another word from him, just his head hanging in disbelief and betrayal. Rod and I were told to stay in our seats, and being commended by the deranged teacher for our bravery in the face of physical punishment, received neither punishment. Cane or lines.

What did this do amongst the ranks? Cause a serious problem? Very much so.

This double-crossing ploy created a long-lasting division among us all. We had to sort things out, but we all knew he played these games to divide the troops.

In stark contrast to the history teacher, our woodwork teacher Mr. Slater, who was also a war vet, was a saint. Slater's trial by fire had made him a kind, patient man. Beside the blackboard on the wall were two old black-and-white pictures of a battleship, and a lineup of a bunch of swaggering jolly tars, with him, at the age of twenty, smiling at the camera, all of them giving the V for victory sign with their two raised fingers: the Churchill salute.

Slater was the most easy going fellow to ever conduct a classroom. If we were late coming, and hurrying down the hallway, he'd shout at the top of his voice, "I'll have your eyeballs on toast, hurry up!" Another one of his famous sayings was "I'll have your guts for garters." He never hit any of us, which scored him big points on our scale of respect. And he refreshingly spent a lot of time answering all the questions we could fire at him about anything, even subject matter that had nothing to do with woodworking. Each lesson started with the class sitting on our respective workbenches, facing the front, while he communed with us with sincere interest.

"What's with your bike, Taylor? I saw you fiddling away with it on the side of the road this morning."

"The gear chain keeps flipping off, sir, but I fixed it up alright."

"What about you, Baker. Did your dad do OK at the Lee Park darts tourney on Saturday?"

"Yes thanks, sir, he won ten quid and brought home the trophy; we're all dead chuffed in our house."

"Well, that's great. He's a good man, your dad. I worked with him building houses before I became a teacher. Say 'well done' to your dad from me, will yeh?"

This was a teacher who could hold your attention for ages, going over such things as the development of working tools from the Middle Ages, to the geography of wood. We learned how to sharpen and maintain all our bench tools and show respect for the workshop, and I think, because of his rapport with his students, woodwork was a place where many of us excelled. Sometimes, larger projects were shared between the metalwork and woodwork classes. One such collaboration was a small steam-driven piston, mounted on an elaborate wooden base. It was a compilation of brass, steel, copper, oak and mahogany, a masterpiece placed in the glass display cabinet for a year.

After one or two more casual comments from the chief, and we were all pulling out the tools and wearing our work aprons, ready to get on with our projects. Mine was the prized possession I'd been carefully crafting over the weeks, my specially designed fishing box. It was held together with dozens of mortise and tenon joints and dovetails on a drawer, plus a hinged padded seat on top and shoulder straps for carrying it while on my bike, off to the lakes or sea.

One unforgettable time in the woodwork shop was when Slater calmly walked from his cutting room at the back with his severed thumb and a big bloody rag wrapped around his hand, explaining with a childish grin that he'd just cut the end of his thumb off on the table saw, and we needed to get help from across the hall. He sat quietly in his chair while our metalwork teacher administered first aid, and a couple of the lads ran to tell the office to get an ambulance. A very calm man, for sure. Some boys puked up on the sawdust floor. The sight was horrible as he placed his separated thumb on his desk next to the pencils. Man, oh man!

46

Your Accent Is Your Fate

At sixteen years, most English kids left school and headed off to the real world, the working world. If a youngster had a relatively comfortable background, the opportunity of furthering one's education would usually be taken care of. And so, as the generations passed, trawling alongside many was the bane of class distinction that had always affected British society. From pretentious accents and pronunciation to never-ending opinions held about the place where you had grown up. Blind opinions by those who had never stepped foot into working-class streets (and vice versa). The old school-tie protocol, with its well-practiced behavior and niceties, was the rough cement that held up the invisible and divisive wall. It had and still has a formidable presence in England. Even today, a person's accent in the UK can closely elucidate not only what town you are from, but also the district within that town.

"Oh, you say you're from Liverpool? Don't you mean downtown Liverpool? Everton, Walton, Bootle, the Dingle, Scotty Road, etc?" As the old saying goes, "Thy speech betrayeth thee."

The inner cities of Liverpool, Glasgow, Newcastle, Birmingham, Leeds, Manchester and the rest of the North had their distinctive dialects, accompanied by their socio-economic baggage. Once you were labeled, "He's from there, she's from there," it was difficult to remove the stigmatization. Class distinction was not imagined or presumed.

That very same class of people who had actually built and held the country together was frequently maligned. These folk were the same cannon fodder sent off to war, while the hobnobs sipped tea and played tennis. The reward of the "hard call" was to grunt one's way to the grave and endure disrespect from the "toffees." The targets were the people like dockers, shipbuilders, mill workers, coal miners, tradesmen and tradeswomen and factory workers, not forgetting the Irish navvies who built the roads and railways. I once stood flabbergasted, within earshot of a man speaking with his high-class inflections these exact words to an elderly lady in his shop. "….but we are above you, my dear."

"I can tell that," she responded. "Looks like you've perfected the fine art of theft as well. Look at these prices of yours!"

There still remains the old-fashioned mind-set that you were usually expected to stay within the class that you were born and raised in. Doctors begat doctors, and laborers begat laborers. Upward mobility through higher education was often looked upon as a slim hope and a financially impossible dream to many. None of my friends at school had a dad who was a lawyer, a doctor, a dentist, a banker or business man; they were all pretty well without exception tradesmen and laborers. Most of these working stiffs rode the buses to their hard graft each morning, and toiled with their hands for a pittance. Menial jobs with meagre wages.

The outlying districts? Now that's where the money was. Areas where their schools had lovely grass sports fields for their locals to kick a ball. In contrast, we had cinder pitches or mud holes where we'd stack our coats in a pile to mark off the goal. We'd watch through the bus windows as we sometimes travelled through the unfamiliar districts, gawking at the differences between them and us. "Look at that house. Did you see that car, wow! Look at those 'toffees' in their nice, clean, school uniforms…"

When I was about thirteen, I experienced what could be called, my "personal accent moment." In English class, at the comprehensive school out in the new suburbs, and miles away from where I first grew up, our ever-so-proper teacher, just one of the many snotty-nosed from some privileged background, asked me to stand up in front and repeat a few words after him to the class. This was to demonstrate to all what a downtown Liverpool accent sounded like. He'd pulled my leg on more than one occasion and wanted to show, in his words, "how a Northern accent, with its special idiosyncrasies, could indicate one's location of upbringing and one's 'claarss' distinction." He was going to show how poor little me would be spotted a mile away, anywhere in the UK, as coming from not only Liverpool, but a central, working-class slum core, like Everton.

Oh yeh? We all thought what understanding would he have of a working-class background? Our eyes often rolled at his polished ways. From the moment I'd arrived at this miserable school, I'd felt detached and isolated, almost like a foreign refugee, with this strong Scouse accent of mine. No other person I knew of had come to this new Childwall Valley district from my part of the inner city, so the local kids' Liverpudlian accents were a bit lightweight. Standing in front of the class, winking at the girls and pulling faces at the boys, I gathered myself together as he started off with his lah-de-dah show.

"Hayes, repeat after me. 'The small girl had lovely fair hair.'" The class, all watching me intently, some sniggering into their hands, listened with great amusement, as I went along with his exercise joke. Looking around, I saw Riley with his finger stuck up his nose, his eyes crossed, wearing a hideous expression, trying to rock my boat. I looked back, unmoved, with my poker face.

I took a deep breath, and out it came: "The little 'Judy' 'ad luvly fer er." That brought the house down. I did my little dance, like I was stung in the arse by a wasp, then waited, standing at attention, for the next command.

"Before we go any further, Hayes, please spare me the agony, we don't refer to girls in this class, as 'Judies.' Understood?" As I looked at him, I'd concluded that, to me, he was a man full of words that meant nothing, a preening parrot on a perch. "A sounding brass, or a tinkling cymbal."

"But we always call them Judies, sir. That's what we call the girls, here in Liverpool."

"All right, that's enough, just repeat the same words I say and stand still and don't start pouncing and performing. Are you feeling alright?"

"I'm feeling the gear, sir. Chuffed in fact!"

"See class, did you hear that waterfall of intelligent language pouring out of this young mouth? The 'gear,' 'chuffed.' What do you think a future employer in London would think of that expression in his"—pointing sharply at me—"job interview?"

"He'd think it was the gear like, Wacker!" was my reply, which brought the house down again. The class went nuts, and his highness from the Tower of London, with his jumped-up attitude towards us kids from the Pool, shouted loudly in my ear, "Get back to your miserable desk and shut up."

As I was returning, I muttered, "I wouldn't want a stinking job in London anyway."

"So what exactly do you have in mind for a career when you leave this bastion of learning?" Spinning on one foot, in his often used pirouette, he stretched his pompous arms in the air. (Funny, but he wasn't the first teacher I'd seen do a spin on the spot. Maybe ballet dancing was a prerequisite for a teacher's degree?)

"I'm going to sea, sir. We've all been sailors in our 'ouse."

"Ah, the Royal Navy. Nice!"

"No, sir, the Merch. On deck, or maybe in the galley with me brother Geoff, where all that lovely nosh is," rubbing my hands in glee.

"Me too, sir!" "And me." called out another couple of boys, as I sat down. "Ah, a room full of 'Jolly Tars.' Off to see the world, '...but what did we see? We saw the sea.'"

And his final comment: "And by the way, son,"—he'd never called anyone 'son' before—"it's pronounced London, not Lundun."

"Yes, sir. Lundun." He rolled his eyes, as I sat staring out of the window, stone-faced and pissed off that he'd tried to humiliate me again, and ridicule my speech. My "Mother Tongue Scouse language."

Stuff him! I thought. There's another big-headed pretender who laughs at the way we talk. He can jump on a train and ride back to "Dear Old London Town" and have tea and crumpets with Betty and Phil.

It wasn't too long after this when I would be facing a bigger obstacle on arriving in Australia. There, no one would understand a word I said. It was, "Come on moit, speak the Queen's Inglish, will yer, or 'owbowt some Fairdinkum Oz?" I had to develop an international tongue as the years went by while I travelled the world.

Unless you're from the Pool, it's not too easy to understand Scouse, such as: "I wus on me tod, leggin' it from a rozzer down the ennog, when I tripped over this jigger rabbit and landed on the grotty deck, you know worra mean like? but I found a tanner, and I wus dead chuffed. Just enough for a three-fag pack of Woodies. It wus the gear, Lah!"

47

A Kick and a Run

Our golf-crazy teacher would always shout Fore as he swung his three-foot-long T-square at the target, your arse. Whoever was getting the punishment of the moment was told to face the open door, bend over, touch their toes and get the whack. Then you were expected to go along with his warped joke and run through the open door, to the laughing applause of some of the class. But, on that day, I just stood up straight, after he hit me, and walked back to my desk.

"And just where do you think you're going? Run through the door!" he called out.

"Fuck off!" was my whispered reply.

"What was that, you damn… Get back here. When I say 'Fore!' you run boy. Do you hear me?" I sat down at my desk and stared into space, only to be grabbed by my coat, and hauled to my feet.

I was a fifteen and could handle myself. I kicked him pretty hard in the shin, hard enough to make him let go of me, grab onto his leg and start hopping around like a one-legged kangaroo.

"You stay right there. I'll be back," he gasped, and limped down the hall to get the headmaster. I quickly packed my books into my leather satchel, slung it over my shoulder and bid farewell to my applauding classmates, who all sent me off with a loud cheer. I headed off down the stairs to the back playground, across the empty yard and over the grassy hill, where I ran off into the sunset.

This was the first time I ever hit back at one of my teachers. To hit back was a final reaction to not only his bullying ways, but an accumulation of anger towards all the abusive teachers I had to put up with since I was eight, and I'd had enough.

My folks only found out about this commotion two days later, when a truant officer knocked on our door and presented a letter from the school, To the parents of Peter Hayes.

My mother received the note, shook her head once more and remarked, "He'll be home in a minute."

Oh yes, I knew my dad would be home soon and be delighted at what I'd been up to; but after two days of going over things in my head about what had taken place in that psychopath's classroom, as well as talking to my mates, I knew I had a good case for my absenteeism. Bullying by that teacher had motivated me, and I was never going back to that bastard's class, ever again.

When my father got home from his long day at work, he liked to sit quietly with a cuppa and read the paper before tea was dished up. Now in his sixties, with four teenage lads under his roof and a fitter-turner's job to attend to each day, the last thing he needed when he got home was another unnecessary problem to deal with.

It was fortunate that he was not a drinking man like some of my friends' parents. He and my mother only sipped a little sherry on the weekends, and after a couple of shots each, the bottle was usually hidden in the laundry, where we boys would find it and have a small nip each.

By the time his tea was poured and handed to him, he had read the Letter of Concern.

"Kicking a teacher? Kicking a teacher?" he exclaimed, and banged his arm across the armchair.

"But dad, he belted me hard with the T-square, across the backside, and because I didn't run through the door, he got really mad at me, and the teachers are always hitting us for no reason."

"They're allowed to hit you for misbehaving; that's what happens at school. We all got it for misbehaving. How else are you supposed to learn? And what do you mean, 'run through the door'?"

"He likes to hit us with the three-foot T-square, like he's golfing, and you're supposed to run through the door when he shouts 'Fore. He's always picking on me and Riley 'cause he doesn't like us."

"Oh he does that, does he? And where have you been for the last two days?"

"Yesterday I went fishing at Calderstone's Park, and today I went downtown to the market to see me mates."

"Well, listen here, lad, there's no more sagging school. Tomorrow you're going back to face the music, so finish your dinner and off to bed."

I was dead surprised he didn't get raging mad and take a swing at me, but I can only think that he was probably empathizing a bit with us boys, because of the daily problems we faced on the street and at school. Things weren't that easy for us.

That evening I made an excuse to go and pick up some homework from a friend and paid a visit to Paul Dale, who lived down the block, and was also having a tough time in school. We'd talked about it before, but now we came to an agreement that we'd run away. We had a choice of heading south, or another option I really liked: the idea of jumping the boat to the Isle of Man, or even Ireland. We didn't have enough money for the fare, but we'd heard how easy it was to sneak on board those ferries at the Pier Head, at nighttime, and I was very familiar with the docks and the Landing Stage at the river. With a clean getaway, and a couple of quid in our pockets, we could probably get a good start and score some work over there. So we arranged for me to meet him at his house at the end of the maisonettes at midnight, and we were going to get out of town. While everyone was asleep, I quietly packed a bag and took some of my fishing gear, including my handy telescopic fishing rod, and silently exited the house. Down at Paul's, I stood waiting for ages and began throwing small stones at his bedroom window, but he wasn't showing. So, knowing his family kept a key on a string inside the letterbox, I let myself in, but quickly got out when I heard some commotion upstairs. I didn't want to be caught sneaking around, I might get a broomstick over the head.

Forget it, I thought. I'm not waiting around for him. I'm off! Looks like I'm doing this on me tod. So down the dark rainy road I went, a bag over my shoulder and my rod in hand, trudging in the direction of town. I stuck out my thumb for a lift as the occasional car went by. It wasn't long before I'd scored three lifts from sympathetic drivers, as they saw me standing under the streetlights getting soaked in the downpour. I finally arrived at the Pier Head docks. I checked out the locked gates and high fence that blocked off the ferry entrance and began tossing coins in my head: would I head south instead of aiming for the Irish Sea route. Maybe Wales or Devon would be a better place to end up. But it had to be by the sea. I couldn't abide the idea of being inland. So with this change of mind, I cadged another ride back to the entrance of the Mersey Tunnel, and waited as cars and lorries pulled up to pay their fees at the toll gates then jumped into a car with a European fellow behind the wheel.

He said he'd only been in Britain a couple of years, and was on his way to work at the Cardiff docks, in the south of Wales. He said he was leaving his family here, back in Bootle, till he settled into his new job, operating a crane, loading coal into the ships. He didn't appear to have the brains or the personal skills needed to push a broom in a straight line, never mind loading coal into the hold of a ship, but he said he'd done it for years, back in Transylvania, or wherever he came from. I noticed the back seats of his ratty car were full of bags and cases, and I squeezed my haversack on top of everything, but kept my telescopic fishing rod in hand. I wasn't too impressed with the way he looked, the state of his messy car, which stank of dirty clothes and had a brown paper bag jammed with rotten food in the front. Still, it was a lift through the tunnel, and that was a start for my quest to nowhere. I also had a weapon in hand, in case he was a bit loony, and needed a good jab in the eye.

"And how far are you going, son?" he asked. I decided within one minute, I wasn't going far with this creepy guy, and came up with.

"Oh, I'm just heading to Birkenhead, to meet up with some mates."

"Looks like you're going fishing?" he added.

"Yeh. Over by West Kirby." (Which, I knew, was the opposite way from where he was going)

We hurtled through the bustling traffic in the dimly lit, smoky tunnel. He knew I wasn't too chatty, so he just kept quiet from then on, and I was leery of the scruffy guy, with the nervous twitch. As soon as we exited the tunnel, I grabbed my gear and bid him farewell, and watched as he drove out of sight. My thumb went up for the next lift, but I stood there for ages like a drenched rat. One old guy picked me up and took me a few miles, and then again, I stood under a street lamp, cold and soaked to the skin in the pouring rain, until a young couple pulled over, and I jumped in. This time it was totally different, and after a few miles, we pulled over to a roadside café, on the outskirts of Chester, for a cup of tea and some toast, which they gladly bought for me. I think they knew that I was running away from home, and began quizzing me a bit about my travel plans. First, they asked how old I was, which I responded with "Just turned seventeen," and was working at a butcher's shop (I was still fifteen.).

"Well, what's the plans for your fishing trip, in the wild, blue yonder?" the bright, happy couple enquired, noting the rod in hand.

It's amazing how fast the mind can spin, influenced by a few brief words that hit the mark, like "wild, blue yonder." A potpourri of images flashed through my head. Running off to Ireland, or to the Isle of Man. Stowing away as a young boy might have done at a sleepy dockside onto Captain Kidd's ship, a couple of hundred years earlier. But this time it would be disappearing into the fog of night, behind walls and gates, onto the Irish ferry. Mixed emotions ran through my mind. I was sick to death of friends that let me down, and the ones I was hanging out with on the streets. I was sick to death of the unnecessary conflicts with the bastard teachers who delighted in making theatre in the classroom at your expense with corporal punishment, in front of an audience of kids who never got hit, but always cheered.

It was a constant struggle for me to envision a positive plan for my future when school was, thankfully, over. I began recalling the occasional escapes and holidays from the city: my trips to the seaside, countryside and rivers, to fish and catch a close-up view of nature. All these thoughts, and more, flew through my mind at the speed of light. Words were branding themselves in my mind. Wild, blue yonder.

"My fishing trip?" I finally responded, as I gazed at the sunrise appearing over the slate roofs of this unknown town, half daydreaming.

"It's more like a trip to see what the rest of the country looks like, and I'll do a bit of fishing if I can, but I'm only going for a few days, and then back to Liverpool. Then me and my mate, Paul, will be going to Ireland to see his brother."

But we were now in Northern Wales, and a road sign "Wrexham 5 Miles" glided past. The rain was over, and everything looked bright, shiny and refreshed. They dropped me off in the town center, then returned to the main highway to continue their journey.

By now I was really hungry, and in just a matter of minutes, my supply of cheese, buttered bread and a couple of pickled onions was gone. I took all the money I had when I left home, just a couple of quid, and now I needed to get some groceries for the remainder of the trip, so I bought a couple of things to eat at a corner store. As I was leaving, a man ran past me into the shop, he'd left his motorbike running just outside. For one moment, I thought about jumping on the machine and taking off, and as I walked past the idling bike, I put my hand on the crossbars, squeezed the hand brake a bit, and shook my head in disbelief. No, I wasn't that desperate. It was a stupid idea.

I walked into the shopping area, where I found a comfortable bench in a park and stretched out for a rest. I fell asleep and was woken by the sound of little kids shouting and playing nearby. Now it was late afternoon. I'd slept for hours and woke up with a stiff neck. What to do? My head swam with thoughts that I was heading the wrong way. I needed to get back and meet up with Paul, who may have simply made a mistake and forgot to get ready for my arrival. Maybe he was all prepared to go, but things screwed up? I gave him the benefit of the doubt.

All right, I'm going back. I convinced myself, and off to the highway I went. The sun had gone over the hills as I stuck my hand out, this time heading north. I'd had a good day out with a bit of adventure, and now I was prepared to go back to Plan A, the Emerald Isle. One of the amazing things about this trip was that it took me hours, and many lifts, to get this far, waiting in the rain, but the return home came easily. No sooner was I standing at the highway, than a huge truck pulled over and took me to within two miles of my home. The trucker was delivering goods to the other side of Liverpool, but had to drive past my district to get there. I jumped out at the junction at the top of Childwall Valley. The junction we called the Five Ways, and I found my way to Donny's place, a good mate of mine, who lived just half a mile from my house.

Donny Stewart lived with his grandmother, because he couldn't get along with his own parents, but wouldn't run off with me and Paul. When I asked him, he said he was very happy living with his gran and had no reason to leave town. With a little bit of coaxing, he convinced the old girl, and I was allowed to crash out at their place for the night, and was also given a great dinner to boot. We talked about my travelling day and the plans I had to carry on, and he wished me the best but said I should be leaving in the morning. He didn't want to get on the wrong side of his gran. She was suspicious about everything, and kept on staring at me, and forgetting who I was. This, after I'd been visiting them for five years.

"Is that your aunty Flo's son, Donny?" pointing at me.

"No, Gran. It's Peter, my friend from school. You remember."

"Oh, Peter, that's right, from across the street."

I'd always lived way down the road, but she'd probably ask, "Which road?" I don't know how he did it, but maybe he stayed because there was nowhere else, and she was a really good cook?

The next morning, about 10 o'clock, I was strolling down the road towards Paul's place, knowing that everybody was at work, his parents and my parents, and thinking if he wasn't around, I'd leave him a note in his letterbox and tell him I was back. Out of the blue, a car pulled up beside me, with my folks in the back seat, and the truant officer driving. My dad jumped out and, in a very kind, consoling way, asked where I'd been, and to get in the car for a lift home. I couldn't believe it. They were cruising the streets looking for me two days after I'd taken off. Back home, in the kitchen, while my mother was making me some breakfast, the truant officer and my dad persuaded me to go back to school that afternoon.

"They'd better not think of caning me again," I warned them. "I'll do more than kick someone, and I'll be gone for good if they try that."

"Oh no, son. It won't be like that," said the TO. "You'll just be told off, that's all, and you'll have to write those exams you missed, to catch up."

My dad added, "It's OK lad. You tell me tonight when you get home what they said. OK? Go back and face the music."

"Fair enough, I'll go back."

I walked up the long hill to school, showing up first at the headmaster's office to apologize for the false parents' letters I'd forged and presented to keep me off school (which caused me to miss two exams) and promised to give a written apology to the teacher I'd kicked in the leg. Then I made my way to the math class and found my seat. All eyes turned, and a few welcoming comments hit the air: "Hi, Pete." "Hiya, Digger."

And another one from the hard-arsed teacher, "Oh, there you are. Our runaway rabbit!" He'd say anything to make the class laugh with his sarcastic jokes. "I suppose you've had a chat with the headmaster?"

"Yes, sir."

"And did he reward you for your absenteeism and the fraudulent doctor's note?" he asked.

"I'll have to write the exams tomorrow morning, sir."

"And that's it?" as he leaned on the desk. "Looks like he's left it up to me then?" and he reached for the cane. This sadist was under the misconception that I was actually going to submit to punishment from him. Fat chance, hombre! I was ready for some conflict.

I sat slouched across my desk, and stared back with rebellion. Then a girl in the class, Ginette Reddy, a lovely girl I had become a little close to on a few occasions, shouted out, "Leave him alone! You're always hitting everyone!"

I was pleasantly surprised at the outburst, and gave her a smile and a wink as she faced down the teacher on my behalf. Man, I was deeply warmed by her intervention on my behalf. I had great feelings for that lovely redhead who sat by the window. I wanted to go steady with her, and when we had our moment of passionate kissing by the gardens at the back of her apartment building, under the stars in the summer, something really clicked. But, to my misfortune, Ginette had a boyfriend, who was out of town for a while. She told me she was always lonely, and wanted a guy to hold her close and make her feel wanted. That was me, I told her, and we planned to meet at a later time, but that never happened. Her university boyfriend was back in town. But right now, she was shouting at the teacher on my behalf, and that was the gear. Our eyes met for one long moment, while others watched, and then she became dismissive. It's all complicated, teenage love, isn't it?

The stick was withheld, and I was sent to the back of the room and allowed to read up for the next day's exam. Paul Dale and I didn't talk much after I'd told him he'd let me down. His pampering dad bought him a brand new Norton Commando 650cc motorbike for his sixteenth birthday, which in a couple of months was a tangled mess. Paul was let off with a couple of broken bones, and a deflated ego. Billy and I enjoyed our road fun on his two motorbikes. He let me ride his Matchless 250. Everyone at that time was in the bike mode. If it wasn't the scooters, it was the motorbikes. Even my brother Dave scored an Italian Gilera 175cc. It was lightweight, but man, that thing could take off.

48

Winter Night Burglary

n 1965, there was an interesting show on the telly that described in great detail how houses were burglarized and "How to avoid this happening to you." This one-hour documentary, complete with a cast of characters, should have been called "101 Tips on How to Successfully Rob a Place and Get Away with It." This informative show went through, step by step, how things were done, and there must have been thousands of young scallywags all over England who watched intently that night, even taking notes. What a gift to the idle thieving hands of the wayward youth. A free lesson on the literal ins and outs of ill-gotten gain.

At school, it was the talk of the day. George, or Big G as we called him, was excited about getting into the biz, and a few days later, we thought we'd give it a go.

Jack Frost had done his bit, and it was a bloody freezing night when my crooked buddy came by. The streets were like skating rinks, and we weren't exactly dressed right for the elements, but off we went anyway for a pint, for Dutch Courage, not forgetting to each bring along a small canvas bag for slummy.

After walking into the higher well-off district of Woolton, and trudging through six inches of snow, up and down the fancy roads lined with expensive houses and flashy cars, we spotted a target. The driveway was empty, but a couple of outside lights were on and a Christmas tree was lit up in the living room. The front door, by the driveway, had two large stained glass windows either side. It was about

9 o'clock, a perfect time for a break-in, because, if people go out for dinner, a flick or a drink, two hours earlier, they don't usually get back till eleven or later. The procedure, as we both had learned from the documentary, was to go straight to the front door, knock or ring the bell and if someone answers, just make out that you were looking for Susan this or Tommy that. Our story would be: We were stepping out and wondered if they were home, then to our amazement, we'd realize it was the wrong street. An Oscar-winning bare-faced act. G and I had practised our poker faces from an early age; to act at all hesitant or suspicious would send off alarm bells, especially if a neighbour was watching through the windows. If someone did answer the door, it was good to walk calmly away, and get the hell out of the district fast. Everyone in this district had phones, not like our crowd, and they could have the heat turn up at the door very quickly. After three knocks and rings, it was obvious that no-one was home, or they were deep sleepers, or they were already phoning the rozzers. You'd have to make an educated guess.

Our next move was to check for a key. It always amazed me how many people kept a key on a string, just inside the letterbox, or under the mat or plant pot. In Liverpool, you're playing with fate if you do things like that, unless you have a big quiet dog lying on the mat in the hallway.

This target house was completely secure, so we walked around the side, through the garden gate to the back and peered through the windows. Our feet made deep furrows in the thick snow. There was no sign of anybody, but a kitchen full of large and small silver and gold trophies glinted as the moonlight shone through the windows. After all the doors and windows were checked, the only way in, without forcing a door, was above the kitchen sink where a small awning-type window was slightly ajar. It appeared to be barely big enough for me to squeeze through with my thin build. With a leg up from George, I balanced on the window ledge and pushed it open as wide as it would go, took an estimated guess and jumped back to the snowy ground. "I can get through, no problem," I whispered. And within a moment, I'd taken off my thick overcoat, jacket and sweater, stripped down to my thin shirt, then I was back on the sill fully extending my arms through the window and barely squeezing my upper body through, as George pushed on my feet from behind. I began to panic a bit as the entry got tighter and tighter around my waist. Then suddenly, on goes the neighbour's upstairs light, which illuminated the snow-laden backyard just like a fairground. Here I was stuck halfway in a window, my head getting warm and my arse freezing off.

George let go of my feet and slid close to the wall while I gasped for breath, holding my legs still for a good long minute, till the light went off again. Man, this was getting a bit hairy, but with a bit more shove and a wiggle, I could now reach the countertop with my hands, and I did a controlled vault down onto the kitchen floor. Now, with fingers crossed, hoping nobody was waiting in the dark with a heavy poker in hand, or worse, a long-toothed canine, I tiptoed across to the back door and unlocked it. George hustled in with my clothes, which I put back on, shivering in the dark. Then we proceeded, as we'd learned from our telly lesson, to find and slightly open two more places of escape. We choose the front door and a larger window in a side room, still keeping the kitchen door unlocked. It was always the first thing to do upon entering a prize (a pirate's term), just in case someone comes home sooner than you expect. Big G slipped quietly upstairs to the bedrooms, while I started looking around the living room.

People often keep items of value in a special drawer in their bedroom sideboard. Also, some have a predictable little hiding spot to stash a bit of cash for emergencies; yeh, like our emergency for needing some loose change for our smokes and beer. So, with this assumption, all the drawers were pulled out and put on the floor or bed, their contents pushed aside to find any hidden special thing.

All items of interest had to be as small and as light as possible, and we began to throw this and that into our thin canvas haversacks with the laced-up top. A nice-looking mantelpiece clock was the first in my bag. Tiny and round. Next, a shiny cigarette case and lighter, followed by a couple of small antique candlesticks. There was nothing in the drawers of a well-polished oak sideboard. It was off to the kitchen next, where I found an overhead cabinet stuffed with all different types of booze. I took a good slug of Harvey's Bristol Cream Sherry, one of my favourite drinks, while I surveyed all the trophies lined up along two glassed-in shelves.

It was at this moment that I knew I'd crossed the line and was now becoming the despicable thief, playing with the belongings of others. Familiar words began ringing in my head. Words like "the lowest of the low." After being brought up by honest Christian parents to be a good lad and show respect for other people's property, here I was now doing this. I had a sick feeling in my stomach. As a tiny boy, I was always concerned about being honest. The school environment, Sunday school and my parents and teachers drove this attitude into my head. Honesty was always the best policy. At one time, when I was small, I found a shilling on the street and turned it in to the nearest shop. This pleased my dad when I told him and also made the shopkeeper glad. I received no ice cream from him for my honest deed. But I was taught never to expect a reward for good behavior.

Now, as a teenager, things were different. I'd become street-savvy, and the seeds of wrongdoing were now well planted. The older street mentors were always available to give lessons, and at fifteen, it seemed I was enveloped in the world of crooked behavior. I had garnered enough moxie for gathering the ill-gotten gains I thought I needed to keep me in good clothes, smokes and fun. But here, now, gazing at the glitter of these trophies, the rewards of someone else's achievements, I was facing the bitter pill of shame and the decision to jack out immediately. This was more than just stealing a packet of fags from a shop. These objects held personal attachment, the result of someone's hard efforts. It was like treading on your granny's grave.

Unfortunately, another feeling won out that night. It had gnawed away at me over the years: the torment and inferiority that poverty brought and the socio-economical differences between the posh crowd and our mob of sweaty losers. In reality, there was no love lost between us. To take a bit from them was more than just getting stuff; it was, in a way, getting even. Stealing from our own was looked down upon, but taking from those whom we regarded as the upper crust was not always seen as the same crime. Some even admired it. But this inexcusable sentiment was not held by everyone.

I froze for a moment, gazing at the glittering trophies, and restrained myself from taking any of them. This was a line I wasn't going to cross. Instead, I began rifling my way through the kitchen drawers, when the shadow of George crept around the corner holding a large nice-looking leather case full of brand-new silverware.

"Look at this slummy," he whispered.

"Bloody 'ell, where was that?"

"Under the fuckin' tree man. Merry Christmas!"

"You robbed a Chrissy present?" I snarled at him. "Don't do that, you bastard!"

"You shut yer gob! These people 'ere are the bastards, mate, not us." He noticed I was leaving the small trophies alone, so he barged in and shoved a couple into his swag bag. "Come on, then, grab the stuff. Come 'ed," he growled.

As we were finishing our yap on the subject of ethical theft, a set of headlights suddenly turned into the driveway, and a car pulled up in a hurry outside the main door.

"Shit! Get out!" he said.

With our slummy bags thrown over our shoulders and the leather case held tight under George's arm, we scarpered out the back kitchen door and across the snow toward the high fence, which backed onto a park. Halfway across the fancy garden, a snow-covered statue stood in the middle of a small, shallow circular pond. It seemed like an easy obstacle to cut across rather than dodging around all the wrought-iron garden furniture. I took the shortest route, straight across, only to find myself ankle deep in freezing water and snow, but with enough momentum to scurry on to the fence. The man of the house was right on George's heels, and he was gaining ground. Throwing the bag of swag over first, I then hurdled the six-foot fence and watched, as George flung the box of silverware, hitting the man squarely in the face. He dropped with a howl onto the snowy ground. As I vaulted over, my left shoe came off in the garden. Big George was right behind me and lumbered over. And we were off, stumbling through the woods, me like Hopalong Cassidy, with freezing wet legs and one missing shoe. Fortunately we were assisted by a bright moonlit snow-carpeted pathway as we continued running down back streets and alleyways, finally cutting into a shed, in a dark lane, for a breather.

"Fuckin' hell, man, my foot's falling off. It's killing me," I complained.

"Here, use these," George said, consoling me as he removed both shoes, took off his two socks and gave them to me: he, now wearing shoes and no socks, and me, with two socks on one foot and a shoe on the other. A half-on, half-off circus act. Again, this was one of those crazy bonding moments of the two lost "Thieves of Bagdad." As we walked, as cool—or should I say, frozen—as cucumbers, out of an alleyway, an old couple, walking their dog, paused to say hello. Looking at our shoulder bags and our breathless appearance, the old fellow came out with,

"Funny night to be kicking a ball, lads?"

"We had an inside game tonight, mister," I replied.

"Did you score?" he carried on.

"We always score, ha!" I answered, as we hurried along.

"Good lads, keep scoring. You might turn out like Stanley Mathews."

Off the old folks went with their fat old dog, which paused for a piss on the lamppost. We laughed over his "Did you score?" comment.

Within moments, we began to hear the approaching ring-a-ding-a-ling of police cars, followed by an enormous booming explosion in the distance. This was the night, when part of the ICI chemical factory blew up a few miles away. The cops were now redirected to the scene of the accident, so we could take our time, and ambled home through the side streets, my foot now numb and feeling like a lump of wood on the end of my leg. After a long downhill trudge, we were back in our district, where we paused at John Riley's place to stash our two bags deep within a thick overgrown hedge by the side of his house, to retrieve in the morning.

"Did you score, Pete?" was the parting hilarious remark from George.

"See yer tomorrow." "Not if I see you first, yeh bastard." Our usual banter.

As I limped on through the thickening fog, I looked back, and there, under a street light, was George, further down the road, his arms around two girls we knew, swaggering around like "King Dick." There were lots of kids on the foggy streets that night, just loafing around as usual.

He'd better keep his big gob shut, I thought. Georgie boy was a well-known braggart, and the girls always clung to him for free smokes and favours. At home I crept quietly through the front door, as everyone was laughing in the living room, watching something funny on the telly, and off I went upstairs to the bathroom, washed and soaked my feet in the bathtub and put a couple of plasters over some small cuts. Finally I slid into bed. As I lay there, my heart still beating from the evening's adrenalin rush, I could hear the passing cop cars hurtling up and down the streets, chasing shadows and waking the district with their little bells. Ding-a-ling-a-ling.

49

Playing the Game, Paying the Price

The next Wednesday afternoon, in the middle of classes, a messenger came in, dropped a note on the teacher's desk, and I was told to pack my bag and report to the office of the headmaster, Mr. Drew. As I walked in, who else would be there, standing with a policeman, but my big-headed mate George.

"Please accompany this officer to his car. There's apparently a few questions you both need to answer at the station."

"What do you mean, sir? What's all this about?" I asked, as we were led out of his office and down the hall, under the watchful eyes of kids and teachers.

"In the back, boys. This won't take long. Just an enquiry, that's all," said the boy in blue.

Down at the cop shop, an injured man, who I wouldn't have recognized in a million years, seemed certain he could identify the two culprits that broke into his house. The middle-aged fellow, sporting a black eye, looked along the lineup of eight boys, all about the same age. Scrutinizing us, we turned, slowly around, one by one.

My heart slid up to my throat as he paused at George, pointed his finger at his face and shouted, "That's the young bastard who did this," indicating his big, bright shiner. Then walking past two more boys down the line, he stopped at me, pointed and said, "And that's the other little fucker!" The officer escorted him down the hall a few paces and lightly, but firmly, reprimanded him for going overboard with his language, while the other bobby took George and me aside into the interview rooms.

We were put into different rooms, questioned separately and then allowed to sit together alone, for a few minutes, to sort out our story. George was allowed to smoke, but I was told I couldn't, still being fifteen.

There was, of course, an unusual looking mirror in the middle of the wall, and we realized they were probably listening to every word, as well as watching us. We'd already rehearsed the story over and over a few times. "We'd gone out for a drink on the night in question, and had taken a bus downtown to check out the action."

The cops pulled our story apart piece by piece. What action, what club? What band was playing and where? What people did we meet? Were there witnesses to verify our story? Amazingly no? How about the left shoe they picked up in the garden that was my shoe size? And I was thinking there was a squealer out there who'd listened to a bragging Big G? I could see a checkmate coming, and began to weigh my options. After lots of puzzling questions, they gave us the ultimatum to come clean or face a stiffer charge and a worse penalty. We were given five minutes alone again, and so we decided to admit to common assault, while in the process of a robbery. This time we both lit up a smoke. I wasn't concerned anymore. I needed a drag. George told them he had reacted impulsively and slung the case of silverware over his shoulder when he was running, and didn't mean to injure the man. "Oh yeh? Just a random throw, right?" was the comment from the officer. We were advised to both plead guilty to an array of charges.

My parents were angry and upset about all this and kept shaking their heads whenever they saw me. They told me to straighten out and asked, "Who are those guys you're hanging out with?" "What family does he come from?"

Next day we arrived at court in our best suits, and the charges were read out: breaking and entering, unlawful entry (which I thought was the same thing, but apparently wasn't), destruction of property, theft; robbery with violence and assault causing grievous bodily harm went to Big G. The list was long and brutal, and after we adjourned for lunch and returned to our seats, we were given the goods.

George received a fine and a six-month term in an adult jail, because he'd just turned seventeen at the time of the crime, and had a string of previous violent offences. As an accomplice, but not responsible for the violence, I was given a small fine, and had to report each weekend, for three months at a youth correction center in Woolton, plus serve a six-month probation after that.

The worst offence, of course, was the violent act and injury. The robbery itself was handled separately, with a requirement to return the stolen goods, which were now stashed away in a friend's attic. We thought!

Our pretend-friend, Johnny Riley, had only put part of the swag in his attic. One or two small items, such as the silver cigarette lighter and radio, he'd already flogged to a fence he knew, and given us a few bob each, but the other bits like the two gold watches and a gold-plated hand-sized trophy, a couple of silver serving pieces and the small camera were still in the swag bags in the attic. Riley was stupid enough to be caught by his equally crooked dad, after he'd been checking out our stolen goods and was halfway down the attic ladder. His curious old fellow quizzed him on why he was up there. I imagine it was like a modern-day replay of the Artful Dodger trying to pull a fast one on old Fagan, his boss. Johnny's bullshit didn't work on the old skiver, and he found the shiny goods and made a few bob himself. We told the law that we'd dropped off the goods in a hedge at Riley's place, but, upon searching the privets, they found nothing.

Now Georgie boy and I were accused of a false statement to the court and threatened with defamation of character toward the respectable Riley family. The burglary victims added up the value of the stolen goods, and that was handled separately, out of court. More cash payments for my sins. My twenty-pound fine came out of my own post office savings account, money I'd been saving for other things. I had a few quid in there, that I didn't tell my folks about, especially the big winnings from the year before. I was a good saver and had my ways of finding a bob here or there, plus the butcher boy money kept coming in every weekend.

We never did find out who fingered us with the burglary. It could have been a snake called Riley.

50

Redemption

I was stupid to get involved with this thieving rubbish and allow Big G to have such an influence over me. Now I'd have to spend the next three months of weekends at a run-down youth correction center in Woolton, Friday 6 PM to Sunday afternoon. That meant I had to tell my boss at the butcher shop that I couldn't make it for a while, and risk losing my part-time gig for good.

George's sentence was six months straight time in the Hard House, just outside of Manchester, a place that turned him into a tougher, meaner fellow who I didn't bother associating with any more. I followed my folk's advice and tried my best to steer clear of the troublesome crowd and became a bit reclusive.

My first visit to the young Ugandan-born probation officer was at his Wavertree Road office. It was an illuminating experience to say the least. Mr. Bruce Thomson was refreshingly inspirational; all we talked about for the first ten minutes was football and the Mersey Beat music scene, and he was mad about the local bands.

This big black African man had three scar lines across each side of his face. I'd seen this before, and I'd heard that it was traditional marking done to a child to show a person came from a certain tribe. He had an interesting accent and spoke better English than most people I'd met, and there was no beating around the bush with him.

After the unexpected friendly chitchat was over, he offered guidance and strong advice, the clearest words of which were to stop hanging around with the wrong crowd and choose my friends more carefully. It's a difficult position to be in sometimes, to want to be part of the cool crowd, yet to also want to separate oneself from the selfish and negative behavior. Especially when you become ensnared within a horde of intimidating tough lads who expect compliance with their troublesome ways. The older ones leading the younger down the garden path. Try this. Do that. Or else.

On the street, it was commonplace to hear all sorts of stories about lads scoring money and stolen goods from break-ins, inside jobs, outside jobs, houses, shops, even churches. (I once ran into a Catholic church, on a dare, kicked the confessional money box off the wall and ran out with it, divvying up the dosh amongst the gang.) Someone paid for their sins, and I collected the tip.

Funny enough, our crowd all seemed to wear swanky cloths and fancy shoes. And where did all the money come from, you might ask. Knocking off, or gambling, as simple as that. Pocket money from our parents? You must be joking. A part-time job or paper round? Ha! Everyone I knew was on the make and take. If it wasn't tied down, it was fair game.

Mr. Thompson had given me the address and the times to turn up at the funny house in Woolton. I remember the first Friday afternoon when I arrived at the makeshift Youth Correction Center near Quarry Drive. A bunch of other boys were arriving at the same time to do the weekend routine of classes and social/cleaning duties and detention. Two of us were brand new, and the others were returning.

We all stood loitering around outside the big wooden doors, waiting. A couple of lads cadged a smoke off me. I'd brought some extra cigs in my bag, knowing there would be a need. Shortly after, Timothy Speers and a couple of other boys and me were called in to register and meet Mr. Trent, the man in charge. We were shown to the assembly room and our dormitory, where we dropped off our haversacks. Those two other lads, who kept quietly to themselves, disappeared on the first night, and we never saw them again. The story circulated that they'd took off to London, the large city of anonymity, and were well-known by some of the other scallywags who'd been through these revolving doors. Some kids were just your regular lads who'd messed up once or twice, but others were desperate hard boys, usually from troublesome families. We had to sign in when we arrived, and sign out going home on Sunday afternoons, then it was home sweet home, to sleep in our own beds again after two nights in a cot.

This was all happening just as Fred and David were heading off to Australia on a job transfer and Geoff was still out at sea, probably in the South Pacific. So these months of trial and tribulation had to be managed on me tod. My folks were quietly supportive and I was glad they didn't make a big deal out of it.

The Woolton Center was an old damp building, with the usual turn-of-the-century toilets and one large communal shower. The dining room was just like back at normal school: long wooden tables with eight chairs. But the food was a little different. Here it was great: a good hearty breakfast, sandwiches for dinner and a tasty hot tea, like spaghetti or cheese pie, at 5:00 PM. Before bed, we had crackers and cheese and a mug of hot chocolate. Unlike regular school, there was no corporal punishment here, like the stick for bad behaviour, just a quiet, empty isolation room where you had to cool off, sit on your tod and read a book or magazine.

On my first night, a big lad arrived at the dining room a little late. He'd just spent a couple of hours in the Quiet Room and was now back with us for his evening meal. Hopefully, with a better attitude towards getting along and following the rules. I ate my dinner quietly and kept my head down, as I was surrounded by intimidation. If a lad really got out of hand, he was restrained, the police were called, and he'd be sent off to the local cop shop, to the cells. So it was smart to keep your gob shut and not rock the boat. I just wanted to get it all over with. It would only be three months on weekends. There was no such thing as communicating with the outside, because none of us had phones at home anyway. There weren't any shoulders to cry on here. But, it must be said, the environment was very civilized, and we all talked to each other with respect, and respect was expected back.

Mr. Trent, the head cheese, was an ex-soldier and an ex-copper, a double EX, and you could see he was a very tough man. He kept his small black book handy in his inside pocket, pulling it out to record the good and not-so-good behaviour he observed while passing through the facilities all day. The back door led to the tarmac exercise yard. At one end was an undersized footy goal painted on the tall brick wall, and at the other end was an old outside urinal, surrounded on three sides with short steel walls for a bit of privacy. This whole facility was old but clean and tidy, and guess who kept it shipshape, with brooms and a hose? We did.

This place rang with the resonance of a military environment, and was run in that fashion. It would be the first and last time for me in a joint like this, and if I had come to my senses that night of the robbery and George hadn't hit the guy in the gob with the silverware case, I wouldn't be in here now. I raged inside over this senseless situation, but only had myself to blame. I just had to get through this. I wasn't a shy boy, so mixing in and cracking jokes to break the ice was easy, but it just covered up my great sense of sadness and loneliness.

At about 9:30 pm, we all met at the small assembly room and were led through a prayer about God's love and our undeserving selves. Then at 10, it was lights out, and no more noise was allowed. We whispered to each other in the small dorms, which had eight to a room. The only sound you could here was Trent listening to the bbc news over his crackly wireless radio in his room down at the far end of the hall. After the quiet chat back and forth, we were off to sleepy time, just like little five-year-olds back at Plumpton Street Nursery. Eight sleepy teenagers all tossed and turned, snoring and farting our way to 6 am, when that bell started ringing, and the doors began banging and slamming open down the hollow wooden hall.

"Up, boys!" We all had to wear the long-sleeved blue shirts issued on our arrival, our own grey flannel trousers and black shiny shoes that we had to keep polished. Like I say, regimentation. This was no problem for me, because our house was very orderly, with our ex-army dad running the show.

We were also lent a dark blue pastic mac for when it rained, and a large white towel to be turned back in to the laundry on Sunday afternoon.

It was Saturday morning, and after a quick tidy up and a splash on the face, we all lined up behind our chairs in the dining room and said Grace: "Dear Lord, bless this food to our bodies, and we to thy service. Ahhhhh Men!"

Breakfast was brought out on trolleys by little old ladies with big friendly smiles. They put large pots of porridge and scrambled eggs at the end of each table for us to divvy out, fill our plates and bowls and dig in, followed by a plateful of toast with jars of marmalade and jam. This was as good or better than most of us got at home. There were about two dozen lads, and so, one of the tables of eight stayed behind after to help clear up the dining room. We all rotated with each meal, but at noon, dinnertime, everyone cleaned up his own mess.

After breakfast each day, we assembled in the main hall and went through the usual Christian school rigmarole. The Lord's Prayer then a hymn, "Let us with a gladsome mind..." or something like that, a brief message of edification from the scriptures, for our young hearts and minds to swallow and follow, and then the day's program. Saturday mornings were reserved for classes in the main hall. It was all general knowledge stuff for our age group, but a few didn't have a clue about what was being taught. The usual geography, history, English, math lessons etc. were, to most, just a repeat of what we'd learned years ago. I was amazed to be sitting in a classroom with some lads who'd had the lowest level of learning you could imagine. They'd ask simple questions, and it became no longer humorous, but embarrassing, to listen to them. Boys my own age showed difficulty, not only in writing skills, but just speaking the English language. Were they just pulling the teacher's leg or actually teenage dropouts? They were dropouts, and this was a big eye-opener for me.

Some boys at sixteen found it hard to read a paragraph, do a simple sum or understand a map of the world. I began to realize just what sort of backgrounds they were coming from: poverty, ignorance and abusive parents who seldom were around to offer love or guidance. Some of their parents or siblings had criminal backgrounds, and the neglect had left them injured on the inside. The flotsam and jetsam of a dysfunctional society. I didn't have any excuse for being there. My folks loved and cared for us boys. I only had myself to blame. Not like these poor lads.

In our dorm, one boy called Henry stuttered and stammered so badly it was hard to talk to him and keep a straight face. He was a great person with a tremendous wit, but his speech came out so slowly that when he cracked a joke, you had to wait quite a bit for the punchline. He couldn't handle the "th" words, and with self-effacement, he'd tell us how his mother would send him out for the messages, and he'd ask the grocer for "a fick and a fin and a pint of mink." To which we would all laugh along with him, having heard it a few times. He was referring to the loaves of bread you could buy, which at one end was sliced thickly for toast, and the other end thinly, for sandwiches, plus a pint of milk. His nickname became Fick and Fin, but he didn't mind that. Some boys, to their misfortune, took it a bit too far, just to have a laugh at his expense, but Henry was nobody's fool. This young fellow was the eldest of no less than nine kids, and it may have been the case that there was not much time to give him the attention or support he needed. One tall boy we nicknamed Lamppost, straightening out for robbing cars, took his mockery a bit too far with our mate, and within five seconds, he was flat on his back with a broken nose and a sore pair of nuts. It came out that Fick and Fin was the son of a retired, professional boxer, who'd taught him a few moves early in his life. He didn't mind you pulling his leg, but there was a limit. Respect was given and taken. Fick and Fin spent the rest of the day in the Quiet Room, and Lampost went off to get his nose fixed, and learned in no uncertain terms, to keep his gob shut, and became refreshingly quiet after his painful awakening.

As the weeks trudged along, and my unfortunate episode was nearing its end, I came down with a bad case of bronchitis, and was sick as a dog. I didn't go to regular school or the weekend center for the last three weekends, and was told by the probation officer not to return for further visits to Woolton. "You don't need to go there anymore Peter. There's no problem, your time's done," were his welcomed words over the phone.

When I was as right as rain, and my chest had cleared up, I felt a massive load had lifted off my shoulders. What a relief to be back to some sense of normalcy, with family, friends and my part-time butcher boy job still waiting for me.

I'd learned my lesson. At school, the expected bantering never seemed to end, until finally I calmly told the enquiring mob, "I won't be going back there, and that's that. It's full of hard lads, and you don't want to be stepping into that nuthouse." They all laughed, but it was like talking to a brick wall.

My time at Gateacre Comprehensive School was nearing its end, and I couldn't wait for the last bell to ring and for me to get on my bike and tell the whole place to Fuck off! I hated it there, and during the last week, after I received my certificates to move on to whatever awaited me, I wanted to leave a small token of appreciation behind. Something that would say See yah later, suckers, to hell with you all. I'd been in this dump for five years, and I could only count on one hand the times of joy and happiness there. Times like performing at the Christmas party, where I was dressed up like a Mexican and mimed to the Speedy Gonzalez record, with a real lit-up Cuban cigar in my mouth. The next day some girls wanted to date me. I felt like a star on stage. Or when I won the twisting contest with Pat. But most of the time, I felt I was in the wrong place with the wrong crowd. This crowd knew nothing of the slums of Everton, and I was a fish out of water trying to fit in, and I didn't want to fit. Now as a sixteen-year-old rebel, I wanted to get even with the teachers that had bullied me, knocked me around and tried their best to embarrass me in front of the class. They would be on the receiving end before the week was through.

One particular sadist, the math teacher, who'd caned girls as well as boys, was up for his due reward. I didn't know where to start, but one morning he was the yard-duty teacher, and we boys had all lined up and got our small bottle of government-issued milk and were hanging around while he was across the yard, leaning against the brick wall, having a smoke. I scored two bottles of milk and started to sip from one, and while he was looking away from us, I threw the other full bottle at the wall just above him, smashing and spraying milk and broken glass all over his head. He screamed with fright and ran over in our direction looking for a suspect. I just stood there sipping away on my drink as he checked around to see who didn't have milk in his hand. He then ran over to another group of boys, like a chicken with its head cut off. We all burst out laughing, as he ran into the building, shouting and howling and mopping his head. What a laugh that was.

This same math teacher commented that he was surprised I'd

passed the GCE exam in mathematics. "You must have done a good job of cheating," he said. He didn't like the way I applied geometry to solve my algebraic questions. A man who'd walk in the class and say, "My wife and I had a good argument last night. Don't any of you get on the wrong side of me today." A real "nowhere man. "

The crazy female French teacher who had slapped a girl twice across her face in front of the classroom for cracking a joke was also on the hit list. Once she'd overheard me talking about her husband, who also taught French across the hall, and threw a blackboard duster very hard across the room at me. I'd ducked, and it hit the girl seated behind me right in the mouth. She needed stiches when they got her to hospital. That wooden duster was meant for me, and that girl with the split lip was a friend of mine, and for all that, the teacher was only slightly reprimanded. So, while she was busy having her lunch, her briefcase was filled with a bucketful of water and glue, and all her paperwork and personal stuff was wrecked. Her desk draw was also filled up with red enamel paint from the woodwork shop. I think she was let off lightly.

During that week, a few of us continued to pay our respects to the miserable sods who didn't deserve to be called teachers. They were more a hindrance than a help to our education. A few months earlier, one very disturbed teacher had tried to commit suicide after locking himself in an office. He left on sick leave.

It wasn't a happy place, and I'm amazed how the mad behaviour went on for so long without the authorities putting a stop to things. I know some parents pulled their kids out and sent them elsewhere. My parents never stepped once into any school I ever went to, except when mum came to Heyworth primary to see me sing when I was six. That was it.

On that last moment in form school, I said goodbye to my half-dozen true friends and never looked back. I didn't want to turn into a pillar of salt, and in a few months, I'd be sailing off to another world.

51

The Lucky Phone Call and the Apprenticeship

Finally through with school at sixteen and a half, I started working full-time at the butcher's shop on Wavertree Road, but took some time off to search for something that had a more technical lean. Billy Watloe had just started a plumbing apprenticeship, another lad was getting into surveying, two others I knew had started with the post office in the telephone department, but I still had that yearning to go to sea. My older brother Geoff was in the Merchant Navy, in the galley, and that year he was doing the Aussie–Kiwi run, and I wanted to join him. Over his two and a half years at sea, he'd sailed around Africa and been picked up at the dock in a Cadillac in New York with his adoring Yanky girlfriend. Now he was enjoying the balmy climes of the South Pacific. His job sounded like every boy's dream! And all that food! A sailor's position that takes you to exotic places, feeds you, takes care of all your needs and sends your pay home to a bank account that grows and grows. Every port of call offered a new adventure, a different culture and a bevy of beautiful young women to meet, and fall in love with for a short time.

My boss wasn't about to give me better hours or a raise in pay anytime soon, and things were getting stale for me, so I wanted to move on. After I'd signed up for the Merchant Navy, passed the short interview, I reported for my training at the National Sea Training School at Sharpness, Gloucestershire, onboard the training facility ship, the T.S.

Vindicatrix, affectionately known as the *Vindi*. It was a historical place where it's said seventy thousand young salts, fifteen and sixteen years old, got their start.

Geoff had won a bronze medal for boxing on the *Vindi*. A natural fighter, he rarely lost a scrap. He encouraged me to get into boxing, which I did for a while. At the boys' club, I did some training and ran ten miles every second night. We'd skip and shadowbox, much to the amusement of those who thought they were too cool to get onto the team. I was a lean boy, and could handle myself quite well, but shortly after starting with the gloves, I paid the price with two whopping shiners in one week. In one scrap, I'd embarrassed an older boy in the ring at the boys' club. I'd put him on his arse with a lucky punch. He waited outside to meet me and verify to the crowd that he was still bigger and tougher. I could have hammered him another time in the ring, but the opportunity didn't come around, and I lost my interest in boxing after a while. Running and gymnastics suited me better.

The days passed, and I only had two months left till my call up to the *Vindi*, when our family was informed that Geoff had jumped ship in New Zealand, and he was to be brought home by a sister ship. There had been trouble on board with a couple of bullies, the drunken head cook and the galley scully. My tough brother had one scuffle after another with the two of them from the time they left home port. He'd had enough after being threatened with a knife, so he and his good friend Luke, one of the deckies, stayed ashore in Auckland, as the ship left, then later turned themselves in to the local police. They were housed in a cell till they were brought home on a sister ship, and Geoff quit the sea, and later began to pursue a religious calling. Now my plans of joining him at sea were blown out of the water. When he got back home, he advised me to first get a trade under my belt and then think about going out on the briny.

"You'll be an officer then, eating at the captain's table, with a better cabin, better money and maybe better company."

My game plan was changing, and the quest for my future occupation seriously needed some redirection. I was driven to find a trade. Blind job searching is a bit like fishing, you send out the hook and you never know what will jump on the line.

At the end of one long tiring day trudging around town, from this company to the next, knocking on doors and making phone calls, I'd finally had enough and headed home. Then, just through curiosity, I picked up a discarded newspaper as I was passing by the ticket window at Lime Street Railway Station. Turning to the job section at the back, I saw a small advertisement for applications by young lads interested in starting an electrical apprenticeship with James Scott, a large firm. They were taking on a half-dozen boys, and it was all happening that week. I checked my change. I barely had enough to take the bus home, but I had to give this a shot. I found a phone booth and called.

A man answered, "Hello. James Scott, Electrical Contractors here."

"Yes," I started, and quickly expressed my desire for an interview. I was speaking a mile a minute when the buzzer on the phone began, indicating I had only few seconds left to put more money in the slot or be cut off. I quickly shouted my address as the phone went beep, beep, beep, and the connection died.

That night, just after tea was over and I was sitting in the front room watching the telly, a knock came to the door, and my dad answered. A man asked if this was the house where Peter Hayes lived?

"Yes it is, and who's asking," dad replied.

"I'm from James Scott, and Peter called our company this afternoon about the interviews we're having for apprenticeships. I think he ran out of change and the phone cut him off, but I drive past this way every day, and I thought I'd check him out. He seemed very keen over the phone."

Dad invited him into the front kitchen, and after we talked for a minute, I took down the information for the interview. So, there it was, by a stroke of luck and the kind consideration from this fellow, I had my kick at the can.

The day came, and I sat the tough exam, along with about fifty or so boys my age, all competing for a handful of jobs. To my absolute delight, I got a letter in the post the next week, inviting me to their offices in a few days to sign my indenture papers to the company, as an industrial electrical apprentice! A commitment that would last five years—a length of time that seemed like an eternity to a boy of sixteen. I was completely chuffed and went out to see my mates that night to let them all know I wasn't left out in the cold. I too would be scoring a trade in something I knew hardly a thing about—electricity? What's that? This was the beginning of what would become my lifetime career, between all the other things I'd eventually try my hand at. But nevertheless, a trade ticket would serve me well in my future travels to three continents. The first thing to do was to score a handful of usable tools, pliers, screwdrivers, etc. and a pair of coveralls for work. Dad insisted that I buy some second-hand overalls so they wouldn't make me stand out like a fresh boy, but rather like a lad who'd been working for a while.

The company had a big job at the new Ford Cortina transmission plant in Halewood, and I was to catch the company double-decker at the Five Ways junction early in the morning. Once there, you punched your card and started your shift. It was a fair walk to the huge new factory from the lunchroom, and lots of fellows would just sit around for a while playing cards and drinking tea till they had to get up and start walking. It was a good ol' union job, and nobody was in a rush to do anything. From the first day on, I was told to carry this guy's toolbox, or fetch this or that for those fellows, help make the tea for the breaks, gather the lists of ordered sandwiches for the guys for their lunch breaks, etc. I learned everything but what the trade was all about. I was told to keep my mouth shut if I saw anything shady going on, like the time when someone borrowed a small crane and lowered another lad over the chain-link fence that was the lockup for hundreds of nice shiny new toolboxes for the factory workers. The young lad tied box after box onto the ropes, and they were hoisted over the fence by the crane driver and loaded into a van to be driven off-site when it got dark. These lads had every angle figured out. Even the time clock for clocking in when you entered the site was manipulated. Everyone had a number and a card, and some guys would clock in their friends in the morning, if they knew they'd be late, or even off work for the day. The job was so big, they might not be missed. Another trick used on the clock was placing a small piece of tape over the square for the minutes and then waiting for the clock to move past the hour mark, and moving the tape again; you could come in late, but your card showed you came in early. We worked five and a half days, which meant four hours on Saturday mornings. For those forty-four hours a week, my pay was five pounds clear, or fifteen Yanky dollars.

The massive construction site was rife with ingenuity and a penchant for mischievous fun, not unlike my schoolboy days. Safety was on the back burner on that job, and foolhardy games were played without much thought for the consequences. All the apprentices had their legs pulled. One trick dished out to me was a little shocking, to say the least. I was told to pull on some stripped wires coming out of a steel box, and as I started to pull, the guys on the other end turned the power on and I got a 240-volt belt, which sent me jumping and flying back onto my arse, much to the amusement of the watching crowd.

That was my initiation into the world of electricity. My lesson was not to trust anyone or anything, when it comes to electricity, but double-check everything. That message was driven home when two qualified men were fried to bits by thousands of volts on the job. Another guy had his head bashed in by his own toolbox, which fell twenty feet off a scaffold. Three guys dead in three months. This was a dangerous place to work, I thought. We also had footy games during our one-hour dinner break, and there were lots of really good players from different trades competing for money.

There were a few mad-hatters on that job, and one journeyman electrician I worked with for a short while kept telling me to join him some night, as he was going to these pot parties where they met at someone's house, played the tunes and passed around the reefers of "Marrydueanna" as he called it.

"The birds love it and fall all over you," he assured me. "You'll score, no problem lad."

He was in his mid-twenties, and I was sixteen, so I was leery of his need to have me join him in all the fun. I stayed with my own crowd, but on occasion bought a couple of purple hearts from him to have my own fun on the weekends. A few of the lads I knew were taking some kind of uppers or downers. We could dance all Saturday night, and I didn't need to sleep in half of Sunday. I was usually going fishing, out and about in the fresh air.

I also had to go to Old Swan Technical College one day a week, from 9 AM till 9 PM. Interestingly, as part of our apprenticeship, we had not only the usual math and other technical lessons, but an English lesson at the end of the day, which involved reading, writing essays and public speaking to the class. The reasoning behind this was if you can't read and understand information, and also convey it clearly so others can understand, you were deemed incapable of becoming a true trades-man, lacking in the skills of communication to fellow workers. All our mathematics exercises were done with slide rule and logarithms tables. It wasn't till 1973 in Canada that I first owned a hand-held calculator.

The Technical College had football and rugby teams that played on Saturday afternoons. I played a bit of both, but wanted to join the footy team in particular. The first day I turned up for a game, the team was full, but the opposite team was a man short, so our captain asked if I'd play for them this time and try out for Old Swan next week. I glad-ly tied on my boots and got stuck in, scoring three goals for the other side, two headers and a hard volley. After that weekend, I was playing for our college, till I left for Aussie in December, and transferred my apprenticeship to Stowe Electric in Sydney.

Part Six

Escape to the Land of Oz

52

Cast Off, Me Hearties!

When a kid is born and raised in a swirling vortex of poverty and adversity, there's a strong likelihood of being swallowed up by such trouble. This can set the stage for a problematic existence, often accompanied by the feeling of a sadly unfulfilled life. To escape such a future requires a courageous decision to relocate. So, when Australia came calling, it turned out to be a timely solution to all our troubles.

"Let's get out of here. Liverpool is going to the dogs, and you boys need a new start." These were words from our dad after my two eldest brothers had already taken temporary job transfers from Lucas's Engineering in Liverpool to Sydney, Australia, six months earlier. This after our Dave had just got over his appendectomy, and we all swore he'd grown two inches in two weeks, lazing around in the hospital bed. He was the tallest of us boys, by an inch or more; we all averaged five-foot-seven. David loved to run, and later became a FIFA referee in New Zealand, where he settled down in Christchurch with his Kiwi wife. He even refereed an Everton game when they visited down under. Dave was smart, fit and always up for a good laugh. Like the time I got a Valentine's card in the post from a girl called Wendy. I didn't know a Wendy, and after I'd gone through a bit of leg-pulling from the family, Davvo, as we sometimes called him, confessed to the lightweight joke

Opposite: SS CERAMIC departing the White Star Line wharf at Millers Point, 1920-1939. It made the Australia to Liverpool run.

in the mail.

The decisive moment to boot it to Aussie came when we received a letter from Fred and Dave telling us they'd like to stay down under for good.

My mother went into a tizzy. "We're not splitting up the family! We're all going!" she insisted.

Funny thing is that before Fred and Dave went to Aussie, Dad had applied, as a family, to immigrate somewhere. Canada wouldn't take us. Dad, at seventy, was too old. New Zealand pretty well said the same, but Aussie said "Come on down! And we'll even pay for your four-week trip by sea." Well, that was an offer we couldn't refuse. But there was a slight hang-up. I still had two months left on my six-month probation.

After we filled out all the paperwork, the time came for Geoff, mam, dad and me to go to the Australian immigration interviews and have our medical checkups. All went fine, except when my mother mentioned to dad, "The doctor said I had the body of twenty-year-old." This caused the old fella to rant on about the doctor being "a bit forward, wasn't he?"

My process was to go before a small board of referees to explain why I should be allowed into Aussie with a black mark against me and a couple of months still left on my probation. I answered a few questions about my aspirations of a new start down under, and my promises to turn over a new leaf, and was told I could go. There didn't seem to be a problem because after just two visits with an officer, Mr. Mackenzie, on George Street, in Sydney, it would all be done.

"Is there something you'd like to say, Peter, before you leave?" the oldest of the three officials asked.

"Thank you, your honours (guessing they were all retired judges). I suppose if this was two hundred years ago, you'd give me a free ticket?" I quipped.

Three sets of judicial eyes glared at me, but one man smiled.

"Close the door behind you."

I was dismissed, and that was it. No more obstructions in our way to the new world. We took the bus home and over a few cups of tea made our plans for the Great Escape from drizzly, run-down, dead-end street Liverpool, where the docks were all on strike, lineups were around the block for sugar, unemployment was growing faster than the hair on your head, and things didn't look very promising with increased criminal activity everywhere.

We were getting out and going to the land of milk and honey where everyone had fruit trees in their backyards and the gorgeous beaches were crawling with beautiful Aussie girls in bikinis. There'd be no more fog or smog and cold wintery nights, and on and on.

I was concerned about dad. He had just spent days in bed with a bad flu, and was coughing his head off. He was now seventy, and I thought he wasn't doing too well with his bad chest, but we hoped that the warmth of the southern climes could only do him better than the damp unhealthy place we lived in now. We couldn't wait to get packing.

As the weeks passed, there were now many preparations to make with our luggage and belongings. For the voyage, we were only allowed so many cubic feet of baggage per person, including our bags we'd take into our cabins. So, after dad made an order, two large wooden crates were delivered to our house, to be filled efficiently to the brim, for shipping, especially with things that we didn't want to buy again when we got there. All necessary bedding, cooking pots and pans, utensils, clothing of all types and shoes—only essential stuff with a capital E. It was like moving house but only to another continent. One grows a strong attachment to objects that, most of the time, are just accumulated unneeded stuff. Looking back at that picking and packing time, I'm still amused at the amount of suits and shoes I'd gathered. The ill-gotten gain of gambling and lifting: Suits and fancy shoes that I felt compelled to drag along. Aussie is not the most comfortable place to dress up in hot tailor-made suits, and I had all kinds: three-pieced, double-breasted, single-breasted, narrow lapels, wide lapels, no lapel, turn ups, no turn ups, Beatle coats. There were shirts and ties, cuff links and fancy footwear, all sorts of stuff—stuff we Mods wore, as opposed to the rocker garb of leather this and that. The days of "Quadrophenia," funny hair, Lambrettas and Vespa scooters, with piles of mirrors all over them.

Aussie's a hot place most of the time, and shorts, short-sleeved shirts and flip-flops are the usual dress code. The main thing that was coming along with me was my Czechoslovakian guitar Geoff gave me, and my fine selection of fishing gear and deep-sea rods. I knew there was great fishing down there. I was going to catch a big shark or two. My hand-made fishing box went to a young boy, Mike, on the next block who I'd taken under my wing when his dad was killed at work. I'd see him at the boys' club, and he wanted to learn more about fishing, so he scored my lucky box.

Besides parting with lots of my own gear, we had to get rid of or sell the house stuff. Mum and dad had made some deals with relatives or friends and workmates to lighten the load. Some guy took the telly. Others took the carpets and beds, the fridge, the washing machine etc. We were beginning to live in an empty house. One night Geoff and I carried a heavy mattress for probably half a mile down the road to an old couple who lived on the third floor of a run-down tower. We humped that heavy load on our heads and shoulders, up three flights and hardly got a thank-you for it. Not even a tanner between us. Somehow dad was given their name, and they were quietly pleased to get it, but no cigar. As we were leaving, I said to the one guy, "All the best to you and your brother." He got a bit pissed off with me, because the other person, who dressed like a man, had short hair like a man, spoke deeply like a man and smoked a pipe like a man, was his wife. I'd never seen such oddballs like that before, and it was a strange thing for me, at sixteen years old, in the mid-sixties.

We also knew a really poor family in the next block of flats, the

Fernandez family: an Irish mother and Spanish father, with eight kids and one on the way. There was always one on the way. The eldest son, nicknamed Ferny, was a very troubled lad with some rough mates who had all done clink time. He was out on parole and showed me his wired-up jaw and missing teeth after he'd had some strife inside with a big bruiser. This family got lots of stuff from us. My dad often showed he had an empathetic Christian heart for those badly done by, and gave them whatever they needed, no questions asked.

Finally, a week before we were to head to Southampton to meet the boat, the two large crates that were jammed to the lid were picked up and sent ahead to the ship. The place was bare, except for my parents' double bed, an old couch and chair that were to be picked up on the day we left and some cooking things to tide us over till the Exodus. We stayed the last night in Liverpool with my mother's cousins, two middle-aged sisters who never married. Their names were Christine and Muriel, always known as Cissy and Muey.

On December 1, 1966 at 11:00 PM, my dad went down t he st r eet to the pay phone, one that was actually working and not vandalized, called a taxi, and we headed off to Lime Street Station. Geoff's girlfriend kissed and cried all over him, and the steam engine blew the whistle and pulled out of the station. I'd said my farewells to a couple of girls and some mates a few days before, knowing I'd never ever see them again. I had no intentions of coming back. It was see-yeh-later time.

"One o'clock in the morning, and all is well!" Except my mother cried all the way to London. We all sat quietly looking out the windows, as we passed through the sleepy, Northern towns and into the quiet black countryside of the Midlands, heading south. It was an uncomfortable ride with intervals of sleep or tea from the canteen carriage. Our stiff necks propped up with coats and cushions.

The first stop was Euston Station, London. A change of platforms was a demanding task, as we were loaded down with big heavy bags.

We took relays to get from point A to point B. During the lugging around, a total stranger offered to carry a couple of bags and helped us a bit. I later overheard my folks referring to him as an angel of the Lord. Are they getting more religious I thought? Yes, they were, and it became more obvious during the voyage.

Our ship for the thirty-day, twelve-thousand-mile voyage was the *Fairstar*, one of a handful of ocean liners owned by the Sitmar Line.

My God! I'd never seen a cruise ship that big in real life. It had rows of decks and windows reaching up to her massive funnels, and the lines of windows, stretched from stem to stern, along her freshly painted bright white sides. It was our floating hotel for the next four weeks. The large gangways were high up the side of the ship for the passengers and low to the water line for cargo. Heavy steel bridges from ship to shore, with big arrows pointing this way and that to herd the multitudes of excited passengers and farewell friends to the correct decks; first class was on top, and immigrants on the lower areas. The paying passengers and the freeloaders whose tickets were bought by the Australian government. We had to pay only ten pounds each for the trip from Southampton, through the Straits of Gibraltar, down the Meddie to the Suez Canal, the Red Sea, the wide Indian Ocean, Freemantle on Christmas Day, around the Aussie Bight to Melbourne, and then turn the corner to Sydney. Stepping down the gangway in Circular Quay.

Yes, just ten quid each, and thousands did it before us and after us, because the two spots down under, Aussie and Kiwi, were begging for new people to pull up roots and build a new country and a new life.

After scoring a four-wheeled trolley for our load of luggage and gear, we weaved our way through the gates and ramps, and finally got to the main deck entrance. The welcoming committee of porters and pursers were lined up in their smart nautical garb, while the deck crew, all Greek sailors, helped with directing and carrying our bags down three decks to our cabins. When we got there, Geoff, dad and I, were placed in one cabin with another fellow called Neville, and mum was in the next cabin, with three other women, Neville's wife being one of them. I suppose this all made sense when it came down to mixed sexes, changing and showering in tight quarters. The women could all muck in and the men also.

I got top bunk above my dad, and Geoff, top bunk over the middle-aged fellow. My mother had the good company of a woman her age and two younger ladies, strangers to each other, but within a very short time unpacking and settling in, they were all having one hell of a good time, laughing and carrying on. My dad displayed an obvious curiosity as to why "those women" should be having all that fun, and making such a commotion through the bulkheads? I'm pretty sure mum was glad to have the break from the family, to let loose and enjoy the ride.

Agreements were made for Neville and his wife, Sally, to have some private times together, in our cabin, likewise for our mum and dad. Geoff and I also had to get our timing right if we wanted to bring a little company back ourselves; and believe me, there was lots of company to be had. The place was running mad with teenagers, and it wasn't long before many friendships started, accompanied with the usual gossip travelling from deck to deck. As we threw our bags into the cabins, a voice came over the loud speakers saying we were leaving port in one hour and all visitors and non-travellers were to leave the ship right away before the gangways were removed.

So, off we hurried, back to the main deck, to witness our casting off. This was going to be really great. Leaning over the high rails, and watching the ropes being let loose and pulled aboard, I joined in with the hundreds of others in throwing dozens of colourful streamers from the ship to the throngs of people at dockside, who also threw lots back at us. People began throwing all sorts of things. A few hats sailed across from the ship to reaching hands, and even a couple of toys and a small teddy bear was tossed for a little girl. A couple of the ship's crew walking along the decks handed out not only streamers and balloons, but small cigars and trinket souvenirs. I scored a couple of cigars for myself, telling the decky I was getting the second one for my dad. Dad hadn't smoked for forty years.

We tied off colourful ribbons along the rails, and as the ship pulled further out, the streamers all began stretching and snapping and floating through the air—tissue paper waving farewell. Finally we were severed from our port, the historical Southampton. The music played over the loud speakers, and it was like New Year's Eve in Piccadilly Circus. A fabulous conclusion to a long tiring day: taxis, trains and now this big beautiful ship. The tugs were pulling and shoving, the ship's deafening horns were blasting away, and the world felt so alive and so was I. My folks looked back to shore across the boiling harbour, with its foaming briny and piles of flotsam and jetsam bouncing off the sides and wharves. Mum forced a smile in my direction, her teary-eyed resolve, and the old fellow was smiling wide and laughing with the anticipation of yet another adventure in his long, eventful life. Soldier, sailor, football player, ARP, fireman, labourer, machinist, tough-nut Bible student and teacher, and now an immigrant.

We were off, as the large tugboats, one by one, cut loose their lines and took us out into the harbour and the waiting sea. An announcement came over the speakers: our evening meal would be starting in fifteen minutes. Before I headed downstairs to clean up for dinner, I stood there on that windy outer deck and bid farewell to the country of my birth. I felt a bit melancholy for a moment, thinking of what I was actually doing. Leaving all my mates behind for good. The dirty old town where I'd grown up. The ins and outs, the poverty, the trouble everywhere, the pubs where I'd sat and drank my share of brew from the age of fourteen. The electrical apprenticeship I'd started five months earlier, and was now transferring to the new world down under. I reflected on all these things.

A young couple standing next to me asked, "And where are you from, lad?"

I replied, "Liverpool," and walked on, with nothing left to talk about. I was famished, longing for dinner, and at the moment, that was more important than idle chat. It was about four o' clock in the overcast afternoon, and the sun was dropping fast. The dependable and predictable rain of England was kissing me goodbye.

I've always had an affinity with the sea. I feel a soul relationship and huge respect for our great mother ocean—a sort of gentle tug of the calming company of her waves and her deep blue eyes. My granddad, Charles Edward, was just a stripling when he took off as a cabin boy from Danzig, a town on the Baltic Sea. My dad and brother Geoff were also sailor boys, in the Merch, and Fred did a trip once to Gibraltar with the sea cadets.

I always feel at home "out on the briny with a moon, big and shiny" as we steamed our way, out into the deep, leaving a long plume of black diesel exhaust behind us in the sky; we were, as they say, really "sailing off into the sunset." The dimming orb of the sun was swallowed up by the cloudy horizon on our starboard side.

This was a far cry from sailing on our "Ferry Cross the Mersey" to New Brighton (as Gerry Marsden would sing). Here was a floating town, complete with dining rooms, drinking lounges, the nightclub/pub with dance floor, a disco clubhouse for teenagers called the Jungle Room (which had a juke box and dished out soft drinks), two swimming pools (a small one for the little kids and the other for bikini spotting and doing the laps), a small gym for working out (which I did every day to stay fit), a movie house where you could take the girls for a kiss and a cuddle in the back row, the laundry rooms down below on level D. The outside decks were marked out for cruise liner deck games, plus there'd be lots of lazing around in the, soon to be, warmer climes on the hundreds of candy-striped deck chairs. Initially, there was an awkwardness in the confines of our cabin. The average rooms were sufficient for sleeping and escaping the crowds, but showering, changing and sorting out your stuff had to be well choreographed. Showers were to be brief, laundry was kept in separate bags, the beds made as you were leaving for breakfast, the tiny desk at my end was cluttered with books and small personal items. We four had all agreed on what time we'd set the old alarm clock. Guess who was the closest to reach out and turn the thing off? Moi.

Nobody wanted to be late for breakfast, so punctuality was the name of the game, and we needed to get cleaned up and dressed with some kind of order. The window of opportunity for any meal was about an hour or so. Everything on a ship had to be "on time," and there was no room for dawdling or special allowances for daydreamers who complained about not getting a meal. If things were cleared up in the restaurant, you were lucky to find snacks and sandwiches.

Neville, to our great convenience, was usually up and out, even before the screaming alarm clock went off. Like a cat burglar, he was dressed and off for breaky with his wife, while we were still snoring away.

The first day out, dad wanted to check on our two big crates that were sent ahead of us. After a long search on a couple of upper decks, we found them jammed into a space behind a wall, just out of the weather on the main deck. They were stowed and tied off with dozens of other boxes and bags. Ours was shoved right in the corner, nice and safe from the elements.

Neville, our new-found friend and his missus were from Newcastle, and I loved listening to his strong Geordie accent as much as he had a few laughs over my Scouse one. He'd come out with some *risqué* jokes in the cabin that my dad didn't care for. But me and Geoff had a hell of a good time with him when we'd find him in the pub, or having a smoke on the outer deck. He and his wife were a typical "fish and chip" couple—she was short and round, and he was tall and skinny— Jack Spratt and wife, and boy did she enjoy her brew! The poor old girl was not too amused to find out that the ship had not one bottle of Newcastle Brown Ale on board, so she had to get by with her Guinness and Scotch, and the usual lager like most of us.

As we began our course across the British Channel and into the mouth of the Bay of Biscay, the weather began to turn ugly, and by now I'd met quite a few teenagers to chum around with. We'd had some times at the Jungle Room milk bar (only a few indulged in the milk shakes, most preferred pop or a real drink back at the bar), and the juke box tokens were given out freely to play the tunes all day long, if you felt like. I think the most played record in the box was "Good Vibrations" by the Beach Boys. We danced and dreamed of all the surf beaches we would soon be on. There was quite a mix of us from all over Britain: Scotland, down to Devon, with all those lovely accents spoken by all those lovely young ladies. This was going to be a really good trip, and I was glad I brought my Old Spice aftershave along.

53

A Hurricane and an Arabian Diamond

In the afternoon of the second day out, an announcement came over the airwaves that all access to the outside decks would be closed off and the bars would be shutting down due to rough seas ahead. Before all the doors were closed, a handful of us decided to nip off to the swimming pool and have some fun while the waves began to rise. We met at the pool, swimming gear on, and in we went. As the ship rose and dove with the huge waves, we were knocked around like a cork. One end of the pool would tip, and we would be sitting on the bottom at the empty shallow end until she lifted the other way, and we'd get bashed against the wall of the pool, or tossed right out. Two minutes of this, and we were ordered out in Greek English. Another half an hour, and we were all changed and back in our usual place, the rallying spot, by the ship's shop/boutique and lounge. I had a couple of quid on me, so I decided to have a quick brew as the bar was shutting up.

"See you later," I said, as the others scarpered off, and I wandered inside, spotting Geoff and a dozen more standing at the bar with their last orders.

"This is great lad," I said, as I approached my brother, "look at those waves over the bow."

"Yeh, it's great alright. We're heading into a hurricane. This place always has rough weather," he replied, being familiar with the Bay of Biscay, renowned for its heavy seas. An old lady in front of me turned around from the bar with a small tray full of drinks; her intentions were to cross the polished dance floor and get to her table. Next to her was an old fellow with an obvious sense of excitement, who found a chair nearby, one with wheels on it. He persuaded her to sit down, while he would wheel her over, her arms full with drinks. She sat, and as he started to walk her over the slippery wooden floor, he let go, and she continued across, lifting her feet and gliding a good twenty feet, as the ship tilted in her favour. She was caught by someone else on the far side and stood up, and walked to her table, unaided, without spilling one drink. All those watching gave her a standing ovation as she sat down, raising her glass in a "Cheers, everyone."

Geoff was next in line, and I knew I'd be cut off, being too far back in the crowd, so he scored me a brew, which was gone as fast as you could say "Ship ahoy." I was back in the cabin for a short break before it was time for yet more food, served by our Chinese waiter. All the cooking and serving was done by a Chinese crew, and the deckies and officers were all Greek. Quite a mix. This hurricane thing was not such fun anymore, with the dipping forward and back, plus the shake and shudder of side waves banging the hell out of us. People began to puke up all over the place, falling over in passageways, and moaning as they headed for their cabins.

Another announcement blared: "This is the captain speaking. As you are well aware, we are passing through the edge of a hurricane, so everyone is advised to remain in their cabins until further notice. Dinner will still be served, but you can also have sandwiches delivered to your cabin by the crew." My stomach told me "get back in your bunk and wait till your cheese sarney and cup of tea arrives." As the *Fairstar* danced and buried her bow, I buried my face into the toilet bowl after eating half a sandwich, then clambered back into the narrow bunk and tried to think of solid land. In walked dad, grasping for cupboards and railings, and slung himself on the bunk below me.

"Ah, this takes me back to 1919 in the South China Sea."

I'd heard the story before, but just to keep my mind distracted, I asked him to tell me again how he ended up on a tramp ship, stopping from port to port, from Liverpool to Vladivostok.

"I was seeing off my brother-in-law at the dock. Arty was your Auntie Lizzie's husband, and was an AB.

"That's an Able Bodied Seaman. Right?"

"Right!"

He had signed on a tramp/cargo ship, with the Blue Star line, that was heading to Russia, Japan, China and a few other places and was going for a year or so. I was still full of adventure from my time in France, Belgium, Egypt and Palestine and was ready for some more travel. I think I needed to get away and see the world a bit more, like your granddad."

He told me that two men hadn't turned up for the trip, and they were weighing the hook within the hour, so would I like to come along, just for the hell of it? They were leaving port on the tide, at midnight. So I had to make my mind up on the spot. They only wanted seasoned men for this trip, so because I'd not sailed on a merchant ship before, he told me to tell the captain that I went down on a ship that was hit at the end of the war, and all my gear and papers went down with it too. The name of the ship was the *Kirkland*. So I put on the face and talked to the skipper, who quizzed me on ship's knowledge, which I knew a lot about, and he took me on and I signed up. In the morning, we were out in the middle of the Mersey, and I was rubbing the decks with a "holy stone" with the rest of them. Arty was on deck with me, and I was in my new suit with the legs rolled up, scrubbing away. That was the first day. From then on, till we got to Italy, I was shoveling coal down below. A hard job. Then, lucky for me, Arty put a word in for me, and I was put back on deck. I got along well with the old skipper, who told me he knew from the beginning I didn't go down on any ship, but liked my attitude and big arms. Muscles from moving sixty-pound shells in the heavy artillery for four long years. He also liked the fact that my dad, your granddad Charlie, was a "true sailor," he said. "Sail and steam," just like him.

"Why do they call it a tramp/cargo ship?" I asked.

"A tramp/cargo ship travels from port to port, picking up goods from one and takes it to another, and all the time, the company you're sailing with makes money on the deliveries and also buys and sells the cargo as well. These shipping companies make lots of money tramping their ships around, and we had loads of fun doing it. We brought back cargo from everywhere, which was sold in Liverpool, but we also left home port with a good pile of cotton and sugar, and some big machinery that we took to Italy, on our way through the Meddie. Ships don't travel empty; there's no profit in that. We took the Suez and Indian Ocean around to some small ports in Indonesia, up to Yokohama, Japan, where hundreds of women loaded us up with coal. They carried all the coal in baskets on their heads to the ship's hold. It took them all day. Then we went up to Vladivostok, but had to lie out a few miles 'cause the civil war was going on, and we could hear the firing on shore. They came out with barges to pick up a pile of steel we brought all the way from England. We turned south, and pulled into Shanghai for a week to get some repairs done on the engines, and that's where I picked up that small opium pipe."

"The one we used to pretend to smoke when we were kids?"

"Yes, the same one you found a tanner in the flip-top case."

"We went further down the Yangtze Chiang River to do a pickup, and that was where we ran aground and the engine room caught fire. We put the fire out, but now we had to go back to Shanghai for more repairs in a dry dock. A couple of tugs dragged us back, like two snails dragging a shoe. It took us forever. Another two weeks there and we were out in the South China Sea, when we ran right into a typhoon, a bit like this one, only our boat was a quarter the size of this. Most of the deckies were in the galley, out of the storm, and my brother-in-law was on his knees praying for God to save us all from drowning, while I was sliding up and down the galley counter, having a great ol' time as she lifted and dropped. Boom!"

"Didn't you nearly drown somewhere?" I asked, as the *Fairstar* began shaking even worse, and I was hanging on to my guts.

"That was while we were anchored in Genoa, when me and another lad were on a plank slung over the side, painting the front of the ship. He leaned back against the ship, to light up his fag, and the plank swung out, and the two of us fell into the drink. He couldn't swim, and he was behind me with his arms wrapped around my neck, and I was trying with all my might to get him off, but we kept going down. I was praying for my life. Then, a pilot, who lucky for us, was rowing by at that moment, hooked the back of my coat and pulled us into the rowboat. That was another close one. After getting wounded twice at war, the last thing I needed was to drown because some idiot spills the plank. That's why I believe in God, son. Yes, Genoa, that's where they caught me trying to smuggle a set of Italian dinnerware home for my mother. I borrowed an extra-large overcoat, and the pockets and lining were full of plates and cups and saucers, but the two guards at the customs bridge took me aside because they thought I was walking funny. It could have been worse, but they just made me pay the duty and let me go. My mother had that set of china for years. Anyway, I thought you were going to sea with Geoff? What happened there?"

"You know." I said.

"Now enough of all that," he continued, "are we going to get another sandwich, or what? It will settle your stomach and I'm still hungry."

"OK, dad, I'll try it again."

This time in the dining room, we scored some more sandwiches to take back, and I managed to hold things down, and sipping the hot tea helped. That night the sea was so rough, I was thrown out of my bunk and belted my head on the desk below me. A little cut over my eye, but after a cleanup, I was back to sleep.

The next morning, it was all calm, the cabin was empty, and I guessed everyone was at the dining room. Sure enough the place was packed, and they were all staring out of the windows at the flat calm sea and dark grey band of cloud all around us on the horizon. We were now in the eye of the hurricane and had to sail through to the other side of the calm. After making a mess of some clothes during my heaving up, it was time for me to get some laundry done, but soon the ship started pitching again. Up and down, shake, rattle and roll. To negotiate the stairs down to the laundry, all I had to do was wait till the ship lifted for'ard and jump half a dozen stairs, which were approaching horizontal level, and as they tipped the other way, the stairs became a ladder. The laundry was closed, as I should have guessed, so now I'd have to wait 'til we got to calmer waters, when we'd pass Gibraltar and enter the Meddie.

The weather improved, and we were soon all back in the routine of eating, drinking, walking the deck, hanging out with friends, swimming, reading, working out in the gym and lazing in the deck chairs. It was late at night and still very warm when we reached the end of the Mediterranean.

We were now putting into Port Said at the mouth of the Suez and tied up to a long floating walkway leading from ship to shore. We were only allowed to disembark for a couple of hours and return in time for our ship to get in line for the canal. It was before midnight and the town was very busy. We joined the madding crowd, and walked down the gangways and along the floating pontoons lined with Egyptian bum-boats. It was good to be on terra firma once more.

The curious merchants sold everything from carved wooden camel seats, to Spanish fly, a drink that's supposed to turn your well-behaved girlfriend into a sex-crazed woman who'd tear your clothes off and pounce on you. Actually, as any world-travelling sailors will tell you, it's just a small glass jar half-filled with camel piss. There were wide varieties of hand-made leather bags, pottery, cheap jewelry, plaster-of-Paris Bedouin heads, silverware, glassware, and naughty pictures of nude Egyptian women. I was even asked if I would like to meet a nice Egyptian girl.

Geoff and his young lady friend walked with me for a while, as we weaved our way through the streets where "The Arabian Nights" came alive. The wide walkways and dimly lit dirt streets were thick with venders selling their wares, so I ended up buying a watch for two quid and three packs of smokes. American Virginian tobacco cigarettes were pricey and were a good bargaining chip when dealing with these well-versed Egyptian salesmen.

The watch had a beautiful Omega face, but I found out three years later, when it died, that the inside was a Timex. Still, that was a good run for a cheap watch. After Geoff's lady friend had rejoined her folks for a short stroll around, we walked off together to a place he was familiar with from his travels through the Suez, a small corner place that served beer in a two-handled pint glass. The idea was to share the brew with your friend, each one having his own handle on the glass.

It was Egyptian beer and very good, good enough to call for a second. The Pharaoh's brew, the staple of the pyramid builders. A minute went by, and who should be walking into the bar but a handful of Liverpool and Scottish lads I'd met on board. Geoff decided to leave our gang of troublemakers and catch up with his lady friend. My folks returned to the ship and their respective cabins.

"We've got half an hour left before we've got to get back, so let's have a quick one for the road," someone suggested. It was a hot thirsty night. Done! Down the hatch, and off we went, shuffling, as teenagers do, back to the boat, down a couple of dark streets, where we came across this tall Egyptian guy standing in a shop doorway, completely dressed in black robes, including the headgear, like the famous Saladin.

"Want to buy a diamond?" he asked.

What a joke, we thought, as we all started laughing our heads off, the way young inebriated louts do.

"Sure, let's see your fuckin' diamond, Abu," someone said, as we followed him into the doorway of an old shop. You could tell something dodgy was going on, as he started to pull a large outrageous piece of cut glass, probably a rhinestone, out of his pocket. Just then, behind us, two big guys, also dressed up like Bedouin nomads, crowded us into the doorway. Suddenly they started pushing us and asking for our money, and just like that, the fight was on. We started kicking, punching, shouting and cursing, and luckily for us, a few of our lads could give it out. A handful of us Liverpool and Glasgow boys who had seen a rumble or two. The two biggest lads picked up the diamond trader and threw him through the shop window, with his legs hanging out the front. And as this was happening, a short shiny knife fell to the ground, and the other Arab guys immediately scarpered as two Egyptian cops pulled over on their vintage British motorbikes. They attended to the injured guy whose legs were a bit cut. Lucky for him he was wearing many layers of pants. A couple of our lads legged it out of sight, down the dark lanes, while the rest of us were escorted back to the ship, after the cops had talked over their radio with their boss. We heard one cop talking to the other about the old guy, and it seemed he was well-known to them. Back at the ship, we were met by a couple of the ship's officers, who gave us the low-down on how we could have been arrested and left behind in an Egyptian prison. "Think about that," they said, "an Egyptian prison."

But after we all gave the same account of self-defense against Ali Baba and his forty thieves, we were dismissed and sent back to our cabins with a reprimand and a promise that we would not leave the ship in the next port. We boys had bonded that night, and palled along throughout the trip. The only real injury I got was a good boot to the leg, and some cut knuckles, and I know we gave them far more than we got. As for the thief of Bagdad? The poor geezer was probably stitched up a bit for his efforts. Maybe he should stop selling diamonds?

My folks calmed down after me and my mates explained the whole story to them, and all things returned to normalcy, just like that hurricane passing over. In the evening we entered the canal, and by breakfast the decks were full of passengers enjoying the view of desert from both sides. We were cruising down the Suez in the blistering afternoon heat. It was an interesting experience, cruising down this salt-water highway, half a mile or so behind the next ship, gliding silently ahead of us. A lineup of ships all heading south. From the deck, we witnessed a fantastic sight as a dozen Arabs on horseback, dressed in their native clothes, galloped up to the edge of the canal on the western side and stood there, fully mounted, waving at our ship of fools, as we passed.

Another amazing moment happened at the southern end of the canal, when we pulled into Port Suez in the middle of the night. Anchored off the port, a half-dozen small fishing boats formed a large circle with a shallow net connecting boat to boat. The sea was dead flat and beautifully illuminated as each boat, with its small lantern on a pole over the bow, rowed, closing the loop of net, with drummers banging away. Then the sea began to boil with a large silver cloud of small dancing fish!

This sight appeared in the heat of the Middle Eastern night, under a wide, clear sky, emblazoned with a myriad stars and a brilliant orange moon. These same stars were gazed upon thousands of years ago, when generations of high priests of Egypt sat, studied and figured out their alignments for the foundations of pyramids.

There was no shore leave for anyone this time, just supplies unloaded and brought aboard, but the entertainment was not yet over for this stop. In the early morning, after breakfast, the decks were packed again with excited travelers peering and shouting over the side at dozens of small bumboats surrounding the ship. Each boat was sbout fifteen feet long, with one guy rowing or handling the boat and the other doing the selling and bartering. Thin ropes, with small weights attached, were thrown up to the ship's railings, and those who caught them tied them off to accommodate the passing of goods from below to the buyers on the promenade deck. This was a live circus act of shouting, bargaining and sending money down in tied-off bags and retrieving the bought item on the returning rope. After an hour or so, the ship's crew began walking the decks and telling the passengers to untie the ropes and let loose the boats. Bartering time was up. One young fellow was right in the middle of negotiating a deal for a large leather suitcase. He quickly sent down a couple of pound notes, his shoes and his shirt, which were part of the agreed deal. The money and goods were received below, but as the beautiful, camel-skin suitcase was being attached to the rope, the ship's horns began blasting away and our huge vessel started moving forward. The poor boy in the rowboat began giving it his all, trying to keep up, but we were now beginning to tow his small boat out to sea with us. Dozens of people began leaning over the side, shouting and cursing for the trader to cut his line. With both the Englishman and the merchant pulling hard, the rope snapped, causing the suitcase to fall into the sea and be retrieved by the Egyptian. He began laughing and cursing the "stupid bloody Englishman" and waving his hands, and shouting "Fuck off Englishman, ha ha!" Some angry onlookers from the upper deck began throwing oranges, apples and even ashtrays down at the poor fellow, as the whole crowd screamed with laughter. The merchant was now heading to shore, and well out of the range of the fruit missiles, but the chaos on deck caused such a commotion that the poor shirtless, shoeless recipient of high-seas piracy was taken aside by two of the ship's company and told to calm down. He was raging mad that he'd been ripped off by that gippo pirate, as he called him. For the rest of the voyage, it was hard not to smile a bit every time he was seen on deck or at the bar.

A few miles further down the Red Sea, we turned left at Bab-el-Mandeb and arrived at the last port and watering hole before entering the mighty Indian Ocean. We pulled up near the Port of Aden, but no one could go ashore because of the dangerous activity on land. It sounded like gunfire.

We anchored out for a day while things were transported in small motorboats, from ship to shore, and we were treated to a visit by a group of young boys who had swam out to the side of the ship. Their gig was to tread water and dive to retrieve coins when people threw them over the side. Some on board would throw handfuls and watch as these dolphin-boys scooped them up, holding them high as they surfaced, to our resounding cheers. After weighing anchor, we cruised across the Gulf of Aden, and our white hotel was gently coaxed out into the flat blue steam bath of the glorious Indian Ocean until we reached Fremantle, Australia. Our days now became a bit predictable, including the frequent sighting of flying fish and dolphins.

54

Naughty Nautical Manouvers

The swimming pool was the usual gathering place for a cooling off in the mid-day sun, for mad dogs and Englishmen; much like a watering hole in the Serengeti, where one gnu would catch up with the news about another gnu. There were many oversized gnus in polka-dotted gnu suits, plus the young, sleek and shapely gazelles, stalked by the preying cheetahs. Cheaters. Everyone on parade, preened, plucked and primed for the show. And all that sunbathing and burning of white, freckled, sensitive British flesh, slathered with the familiar high scent of summer. Pungent, suntan lotion.

Another big distraction from the doldrums were the festivities as we crossed the equator. Someone dressed up as King Neptune and another as Captain Kidd and prodded volunteer pirates along a plank to their demise in the deep end of the swimming pool. The lucky villains were rescued by a swarm of lovely mermaids, some with eye-catching double-D flotation. Modesty was an unknown practice on this boat. And of course complimentary small glasses of cheap bubbly were passed around at dinnertime, as we cruised over zero latitude.

During the hot afternoon at the lounge, the entertainment committee held a talent contest, where, to everyone's delight, there developed a long lineup of seasoned as well as first-time performers. Participants were encouraged by their families, fans and their drinks. Although encouraged by some friends, I didn't have the confidence and wasn't up for doing anything public, and just enjoyed watching everyone carry on. Neville, our Geordie cabin mate, did a short routine of one-liner jokes, followed by a few individual singers and an amateur magician who performed a couple of card and coin tricks. The star of the show was the eighteen-year-old Liz from London, who had become the ship's darling in short order; everyone knew Liz. She stood up there on the small raised platform. First it was a tap dance as her friend from the ship's band, with the clarinet, played a wild rendition of "Tiptoe Through the Tulips," then, while still catching her breath, she recited some boring poem before she picked up her violin and played "Danny Boy." Luckily for us, we were only subjected to one verse and chorus. The crowd was silent, some a bit teary-eyed because the tune was sad, and others because of the terrible screeching from her bow work. But she won the contest hands down with a roaring applause from the inebriated mob, who were either crying in their drinks or entranced by this buxom beauty. The ship's Chief Petty Officer in his well-pressed uniform presented her with the winner's prize: a pint glass mug engraved with the ship's name and a bottle of cheap bubbly for crossing the equator in style. Now she was definitely the talk of the "Love Boat." The evening was arranged for the King Neptune Ball, and prizes were given out for the best costumes.

The sea was pretty flat for most of the crossing, and the temperature at nighttime was nice and balmy. We sometimes spotted other ships in the distance, their distant lights reflected on a flat black sea. The evenings were pleasant enough for the courting couples to parade on the outer decks and smooch and carry on, in a corner, here or there, or "behind that lifeboat over there." Romance was in the air, and I had my hands full, so to speak.

London Liz had her own special troop of suitors. She could often be seen inebriated at the bar with her arms around the older guys, some old enough to be her dad, and then be spotted other times at the Jungle Room with the teenaged boys. She was only fairly pretty, but very shapely, with a wobbly gait, like she'd practiced for the catwalk at a fashion show. Along with her appearance, there were also the outrageous stories she'd tell her fawning admirers. Her family were paying passengers, but that didn't stop her from sipping booze in the cabins on C deck with the freeloading immigrant crowd, as some put it. One hot night, she and I got a little friendly, It was after the dancing had stopped and everyone was heading back to their cabins or outside for a stargaze. We cruised the deck, had a smoke and were getting cosy when she became distracted as one of the Greek officers walked by. It was obvious our Lizzie had met this guy before, and she was all over the dashing young man in uniform, like a spaniel on a butcher's leg.

"Have to go, Pete. See yeh tomorrow," she said, as off they went, up the stairs to the wheelhouse, I guess for some nautical maneuvers? Passengers were never allowed beyond certain boundaries, but rules were meant to be broken, right? I wasn't exactly heart-broken; and besides, there happened to be one really beautiful girl I had started spending some time with a couple of days earlier.

Laetitia was my very own teenaged Bridgette Bardot, and I wasn't going to share this succulent bowl of fruit with anyone. London Lizzie couldn't hold a candle to Tish, who was very exciting to be with. We were both two months away from seventeen. She was just three days younger than me, a beautiful petite blond from Leeds, and, with her accentuated Yorkshire twang, always had a funny way of putting things. She'd give a wink and tilt of the head if she wanted to go for a stroll or some private time away from the noisy crowd. I had to fight the other boys off as we strolled, swam at the pool or danced to the jukebox in the Jungle Room.

She was an only child, and her family was heading to a small town called Gympie, just north of Brisbane, to buy a horse ranch and settle down. As we started seeing each other on a steady basis, she introduced me to her folks, who invited me to visit them in Toowoomba, Queensland, after we were all settled, and if I had the time to travel the six hundred miles from Sydney, where our crowd were heading.

"I grew up with horses," she told me. "If you come to visit, I'll teach you how to ride." As I said, she always had a nice way of putting things.

"Yeh, I bet you could. I'd love you to teach me how to ride." My response was a wink and a tilt, copying her cuteness. She blushed very easily when I came out with my suggestive comments, and then she'd sometimes follow up with an attempted swipe to the side of my head. She caught me the very first time, but after that, her moves became predictable. I'd duck or weave, lift her up and spin her 'round, and we really enjoyed our little wrestling matches on the bunk, in her family's cabin when her folks were out sunning at the pool, which they did every day. Their family name should have been Mr. and Mrs. Stuck-up 'cause, in short order, I began to realize our lovely Tish was spoiled rotten. They wouldn't have had a clue of the working-class poverty I grew up in, back on Everton Road as I was well-dressed all the time. Still, they did possess those niceties that the upper crust are well practiced at, and my off-colour remarks were silently tolerated. Pip Pip again. The Stuck-up family were lucky enough to have an outside cabin with a porthole, which I'd open to let the smoke out when I'd light up a Players and give my lovely Tish some beginner's lessons on how to hold a ciggie and take a good drag. Her parents were really pissed off with me for introducing her to the sinful world of tobacco smoking. That didn't help our budding relationship, resulting in her cabin becoming out of bounds for this lad. Some parents on board didn't give a hoot about what their kids were up to "on the good ship Venus, by God you should have seen us…"

One notorious cabin became a revolving door for boys and girls to have a quick fling and get out so the next couple could have a secret rendezvous. We even had a few drunken parties there: A dozen legless teenagers all having a mad time, lying all over each other, our legs and arms intertwined like a barrel full of snakes. On one occasion, I brought my beat-up acoustic guitar along, and we all had a merry old singsong, jamming to the tunes and howling out the words. Drunk as a skunk, I hammered away on my axe and sang the only song I could play, "My Girl," by the Temptations. Much to the delight of a wild-eyed, twenty-year-old Scottish girl who jumped on top of me, kissed me madly and dragged me back to her cabin for some private entertainment. I forget what happened next. Wink, wink, say no more. Oh, the inspiration a few drinks and a little guitar pickin' can bring! Tish, my part-time sweetheart, was back in her cabin that crazy night with a bad case of food poisoning, and I was told not to visit by the overbearing parents. So, as circumstances dictated, I found myself in another bunk, taking private lessons in ancient Scottish slang, reminding me of a fishing trip I once took to that wee toon, Dalmellington in Ayrshire. If only Wee Lizzie could see me now, she'd throw a haggis at my silly head.

The *Fairstar* chugged her way across the "flying fish ocean" and sighted land. A voice with a strong European accent came over the air waves: "Ladies and Gentlemen, Australia is within sight. Take a look, straight ahead, over our bow." So, finally, after many days floating on the endless, wide blue soup bowl, we could now see the Land Down Under.

It was a bit disappointing to be brought into dock with just horns and train whistles, when we were looking for hopping kangaroos and the sound of the didgeridoo. There was no chatter of a laughing kookaburra, or the slither of a snake. I would witness all that on later travels up the eastern coast, over my next four years. This was a dockside, just like any other: dirty, noisy and probably the most isolated Westernized port in the world. Many hundreds of miles from anywhere, by sea or land—across the wide desert to Adelaide, one way, or a shark-infested sea to Jakarta the other. Take your pick!

Fremantle on Christmas Day 1966 was hot and sticky, and we were allowed ashore for a day, but clearly told not to be late getting back to the boat as they wouldn't be hanging around for stragglers. Here's where the first load of the British immigrants would disembark, and everyone wanted to stretch their legs on some solid ground, the last place we'd left the ship was that memorable night in Port Said. Our little gang of scallywags went ashore to enjoy a few cold drinks at a local saloon, while crowds of others took buses to Perth for a brief visit. Next, we weighed anchor, and for a few days, we had a rough ride around the Great Australian Bight, then one more stop at Melbourne, where I kissed my Scottish lassie goodbye, then on to the end of our twelve-thousand-mile trip, and the beautiful port of Sydney.

Passing the Heads into Sydney harbour, I was amazed at the striking shoreline packed with incredibly beautiful houses and tropical gardens. Then, sailing closer to port, there appeared the fabulous white shell roof of the Sydney Opera House and directly in front, the massive bridge, the two main iconic landmarks of Sydney's inner harbour. (Just six months later, I'd be doing some electrical work at the Opera House for Stowe Electric.)

We finally tied up in Circular Quay, and this was it; we were here. Fred and Dave were waiting for us four suntanned new immigrants, and with our heavy baggage jam-packed and bursting at the seams, we joined the wobbly legged crowd of disembarking Pommies, shuffling along the decks to the main gangway, bidding fare-thee-well to the smiling crew, kissing the girls goodbye and shaking hands with various friends and acquaintances. At long last, we'd arrived on the shores of this big amazing country, where I would spend the next four and a half years. Years filled with more adventures than I could ever imagine.

As dad and I walked side by side, down the gangway, to the awaiting throngs, he gave me a friendly elbow to the ribs, and looking me squarely in the eyes, said, "Son, always remember you're British!"

Words he probably shared with his brother Ted, that day, way back in the First World War when they walked down the gangway off a troop carrier, onto the shores of France, to do their job for King and Country. An adventurous old man reaffirming to his son, that I was a bit like him, entering into my own new adventure.

Epilogue

Fred and Dave had rented a house on the North Shore of Sydney, so, after hailing a couple of cabs, we crossed the Harbour Bridge for the first time, and ended up at some run-down flea-ridden house in Mosman, a middle-class neighbourhood. It had an old front veranda with a worn-out corrugated iron roof, just as many of the buildings in Aussie had tiled or corrugated iron roofs. Excited to be there, we unpacked a few things, began to settle in, and waited for the delivery of the crates that held all our worldly possessions. To our great surprise, we found lemon and orange trees in the front and back yards, and nobody nicking them, and next door a wide row of banana plants, drooping with big hands of fruit.

The next day was January 1, 1967—a brand-new year in a new country, with a new address, a new direction in life, and I would finally be using my real name, Haase, instead of Hayes. I'd be settling into a new job in three days, and finding new friends and acquaintances. We'd all be handling new Australian money—dollars not quids, which I had some practice with on the ship. I'd have to get rid of some overly warm northern hemisphere clothing and start sporting the acceptable shorts and flip-flops that all kids my age were wearing.

Each morning I'd walk for half an hour over the crest of the Mosman hill and down to my new job, strolling at a casual pace, breathing in all that fresh clean air that was rich with the scents of gorgeous unfamiliar flowering bushes and fruit trees. A complete contrast to the distant world I had left behind with smog and cold damp

Opposite: Me and my Holden, Campsie, Sydney, Australia, 1970

houses. I felt reborn being here, and enjoyed every moment, absorbing every single thing I could in this wonderland. My strong Scouse accent brought a lot of attention in good ways and not-so-good, but I was a quick learner and soon understood how things were said and done.

L-R, Peter, Fred, Geoff, Dave, Sydney, Australia, Jan.1st 1967

I learned to speak with an Aussie twang with "Ow's it gowin' moit? G'day, Fairdinkum" and began to wrap my mouth around the towns and places: Wooloomooloo, Mullumbidgee, Coonabarrabran, Wagga Wagga, and many more tongue twisters. The beaches were hot and fabulous, crawling with the young crowd, surfing and hanging out and having fun. The fishing and sailing were exciting, and the new world down under would also summon another astonishing experience for me.

Over the next few years, I would unexpectedly become involved in religious studies after Geoff and I had joined a local Baptist church our parents attended, mainly because they had lots of good-looking

Sheilas in the youth club. To attend the club, you had to go to their church on Sunday.

My folks were now living the dream of many from Britain, retirement in a tropical country and relief from the aches and pains of those cold Liverpool winters. Dad wanted to keep busy and have an excuse for getting out of the house, so he took on a part-time house-painter's job, but that came to a quick end.

Because we were all living together again, he became the self-appointed family business manager, collecting a bit from us four boys from our weekly pay. We lads had our private union meeting, and Fred, the shop steward, told him he'd only get enough dosh from us to cover our expenses, and his pension should cover the rest. That was fine until, one by one, we all married off and the old folks moved into a small flat on their own. Dave married a New Zealand girl I introduced him to, and moved to Christchurch, New Zealand. Fred and Geoff married Aussie girls and also left Sydney for the north Australian coast.

In 1971, when I turned twenty-one, I flew back to London, UK, leaving my family behind. I eventually walked away from my religious episode. Later that same year I journeyed to Canada, landing in a snowstorm in Toronto, lived in the Yukon for a year, then moved to British Columbia where I've been ever since.

After working as a journeyman electrician and singing in Vancouver nightclubs and pubs for some time, I met my future wife, by chance, on a bus, and we married, had two amazing children and settled down on Salt Spring Island. Many other adventures were to await me.

Now here I am, a double immigrant. Just a Liverpool lad with some early stories, and there were so many Liverpool lads.

Acknowledgements

After years of suggestions by friends and family, I finally began to write down a few of my early stories. This process of memoir was new for me. My way has always been of the oral tradition, or singing, but now with this completed book in hand, a certain convenience has arrived. "Oh, you want to hear that story again? Turn to page number *** It's all there."

It behooves me to thank my parents, Mary and Albert for their love and support and their stimulus of telling stories from the time I could pester them to "say on."

I'm fortunate to have spent the last forty years with the love of my life, a great writer and thinker, Mona Fertig, who enabled me to view the past through the lens of writing, and I embrace the encouragement she gave me in bringing this project to fruition. Love to our wonderful daughter and son; Sophia and Paris, who patiently endured my repetitious stories and readings, smiling all the way through.

Thanks to Ken Rogers for his book *The Lost Tribe of Everton & Scottie Road*, I couldn't believe the similarity of our backgrounds and the familiar stories, and thanks for your helpful blog where I found Alan Bruce, an old classmate from the '50s. Alan has been an exceptional mine of recollection, and along with Ronnie Marshall, sent me some treasured photographs. Ta to my fellow Evertonians, Alan, Ronnie and Ken.

Appreciation to Monika Ullmann and Claudia Cornwall for their manuscript input and Groovy! to Mark Hand for his book design, and Judith Brand for her eagle-eye copyediting.

Magic work! to Bob Edwards of Liverpoolpicturebook.com and to Roger Hull of the Liverpool Record Office, Liverpool Libraries for help sourcing historical Liverpool photographs. The old Liverpool websites were a great discovery.

Li Read and David Gordon, it was fun reading early versions of this manuscript on your radio show *All Things Salt Spring* back in 2009.

Thanks to my three brothers. Cheers lads! See yeh on the swings.

To the town of Liverpool for showing me what "to be, or not to be?"

Last, but not least, thanks to the late John Lennon for his Scouse attitude.

Most of the names in this book have been changed to protect the innocent and the guilty. There's a story down every jigger. If there's any jiggers left!